The Unknown Homeland

The Unknown Homeland

A Samizdat manuscript
translated by Marite Sapiets

 Templegate

© A. R. Mowbray & Co. Ltd. 1978

First published in the United States of America
in 1980 by
Templegate Publishers
302 E. Adams St., P.O. Box 5152
Springfield, Illinois 62705

Translated from the Russian by Marite Sapiets

ISBN 0-87243-082-0

Foreword

A Good Pastor

In the 1920s almost all the churches in Petersburg were still open.
Of these, one of the most popular was the Cathedral of St Sergi
in the city centre, on the corner of Liteiny Prospekt and Sergiev-
sky Street, now Tchaikovsky Street. It was the former church of
the Imperial Guard and in the past it had been one of the most
aristocratic churches of Petersburg. It looked like a palace to anyone entering—with its magnificent carpets, exotic lamps and
Italian-style ikons. On 18 July 1929, the patron saint's feast day
was being celebrated there. I came in at the end of the liturgy;
after the liturgy, as laid down by statute, the Blessing of the
Waters took place. It was read out by a middle-aged priest. I was
impressed by his intonation when reading the prayer before the
Blessing: he was speaking with unusual feeling and inspiration,
not looking at anyone. It was as if he were alone in the church.
I particularly remember the tone in which he pronounced one
phrase from the Blessing of the Waters: 'And submit yourselves
to the Power which washeth away the defilement of our passions.'
After this, the meaning of the rite being performed became clear
and comprehensible to me. I asked what the priest's name was.
A number of voices answered 'Father Pavel'.

Thirty-four years have gone by since then. With their passing
I have changed from a fourteen year old boy into a middle-aged
man. St Sergi's Cathedral has long since been demolished, and
the ugliest, most shameful building has been put up in its place—
it now houses the KGB registration office. The majority of those

who were present at the Blessing of the Waters in 1929 have
departed this life long ago. I was visiting a well-known priest in
Ryazan, when I suddenly noticed a typewritten *samizdat* book on
his table—I opened it. The epigraph immediately attracted my
gaze:

> 'There, beyond the storms,
> Lies a blessed land,
> Where the skies are never darkened,
> Where eternal silence reigns . . .'

I asked my kind host what it was. The priest replied 'A manuscript about a priest, from your part of the country—Petrograd;
he used to serve in St Sergi's Cathedral.' 'What was his name?'
I heard the answer 'Father Pavel'. I spent the whole of the following night reading these reminiscences. The text had been somewhat shortened in comparison with that given here. A page,
which is missing here, had been added at the end. It mentioned
the priest's youthful work on St Symeon the New Theologian,
which he had written when he was a student. There were two
notes on the cover, written by the book's owner, a teacher in
one of the schools of Leningrad: 'I read this book in 1948', and
the second note: 'Read the book a second time in 1957, as a
pensioner. Pasha was a clever boy, but a fool at the same time,
like all men. He fell in love with a girl who was quite unsuited
to him, and then married her.' The teacher's name was given
below, together with the date of her death. She died in 1959.
This was my second meeting with Father Pavel.

Now I've met him a third time—in a foreign land, when I'm
almost seventy years old. I read the book avidly, thinking of
Father Pavel, of the Russian clergy, thinking about the fate of my
native land. 'No town can stand without seven righteous men',
say the sacred writings.* There were such righteous men in Russia,
there were such men among the Russian clergy—that is why

* See also Gen. 18, v. 24, 26.

Russia has survived all adversities, why the Russian Orthodox Church has been preserved, in spite of all persecution. Father Pavel was one of those righteous men. And such men exist even now in Russia: because of this a bright future awaits her.

I strongly advise all those who are concerned with the fate of Russia and that of the whole world, those who suffer because of that fate, to read this truthful book, the story of a good pastor, written by a close relative of his, which draws a living picture of him and the people around him, who passed through such hard times.

ANATOLY LEVITIN
Lucerne

December 1977.

PART ONE

Chapter 1

On a clear frosty, autumn morning, just before seven o'clock, when the wormwood in the ditches was bright with silvery hoar-frost, a long goods-train drew into Irkutsk; attached to it were two prisoner-wagons. It had taken twelve days altogether to get there from Leningrad, not stopping anywhere for long, except in Omsk, with no connections to transit prisons on the way. All those in the wagons were being sent to the Eastern distribution centre so that they could be transported to the distant villages of Siberia. The prisoners had their names called, they were counted, lined up in pairs and led off across the pontoon-bridge over the Angara river, through the lower reaches of the town, towards Ushakovka.

The prisoner-transport on the march was a 'motley crew' – two women from Vologda, convicted of vicious speculation, two embezzlers, a number of robbers and a foursome – a man and three women – with convictions for large-scale burglary. A fat accountant kept falling behind, very much out of breath. He was finding it difficult because of his unseasonably warm coat and he was almost dragging it behind him, letting the full weight of the skunkfur collar drop almost as far as his elbows. Behind everyone else walked a young man with grey-blue lips, who looked ill – obviously a long-term prisoner. His partner on the march was the only political exile – a scholar and priest, who stood out in the procession because of his unusual height and could hardly keep up with the quick pace of the column. Bent double and gasping for breath, he was carrying a small suitcase in one hand and a bundle of food in the other. The robust

1

Siberian morning irritated his chest, which had not yet become accustomed to long walks and fresh air. During the journey he had dreamed of the walk they would have to take from the station to the prison through the town. In six months of imprisonment, he had forgotten what the noises of a town sounded like and his eyes were dazzled anew by the infinite space of the sky. In the prison-wagon, he had thought that, once he got outside, once he was standing firmly on hard ground after twelve days of swaying backwards and forwards on the train – then everything would be over. There would be no more foul air or overcrowding…His frequent spells of dizziness, the tight sensation in his chest, would immediately disappear. However, when he had emerged, trembling and hardly able to stand on his own feet, into the railway yard from which they had been sent off to the bridge, he had felt uncommonly weak, with a heaviness in his arms and legs, as if he had been drinking wine. His head was going round and round and there was a buzzing in his ears. The strange unsteadiness of his body worried him. Would he make it or would he fall down? It did not even occur to him to say anything about his condition; he walked on with only one thought: 'I must, I must last out to the end'.

Siberia greeted its new guests in festive style with a wonderfully fine morning. Sunshine flowed over the town; the roofs and windows glittered. The watery expanse of the Angara acquired a golden sheen. The travellers were enveloped in the cornflower blue of the skies, reminiscent of spring in the Crimea or autumn round Lake Baikal. Unexplored, unknown Siberia gave him a brief smile, like the smile of home. In the hilly outer fringes of the town, the autumn foliage of the trees glowed yellow, like little amber-coloured lanterns. Before them lay the bridge over the Angara; the Angara was foaming and bubbling, its waters blindingly green and transparent. Such a river should be cased in armour, locked in by cast-iron chains, arches and girders, but here it was trustingly bridged by ordinary wooden boards, with dangerously wide spaces between the lower supports. The stony river bottom looked deceptively close – at a depth of nineteen to twentyfive metres.

When they had crossed the bridge, they all suddenly cheered up and began to chat. Perhaps it was because the spray of the Angara had combined with the air to produce an invigorating breath, or because the freedom they longed for had touched their confined hearts – but all of a sudden someone in front began to laugh; one of the boy thieves whispered in a soldier's ear 'Let's have a smoke, old fellow', but the latter snorted, 'I'll give you smoking' and turning to the others, who were falling behind, he said, in the tones of an old sergeant: 'What are you staring at? Never seen a river before? March on.'

It grew hot marching along the river-bank; white dust choked their nostrils. The morning suddenly turned into the heat of day. Everywhere the awakening town began to show signs of life. A woman opened the shutters, rattling an iron bolt. To a keen sense of hearing, which had long been parted from the sounds of daily life, it was wonderful to hear the squeaking of buckets on the end of a yoke, – they were approaching a water-pump. Two small boys, their faces pressed to the window pane, were staring at the column. And all these small novelties of life, the freely-flowing Siberian river, the blue sky, the crowing of cocks, the gold of autumn leaves – all this, like the nearness of freedom, greeted the new arrivals, among them the priest, now falling behind.

One and a half years of imprisonment, alternately in solitary and general confinement, had taken their toll. He had grown weak, he had aged and become feeble, but his spirit was un-clouded. On the contrary, he experienced everything in more depth, more acutely. He had even developed a habit of checking the normality of his own responses objectively, but at this point, the fresh current of life, so powerful and bright, was acting on him like a poison. The same thing happens to a starving man, if

he is given too much food. The morning air, the seething Angara
the thunder of its crashing waves, like that of the sea, the wide
unpaved street, the shutters, the dogs barking, the sound of the
water-jet in the pumping-hut, the sheer variety of this food,
simple to those whose regular diet it was, delicious but harmful
to the prisoner, was almost making him faint. Climbing the hill
towards the Ushakovo pass, he was very much out of breath and
touched his neighbour's hand with his bundle. 'Tired, Father?',
asked the latter and whispered to him out of the side of his mouth,
almost tenderly, 'we'll go slower, to hell with them...' The pair
of them slowed down – the leading guard could not see them, but
the other one, who was walking beside him, immediately
shouted at them: 'No loitering!'

"The old motor's running down for all of us, brothers,"
whispered the pale prisoner. "You know, when I'd been inside
for half a year, in the reformatory, I almost snuffed it. My hands
were weak and trembling, my knees quivered like a nervous
young lady's. But when I was going to kill the wife, I was a man
of steel!"

"But how could you... what did you do it for?"

"Another bloke, what else? Teach her not to be a tramp.
I swung my arm back and let her have it with the axe. She didn't
even give a squeak. All over in a moment. When I think what I
ruined my life for! She painted her lips, shaved her eyebrows,
looked like a clown. And that's what I ruined myself for, rubbish
like that, a bit from the market-place."

It was not the first time in his months of imprisonment that the
priest had heard such speeches and still he could not get used
either to the morals or to the language of those around him. He
understood only one thing: all these people, these pitiful rejects,
were his brothers in suffering and in their common lot; like him,
all of them felt sorrowful; for them too, it was stuffy and crowded
but he could not establish a living link between them and himself
and tormented himself with reproaches about his inability to do

so and the distance he put between them and himself. He spoke simply and peaceably to everyone, but the people life had brought him into contact with did not understand such a quiet and amiable approach. Then he was tormented even more by his alienation from the general level of those around him. He had always been gifted as a wise and discerning preacher, but now he was far from thinking of any sort of evangelism. That belonged to another life, which had rolled up like a scroll before his eyes and disappeared unexpectedly and stormily. In the great cathedral .... before a gathering of like-minded people, it would have been a different matter – but here, his loftiest words seemed insignificant; here, life itself – a life of retribution and repentance – was the active factor.

On the way to Siberia he had got to know all of them and their life-stories. He knew about each man – what he had been and the reason why he was walking beside him, but their artless accounts of theft, murder and dissipation did not call forth reproaches from him. He only felt sorry that he had no language in common with these men, condemned like himself to exile and the loneliness of a Siberian winter, that they could not exchange thoughts, that they had no store of words they could all understand, which would have made it easier for them to live together...

"Hurry up, priest! Look lively!" – shouted the guard.

The day was growing warmer all the time. The crisp, frosty morning had long since thawed out. The sun was beating down fiercely on the open ground. The column passed some new buildings made of hard planks. Waves of sunlight poured through the windows, it grew hot... Going down a little hill, they stepped on to the Ushakovko bridge across the shallow Ushakovka, with its flat banks. A new horizon opened up ahead – they were on the outskirts of the town. It was hemmed in by a chain of hills, of a fabulous blue, which almost merged with the sky. On these light blue heights, the gold of poplars in September shone out ...

Carts and wagons rattled continuously across the bridge – a lorry grumbled past with a load of iron bars, then a hay-waggon swayed over. The scholarly priest was gripped by a strange sensation: his eyes, still not used to the abundant light of day, and his thoughts, somewhere deep inside him, were once again absorbing reality and taking it in, but it seemed unreal, like a dream, a vision, or a fantasy . . . His eyes and thoughts were taking time to awake. In awaking, they were absorbing the new life in a new way. At the beginning of the journey, when he was crossing the bridge over the Angara, freedom had still not made itself clearly felt to him; he had not been thinking about anything except the heaviness of his body and the difficulty of moving his legs, but here, in spite of the hour-long march, he longed for his journey to come to an end as soon as possible – he longed to be free. If he could just sit down on a flat patch of grass, even if people stared at his tall, absurd figure, – there, in the distance, children were swimming . . . he would be able to cool down, get used to things. As it was, he felt agitated and excited, almost intoxicated.

In prison, it had not been so terrible, but now he was struck by the sharp contrast: the drowsiness, illness and darkness of prison were struggling against the great present reality of life: the lorry, the bridge and the creaking wagons. And above them all was the the horizon, the continental sky, with the amber-yellow trees on the blue expanse . . . The cocks were crowing loudly on the hillock beside the buildings. Children were diving, spraying water about. Somewhere he had seen such pictures; somewhere, in some past dream, he had drunk from these bright springs. Then darkness had flowed over him. Later, death had stood aside, after threatening him and granting him a respite. And once again, life – a new kind of life – had unexpectedly been restored to him: a strangely chaotic life, elemental and powerful, able to uphold his failing strength. One had to get used to it, and treat it with care. In its new form and content, it had almost the same effect as strong drink. It had to be taken carefully, not all at once; one short sip was enough for the time being . . .

The bridge shook and rattled. Armed men in a bulky lorry, with pistol-holsters and rifles . . . A military vehicle flashed past, rumbling suggestively, and disappeared behind a two-storey building. This building stood on open ground, its numerous windows, caged in by iron bars, directly facing the bridge. It was the prison, the detention block, or, in other words, the East Siberian distribution and isolation centre.

The column had already crossed the bridge, the guard's hut was not far away. when suddenly, a sound he had not heard for a long time penetrated his consciousness: a churchbell was ringing, the only one remaining in a church which had not yet been closed.

'That's the early service', he thought, "Probably just before the singing of *It is meet and right*". It was amazing how this regular faint ringing had reached the pastor's ears; it was not a minute late, but just before he entered his last prison, it joyfully sang to him of the freedom that was near. To the sound of the bells, the column marched up to the prison and stopped before the main entrance. People shifted from one foot to another, waiting to be assigned to their places.

The most difficult thing was not being able to put his bundle and suitcase on the ground; it was just by the door that his strength deserted him altogether. At last the inspection of documents came to an end. The new arrivals were taken through the first and second barred gates and stood against a wall in the depths of a dark corridor . . . A roll-call of surnames began, assigning each prisoner to his cell. There was some perplexed discussion about the priest and where to put him, as he was not a criminal. All the others had gone, he alone was still waiting to be assigned, brushing dust off his cassock with his hand. "Where shall we put the priest? The second floor's full up. Section 12 – but there are no free bunks in it . . . Well, we can put in a bunk . . . the plank-beds are all taken. That's decided, then – Section 12 . . . There are two other politicals in there . . ."

In the dark corridor, the scenes of the glowing autumn day

disappeared. The usual arched ceiling met his gaze. Two prison
orderlies were carrying along a pail of boiling water – for
morning tea – on long poles. Everything grew small and narrow,
as it had been in the other detention centre, back in Russia. . .

A moment's rest ensued. Suitcases, bundles and bags, thrown
off people's shoulders, were put on benches; people settled down
beside their luggage. Suddenly a whistle sounded, resembling
the furious buzz of an enormous beetle.

"To the bath!"

Once again they were lined up; they were each given a piece of
soap; those who could snatched a change of underclothes to take
with them. Leaving the narrow prison corridors behind them,
they emerged into a backyard between prison buildings, where
two young cockerels were cheerfully pecking at the ground. They
went round a brick wall, near which a black Maria was parked,
covered in the dirt of Ushakovo. From there they went on down
a sloping square between planks, barrels and bricks, along a
narrow alley of the Eastern kind. Were they back in the town? It
was hot and dusty; their legs, which felt as if they were made of
wood, could hardly move . . . They reached the public baths,
which had been open from seven in the morning; round the
entrance, children were gnawing cedar-nuts, while a half-blind
old man was selling birch-brooms. There were also three women
there, selling baskets of wild cherries; one of them stepped back
to let the column go past, and suddenly caught sight of the priest.
Her face trembled, she flushed and tears came into her eyes.
Quickly, taking a rouble out of her apron pocket, she thrust it at
him, before anyone could see, and whispered pityingly, "Here,
father dear, take this, remember the sinner Avdotya in prayer,
remember. ."

If he didn't take it, he would offend her. Should he take it? –
Beside him and behind him were the guards. The priest's face
showed his sorrow and bewilderment; he smiled, thanked her
and immediately looked away from the woman . . . He even

turned his shoulder aside, just so that he wouldn't have to take it. The rouble was taken by the pale man who had killed his wife. He took it deftly, behind the priest's back, – it was just then that they were allowed into the bath-house.

Section 12, Cell 124.

The sunny autumn had penetrated even here, in the form of bright, dusty shafts of light, but the dark room with its plank-beds one above the other, looked even more unattractive when lit up to some extent by the windows. In spite of the usual rule, common to all prisons – a weekly bath – there was no general cleanliness. True, every morning the prisoners took turns to wash the floor. Nevertheless, the newly-washed floor, with its cracks and ancient ruts dating from Tsarist times, was soon dirtied and spat on again. Each prisoner almost made an effort to add to the general disorder. One would spit from above right in the middle of the floor, another would crush a cigarette with his foot, while the guard was looking out of the window. Busy families of bugs swarmed over the plasterwork of the old walls; they were constantly being scorched out with boiling water, disappearing and reappearing again. Getting rid of body lice took less time and was also a more thorough procedure – they went through the sanitary ritual once or twice at most.

On the journey, the learned father had been subjected to a great deal of laughter because of the way he shuddered painfully as one or another prisoner ran his fingers over himself, pinching them together. "Never mind, father", laughed the pale girl-murderer, "You could start by squashing just one, that blonde one with the grey back, or they'll end by eating you alive as well." However, the journey was over, the lice had been liquidated, but now, in Section 12, he was suffering from something else – the continuous talking. He could never hide anywhere from it – morning, noon or night – somehow, unexpectedly, the chatter would begin, because of somebody's

insomnia, or started by a stool-pigeon, or after a summons to
a nocturnal interrogation, which had often happened back in
Russia. Almost everyone talked and talked. . . And it was all so
confused. Even if it had occurred to these people that one of them
was ill, suffering to the point of torture from having to listen to
unnecessary eruptions of words, they would not have cared –
what did it have to do with them? But in conversation, these men
burnt up all they had within them – fear, sorrow, the pangs of
conscience, nightly boredom, the unknown nature of their
sentence – and much else besides. . .

All sorts of subjects came up – anecdotes were told, events
discussed. Domestic life was remembered. People spoke of their
homes, of the children they had left behind. Often they boasted
about the acts they were accused of. In Irkutsk, it had been as
if a demon had suddenly possessed them – the whole band of
them had got together and started telling dirty stories. Market-
place witticisms and ribald songs flowed out without a pause into
the darkness of the nights. In the evenings, they played with
greasy cards to the point of blindness. They reminisced about
their women, cursing in foul language. They shared all kinds of
intimate details, inclining their livid faces towards each other.
Only a book-keeper, a 'former person'*, being an intellectual,
preferred the priest's company to that of the others, but even so,
he tried not to express openly any particular sympathy towards
him, merely throwing a few necessary words in his direction as
they were required.

A certain variety in life, by way of escape from dullness and
sloth, was created by the arrival of a Chinese doctor. He was
brought into Section 12 towards the end of the second day after
the prisoners from Lenigrad had arrived in Irkutsk; in spite of the
overall crowding in the cell, they squeezed it even fuller, putting
in a bunk for him, and the cheerful yellow-faced man moved in

* "Former person" was the name given under the Soviet regime to people
who had held an influential position under the Tsarist regime.

temporarily. He walked about in soft slippers, reacting quite calmly to his surroundings. However, when a soldier came into the cell with a tea-pot, the Chinese doctor livened up, smiled, screwed up his slanting eyes into even narrower slits and asked, "They giving out parcels soon? Want food." He had been brought there from Tomsk transit prison, with the column of prisoners that had preceded them. For twelve years he had successfully been treating the sick with herbs, but had grown careless: he opened a store providing things that were sometimes in short supply at the chemists. At this time he was also charged with being responsible for the death of a child, whom he had been treating for dyspepsia with an infusion of wild sorrel; so he was put inside as a merchant-speculator and illegal medical practitioner. He had relations in Irkutsk and eagerly awaited parcels from them; on the first Tuesday they brought him a raw cockerel, ten raw eggs, some brick tea and a couple of loaves of wheaten bread. He ate the fowl greedily, raw, cutting the bird up with his penknife, sometimes assisting this process by tearing at it with his hands; he also swallowed the eggs raw, but brewed the tea strongly in a pewter cup with the first boiling water that was brought.

The guard on duty, who brought the parcel to the section, was interested in this Chinese custom of eating food raw and, allowing himself a certain familiarity with the prisoners, asked the priest:

"Is that part of their faith then, having to eat cockerels raw?"

In a quiet voice, interrupted by gasps because of the shortness of breath he now suffered from continuously, the priest explained that each nation has its own tastes in food, its own understanding of the body's needs, that this really had very little to do with religion. Perhaps some of the things we ate would appear uncivilized or unpleasant to the Chinese.

The Chinese had obviously understood the priest's words; he nodded and smiled, tearing himself away from his dinner: "Your food no tasty. You no like mine."

The pale man, who was being sent into exile for murdering his wife, pined for liberty more openly than anyone else. In this gaol, he was made use of, being an intelligent, literate and efficient fellow – he was assigned to the parcels section. He had a reason for taking to this work: surely someone would give him something for himself as well, would push something into his hand . . . and how precious that would be. Here he had no relations or acquaintances. As he himself had endured imprisonment and was still enduring it, he felt a lively sympathy for them all. He was not a stranger or one of the locals, but a brother, and so all the women in headscarves, all the men and adolescents who came with their parcels, were like his own people. He talked to them all lightly, a bit coarsely, but people immediately felt that he was sympathetic, that he was one of them. Before half an hour had gone by at his second reception of parcels, he was already in possession of two salted cucumbers, an egg and a piece of dried salmon on a wheat roll. He usually put all the food behind his barred window, declaring it to be 'mine'. He had to conceal his attitude to the prisoners and their relations carefully – or he would have been removed from his post and then he would have been left with nothing but his ration, which would have been a lot of use.

"Who's that for, Mokeyev?" – he would ask, roughly taking the basket – "What are you howling about? Mokeyev's not dying. It's not bad in the hospital. Who's next? Fifth Section? Come back tomorrow. We're not taking anything for the Fifth today. Back off a bit, citizens . . . We can't have this. Come up in order, one by one, anybody who's here by right, don't push. See, you'll be able to hand yours in too, in time. Just wait a bit. . ."

The women called him their 'benefactor'. . .

In the course of a year, prison had whitened the lips and cheeks of the benefactor, who last year had chopped a woman to death in a fit of rage. But this could not be linked with his outward appearance, nor with his somewhat weary, measured voice. From the day of his first appearance at the parcel reception office, people began to call him 'the pale fellow'.

The learned father, in his first days at the detention centre, kept on imagining that his wife had come to visit him, in spite of the complete absurdity of such thoughts. He seemed to be always hearing her quick steps behind the door, her voice, her familiar, captivating smile. However, at this point, admitting the complete illusion and insubstantiality of this mirage, he would crush these worldly, and thus unstable, thoughts by means of prayer.

From the town of Bratsk he was to go – by way of Tulun and Bratsk – to the distant village of Ust-Vikhorevo; this, so he had been informed, was to be his destination. 'Bratsk fortress': that was the name of the tiny dot on the map, on the bend of the Angara. The word 'fortress' had echoes of pre-revolutionary Siberia, of some remote spot, in a starless night. At Bratsk, navigation along the Angara ceased. There would be a jetty . . . it would be springtime . . . His wife would only be able to come in the spring. Here his knowledge of the new journey ahead broke down; unknown Siberia awed his sick spirit with its mountains and vast distances. Everything became unclear, as if in a mist, but he kept on seeing the wheel of the paddle steamer cutting through the grey waters of the Angara.

Although he was a great scholar, a man familiar with books and philosophical works, it was now that he learned to day-dream and ponder. The thoughts that flashed through his head one after the other could really only be described as daydreams. They constantly crowded into his brain, taking the place of books and sermons. The trifling events of prison life flickered past. These amazed him but he did not disregard them. On the contrary, even the most insignificant of them made a painfully acute and profound impression on him. Formerly, life had been edged out of his consciousness as if by giant musical chords. Ready-made analyses had flowed into his mind all at once. He had been seized by the idea of a single, harmonious whole. It was different now, but better, altogether new. He felt he could move the walls apart

and gaze at the vast spaces beyond them. The tiniest signs and
details of a secret, hidden life impressed themselves incompre-
hensibly on his consciousness. He felt it was just about to open
out and shed its light on him. . .

At the parcel reception office, someone had brought one of
the prisoners a bouquet of asters – lilac and pink. . . He felt that
the smell of carbolic in their cell, stronger than that of sweating
human bodies, had suddenly disappeared. He saw before him the
familiar refuge of an autumn garden. Back there, in Russia. The
sunset was fading over the river. The damp shadows of evening
descended. Someone was coming towards him, wrapped in a
shawl. In her hand she held a watering-can; in the flower-beds,
asters were blooming. Nearer and nearer came the light footsteps
of the familiar figure. Already she was no longer in the garden,
she was standing in the cell, exuding the fresh scent of autumn
flowers; on her breast she was wearing a huge, budding lilac aster;
the familiar dimples on her cheeks were trembling; she cast aside the
watering-can and was stretching out her hands to him –'my wife'!

That was one sort of mood. . . Another, more vital and real,
had been with him since his first days in prison. Those first days
had been when his hopes were highest. Of course, his ordeal
would soon be over. There had been some misunderstanding,
some mistake. He had been brought in as a routine check, because
of his faith and priestly office, that was all. . . Feeding on the hope
of a quick release, he loved to imagine himself taking a service
in his great church. Sometimes he saw himself at the altar, sometimes standing at the altar steps with the cross, sometimes leading
the prayers. He had grown so close to his church, that he could
never have imagined being far away from it for long. Serving in
it, offering the daily sacrifice there, and finally lying there in his
coffin, with the Gospels in his hands – he had not imagined living
in any other way.

However, the days flew farther and farther away from the day
when he had been taken from his home. Whitsun had already

gone by, and All Saints too. All the summer feast-days had flashed
by in turn. Waking up in his cell, at night, he tried to work out
when he would be taking part in them: on the Feast of Elijah
the Prophet or the Feast of the Holy Cross. Then he would
suddenly accuse himself, weeping, of pride, impatience and false
dreams, and would begin to pray for resignation, for a cross.

He had been connected with an important trial, as the spiritual
confessor of the aged defendant; and he, whom neither the cell,
solitary confinement nor tedium had been able to break, had
become almost ill after interrogations in which his words were
disbelieved and he was treated as a noxious liar, an unworthy
person. After he had undergone questioning a number of times,
his daily appearances in church, in the form of mystical journeys
there, disappeared from his mental horizon. He also stopped
composing sermons. His mind became deserted, like that of a
poet tired out by creative inspiration, – and different guests came
to him in his cell.

These were golden, detailed memories of his years as a teacher,
which fell into his solitude like gilded nets, fishing out his thoughts
and dragging them off into those clear spring snares. His wife
stood before him, as if she were really there, – and into his
memory flashed that especially bright moment, when he had
renounced his solemn vow and had stretched out his hands to
her alone.

There is a love in this world that is different from all the known
forms of love, when those who love see no limit to their
emotions and do not measure love's depths; they do not want
or desire their own good, but drink more and more deeply
from the inexhaustible spring of eternal love. They pour out
this living water on everything around them, distributing its
beneficial moisture over the dry grass nearby, the dusty roads,
the remote pathways and wilting bushes. The inspiration of
such a love, knowing no bounds or limits, comes from a

different spring, immeasurably great and incapable of drying up, inconceivable in its eternal inexhaustibility. The torrent keeps on spurting out, the clear waters flow forth, quenching the thirst of mankind over the centuries. Whoever finds on his way a golden rivulet of that universal stream, whoever falls before it and drinks from it with eager lips, will drink from its wonderful waters for ever. His soul is fed, his body strengthened, his spirit soars towards heaven; his hopes take wing, his mind is enlightened. That person himself becomes a vessel for the living water; people come to him, drink and revive . . . and in their turn they relive the thirst of others.

All his life, from his earliest childhood, from the moment when he felt a higher consciousness inspiring him, a feeling some people experience more strongly at an early age than at any other time, the child – later the youth – Pavel drank from the wonderful spring of that inexhaustible stream. As an eight year old boy, he persuaded his sister to go on a pilgrimage with him – his nurse's tales of Mount Athos and Jerusalem had sunk into his sensitive soul. Early one morning both children – Pasha* and Masha – disappeared from home. They were found only next morning, tired and hungry, in a forester's hut. Their parents' happiness at finding them was so great that they did not even think of punishment. The forester had brought them to his hut from the crossroads on the very edge of the forest, where, tired out, they had asked him pitifully: "Uncle, which is the road to Kiev from here?" They had travelled fifteen versts from their home and had passed the night on the edge of the forest. The episode was talked about and remembered, as a 'childhood happening', but as if by agreement, no-one in the religious family laughed at them. Indeed, they began to watch Pavel carefully. The boy grew up in a sensitive, spiritually gifted family and, as he said later, 'I could not have been

* "Pasha" is the diminutive of "Pavel."

different' – his whole nature was determined by this. He was not prevented from doing anything, but particular care was taken to influence him wisely, towards attainable goals, to discourage his early dreaminess and unreasonable longing to perform feats beyond his powers. Pavel was a quiet and gentle child. Nevertheless, his parents were afraid that they might be presenting the world with a fanatic or narrow-minded extremist, so Pavel was given an all-round, varied education; he was surrounded by books, though their selection was strictly and secretly controlled by his teacher father. The boy learnt well, though at times he seemed absent-minded and pensive. He graduated from high school as one of the best pupils; it was time to move on to further studies, and the question of going to university arose – his father must have been astounded when his son told him, "Just as you like, Dad, it's all the same to me: God's will be done, but if you're interested in what I want – I should like to be a monk."

However, he listened to his father and enrolled at a university, from which he graduated with a first-class degree from the faculty of history and philology. He was allowed to stay on at the university for three years as a post-graduate student in the faculty of philosophy, in preparation for professorship. It looked as if he had agreed to take the road laid out for him, but at this point he immediately announced to his parents, "Now for the Theological Academy". His parents did not say a word. He was already independent; in addition, they had placed their hopes in his years of study, as a way of putting off his taking of monastic vows, while in the depths of their simple, loving hearts, they looked on every religious and well-behaved girl as a possible match for their gifted son.

Next year, after the first revolution of 1905, he also graduated from the Theological Academy, with the title of Master of Theology. The way to the higher ranks of theological education lay open to him. In the autumn of the same year, he was asked to take a special course of lectures on the history of Russian

religious and philosophical thought at the Women's Pedagogical
Institute in Petersburg; immediately after this appointment, he
was given the post of official lecturer on church law at the Sunday
school of St. John the Baptist, and in the following year, 1907,
he was permitted to teach religious instruction at a women's
high school without first taking holy orders. He found this
arrangement spiritually acceptable. He was not in any hurry to
take holy orders. He cherished another dream, which he had confided to Metropolitan Anthony while he was still a first-year
student, – and had received his full approval and blessing.

In this way, the days flowed past for him. After his graduation
from the Theological Academy, two more years passed. He awoke
to his calling as a theologian and philosopher and matured in this
field. He felt the lure of academic work, of a quiet study and the
opportunity of writing about the infinite from within the narrow
confines of life. He was getting nearer and nearer to the sublime
path taken by his beloved Bishop Feofan*, whom he believed
to be his spiritual patron. He was already dreaming of the Highest,
for whose sake he would be glad to become a hermit. He seemed
to see the morning sunlight shining into a monk's narrow cell,
he heard the sound of the chapel bell, and he felt such a desire
to work for the glory of God, because of his spiritual love for
the world he was leaving behind for ever, in order to make himself more closely responsible for it by means of prayer. He imagined himself writing and working creatively, like the hermit
bishop. At last his first small book, *The Mysticism of Symeon the
New Theologian*, saw the light and was discussed among the close-
knit circle of students at the Theological Academy.

During these teaching years, he had to work hard, both at his
lectures and at the high school, and although he conscientiously
fulfilled his task, the higher inspiration to which he dedicated his
leisure time enveloped him from head to foot; his teaching

* Feofan the Recluse – a Russian 19th century bishop, scholar and mystic,
author of *The Way of Salvation*, an influential work on the spiritual life.

demanded strength, but did not take up all his energy. On returning from his lessons, after resting a while and fortifying himself with food, he could sit down to his writing work, and from dusk till dawn he would stay up, working at his papers, returning to real life in the morning, hungry but happy; when, almost late for his first lesson, he took a quick bite of bread or a cup of tea in the staff-room, how tasty that bread-roll seemed to him! He felt he had never eaten anything so good.

He made it a rule to begin his literary work with prayer and regularly to continue what he had begun, by small, but daily, additions. This immediately bore fruit: the riotous forces of un-bridled inspiration submitted to the quiet spirit of the true artist. At first, his brain had overstrained itself, his hands and feet had got cold, and all this had led to a certain absent-mindedness after working-hours. Now, he learnt to work calmly. Thoughts appeared one after the other, no longer galloping about in chaotic haste, but lying down on the paper in clearly-formulated rows. He now needed to put in fewer and unnecessary explanations; in the spring, after the high school exams were over, he hoped to begin a substantial new work. When he had finished that, he felt that, with God's help, he could leave his teaching post and take monastic vows – mainly with the aim of going into a hermitage and devoting himself to theological writing.

He was already on the point of turning towards that better side of life, which he was finding ever more understandable, but he was still delaying his departure from the world. In the high school where he taught, final exams were being held and were now coming to an end. He was acting as assistant examiner in divinity and history. Reserved and shy by nature, he was inevitably always bumping into a merry crowd of girl students on the stairs or in the corridor, sensing their glances in his direc-tion. He would walk, or even run, past, hanging his head, and often heard their stifled laughter behind him. This involuntary embarrassment was still with him even on the evening when, after being invited to a party there together with the other teachers, he stepped over the threshold of the decorated assembly hall. He had come here, after deciding that "I shall give in today, but this will be the first and last time!" In this mood he appeared at the entrance to the familiar building. But Lord, how strange and elegant everything looked!

Instead of the familiar classrooms, there were comfortable parlours with soft furniture and carpets. The floor in the hall had been polished to the semblance of a skating-rink. His eyes met the flushed faces of his pupils. What was he to do here? Parties, concerts – was this laughter and coquetry really seemly for him now? He had not despised his youth, or its gifts, but at the age of thirty-two he had already wholly given himself to the narrow way he had chosen. Then, as a furture hermit, who would never hear a woman's laugh or see a girl's rosy cheek, he considered anything like this dangerous and unnecessary. What good would it be to him, if in the autumn, the door of the tomb he longed for closed behind him and he left the world of emotions, passion and desires? "Even an impression received only once is reflected in the brain cells, "he thought," and lives on there to the end, to the darkness of the grave. Then why should the brain and heart of a man given over to the power and activity of the Holy Spirit preserve within themselves other associations then those to whom he has dedicated his life?" He saw nothing sinful in the high school party, but at the same time, he considered that everything going on around him was already unnecessary to his existence and cut off from his way of life. It would have been more useful and more enjoyable to spend the day, without wasting precious time and half the night, writing out a few pages from the works of St. Basil the Great, and then to follow his rule of prayer, especially since tomorrow was a feast-day.

Meanwhile, the school hall was filling up and becoming more lively; girls in their last year at school and second-form pupils were coming in with their fathers, mothers and brothers, some

even accompanied by friends of their brothers, pupils from the
boy's grammar school, sailors and cadets. The scent of lilac and
lily of the valley wafted through the air. The lace handkerchieves
and scarves, the elegant slippers, all these young faces, shining
eyes and straight fringes, had the air of a spring daybreak. The
space between the two windows was taken up by a massive
portrait in a gilded oval frame, of the empress in the costume of a
Russian nobleman's wife with pearl ear-rings and a white tulle
headband. They had forgotten to let down the blind on one of the
windows – the May night peered in, a high star twinkling in the
deep blue of the heavens. The headmistress entered, dressed in a
blue dress with a sumptuous bosom, hung with medals; some of
the teachers got up to greet her. He himself bowed from a distance
and then tried to find himself a quiet spot, where he would not be
noticed and where his neighbours would be suitably sedate
persons (as he felt he needed). However, when, contrary to
expectation, the school chaplain, in his elegant silk cassock, sat
down in the front row of the chairs put out for the concert, his
two daughters seated themselves on either side of him. The timid
teacher sought some salvation behind the huge white stove,
which jutted out some way into the hall. He retreated at once into
the very corner; beside him there were still two chairs, which
were soon taken by a gentleman in a judge's dress-coat and his
young daughter. Until the concert began, they talked together in
an undertone, the girl constantly holding back and hiding her
laughter, fearing lest it should escape and ring out through the
hall. The poor teacher imagined that the whole hall was laughing
at him in the person of the blonde giggler. But the girl, young
and full of health, was simply enjoying herself, with her whole
heart ... She was filled with the joy of life; without a trace of
embarrassment or coquetishness she launched into a conversation
with her shy teacher, telling him that she was waiting for her
friend Bodaleva, that both of them were students in the third
class, that they were both 19 years old; after finishing their

studies they hoped never to part and to work together. Again
her bell-like laughter rang out, seemingly without cause, but so
understandable to everyone who looked at her.

The concert began. According to custom, it started with
choral singing. 'We walk to the bright Aragvi for water every
evening' . . . sang the young voices, and the familiar melody
made him feel young, serene and somehow enchantingly sad.
Suddenly, the hall erupted into noise, everyone was clapping,
and he came back to reality. There was long drawn-out applause
for the choir. Then three of his pupils, in their last year, came
forward and sand *The Crucifixion*. His thoughts, confused by
Aragvi and its vibrating sounds of Eastern enchantment, immediately turned in a different direction. The *Crucifixion* was
followed by a sweet child soprano, who gave a pure, clear
rendering of 'In the sunlight, the dark woods turned red'; she
also received a lot of applause. Readings came next; *Thoughts*,
by Shevchenko, and *To my nurse*, by Pushkin. Then there was
more singing – the duet 'Don't tempt me'. The singing of this
duet again enticed his emotions and thoughts, tuned to a high
and peaceful plane, into some domain of melancholy chaos,
somehow ghostly and incomplete. The song poured out over the
hall, like an invisible mist, troubling the soul with its disturbing,
tender unrest. It appeared that, in his comfortable silence behind
the Dutch tiled stove, he had weak defences against his own
newly-born, heavy feelings of longing and melancholy. Such a
mood was not natural to him. It had descended on him as a result
of the varied combination of sounds, of this whole world of
sound and words, an entire scale of moods, expressing the
sorrows, doubts, anguish and hopes of the earth, seemingly
abandoned, sunk in its own passions, invocations and enchant-
ments, but nevertheless an earth unknown and beautiful. Taken
together, all this made his heart beat with a painful excitement
he had not known before. The concert came to an end. In the
hall, everybody began to talk at once and moved aside; the

young people carried away the chairs to their places in no time
at all. The teachers and many of the school-leavers went off to the
classrooms to have tea. The classrooms were unrecognizable!
Since yesterday they had been transferred into comfortable
parlours, with pale yellow and blue lampshades, small divans,
little tables and padded stools. However, in the hall no-one had
time for tea and snacks – the young people were getting ready to
dance. The pianist tested the piano-keys, everywhere there was
the sound of laughter, chatter and merry disputes. . . . And, at
last, the first couples moved off in a waltz. The moment of decision had come. The school's teacher of divinity rose – he did not
dance; it was time for him to go home, to his silence. What else
was there to wait for? Suddenly, a question reached his ears,
addressed by the man in the judge's dress-coat to his daughter,
the giggler:

'Look, Katyusha, look over there, do you know who that
beautiful girl is, the one in blue, looking exactly as if she'd come
out of a picture by Makovsky?'

Katyusha was never short of laughter and at this point, she let
out such a peal that her father was embarrassed.

"Papa, you're incorrigible! My papa and his beautiful ladies!
Well, all right, I'll introduce you."

"Katyusha, I only asked, after all", the judge-papa guiltily
tried to justify himself.

"You asked – so I'll answer. This is my friend Nina Bodaleva.
The one who took the final exams as an external student, but
is now coming to the Institute with me. Nina!" – the merry girl
shouted at the top of her voice – "Come here, over here!"

Bodaleva came across the hall in answer to her shout. The rows
of dancing teachers, grammar-school boys and high-school girls
parted to let her through to the other side of the hall, while those
standing and sitting by the walls cast admiring glances at her.
Beauty is difficult to describe. Chekhov, in his story *The Beauty*,
creates the character of one of the world's enchantresses by in-

sinuation alone – the Armenian girl Masha sows an unusual sadness
in an actor's heart, like the melancholy produced by life in the
hot, dusty steppe. Bodaleva captivated everyone, engendering
not sadness, but ecstasy at her triumphal air, like that of a Russian
swan. It would have suited her to arrange her flaxen hair, now
twisted in a heavy knot at the nape of her neck, in a plait thrown
over her shoulder, or to wear a head-dress with pearls and
pendants, though not one as narrow and fine as that of the
empress in the portrait, just a real peasant headband with twists of
glittering lace and glass beads, above her sable eyebrows and
silky eyelashes, which slightly shaded the brilliancy of her laughing violet eyes. But then, what did she need a Russian costume
for? She looked good in any dress; if such a beautiful girl were to
dress herself in a coarse shift down to her heels, with a blue or
raspberry-coloured kerchief on her head, or with her wavy
tresses simply thrown over her swan-like neck and sloping
shoulders, her appearance would have no need of any artful
toilette or any artificial hair-curling. A healthy, delicate pink
glowed in her cheeks, she had a smile on her lips, a barely perceptible dimple appeared and disappeared on her cheek; her
tender eyes were more blue than her blue dress. Katyusha immediately introduced her to her admiring father, who bent to
kiss her hand, at which the girl blushed all over and became even
more beautiful.

"Why are you not dancing?" she asked turning to Katyusha.

"I don't have a partner", the latter replied unaffectedly,
breaking into laughter.

"Well, then I'll find you one. Or I'll strike off one of mine.
Who can I get you? Oh, but there's a partner for you, right next
to you – Pavel Petrovich! Aren't you going to dance?"

The poor teacher was ready to sink into the ground and disappear in his confusion. He found it hard to raise his eyes. In his
classes at the high school, as well as at his lectures, he had always
been laughed at for his timidity, and vivacious schoolgirls had

tried to annoy him, to make him lose his temper – and one day they had succeeded. He had flared up, flown into passion, and then got up and went towards the door. However, at that moment, he had turned to the class and said quietly and distinctly, his eyes full of tears: "How can you not be ashamed of humiliating someone like this? Let this be the last time it happens!"

The class had fallen silent and the girls had called after him, almost in chorus, "We won't do it any more, forgive us!"

This was no longer the classroom: only one student, Bodaleva, stood before him and summer lightning flashed before his eyes.

"I don't dance."

"Not even a waltz? Just a waltz? How can it be that you don't dance?"

He insisted that he didn't dance. Bodaleva dragged him towards Katya, who fell on his shoulder with laughter, while Katya's father good-naturedly advised him to begin with a waltz, as people suggested; teachers and pupils gathered around them and, finally, Katya dragged her awkward partner into the middle of the hall. If only he didn't fall! His inexperienced feet hardly managed to keep up with the quick, flowing movements of the dance, the ground whirled beneath him, someone shouted "Bravo, Pavel Petrovich!" His name and patronymic offended his ears – it was the end, he was beside the stove once more and his partner, Katya, was no longer sitting on a chair – he himself had been seated, or rather thrown onto a chair. Once again Bodaleva was there; she was not laughing, (he felt like thanking her for that) but, on the contrary, talking to him very seriously: "You see, everything turned out all right . . . The first steps are always difficult. Have a rest now, and later, we'll go into an empty classroom with Katya and show you some of the simplest 'pas'."

"No, no, I implore you . . . I never . . . I don't dance . . ."

All the same he did go into an empty classroom, which smelt of chalk and dust, where maps, globes of the world and blackboards had been piled up the day before, because of the party. It was now a storeroom for school property from all the parlours. The classroom was lit up dimly by a tiny gas socket. There in front of him were all the display-boards, well-known to him from the classrooms where he taught: the Plants of Australia, all the races of mankind, hunters in the Alps. One of the boards informed children year after year about "tornadoes in the desert". Thick and narrow columns of sand were advancing like angry titans upon a lone traveller, who had retreated to the very edge of the picture and was lying at the feet of his camel. Above hung a sky of ominous hues and blue-black clouds. The tornado, with its as yet incomprehensible and unperceived clouds, laid hold of the teacher's soul as unexpectedly as its brother of the sands would have come upon the lone traveller in the Sahara. Katya was called back into the hall. She fluttered out of the classroom, leaving her friend alone with the inexperienced dancer, but bringing their dancing lesson to a sudden end. It turned out that Bodaleva was not so lacking in sensitivity and seriousness that she had not noticed how far her teacher was from being in a party mood. Yes, she had known him for a long time, in spite of the fact that he had never taught divinity in their class, besides which she had started as an external student in the second class, but now, in her higher studies, she had long been attending his lectures on the history of Russian religious and philosophical thought. It was true that she did not think a lot about these exalted questions, but she liked his lectures, she had made notes on some of them; however, he himself did not know her, had not noticed her. Firstly, this was because she had not been a pupil of his at the high school, secondly because . . . because he never looked at his girl students. Why was this? Well, of course, he did look at them, but somehow inattentively, as if thinking of something else . . . And then, sometimes he never raised his eyes at all. Why? Surely this was not a good thing? It meant he had a bad conscience about something . . . That was her opinion of people who didn't look openly and cheerfully at others. "Oh, I'm sorry, she burst out, pausing, somewhat, "I'm being very bold, telling you all this. You're not offended?" Nina asked this sincerely, in answer to which he blushed all over and immediately raised his eyes to her. – "Something on my conscience? You really think I have something on my conscience? Oh no, you're wrong. Go on, look in my eyes, do I have anything evil on my conscience?"

Now they both gazed at each other, staring fixedly into one another's quivering pupils, until she was the first to break off this mysterious and daring communion.

"Well, all right, I believe you don't have anything on your conscience . . . I believe you, you have such . . . such eyes" – she found it difficult to be specific – "as if they had bright little coals gleaming in them . . . you couldn't hide from them, from their sight. You're so quiet and timid, but when I look closer, it's just like coals gleaming in a dark fireplace in winter . . ."

He slowly looked away and finally succeeded, with difficulty, in averting his eyes from her gaze. . . . But why, she asked, why had he chosen to teach such a subject – theology? After all, she had heard that he was by profession a philologist. Why did he not teach literature, or history?

He shyly shrugged his shoulders – a favourite gesture of his when embarrassed.

"You see . . . Well, you know . . . I am, so to speak, a Master of Theology, I recently graduated from the Theological Academy . . ."

So that was it! Now for her reaction! It was as if she had never heard of the Academy. She even felt somewhat embarrassed in front of him. The term "Master of Theology" sounded so strange to her . . . as if she had forgotten it or lost sight of its meaning . . . It was something important and serious . . . She lowered her eyes and sat down quietly, as if in the presence of the headmistress, or an inspector, or with Father Fyodor.

"So, then, what are you going to do in future?" – Her quick, agile voice suddenly broke the silence again. The rapid flow of words, one of her characteristics, did not quite fit in with the flowing movements and stature of this swan-like Russian beauty. It indicated a great inner burning, an impressionable soul and some kind of impetuous feelings in her heart. At any rate, this was how he explained to himself this lively and anxious burst of words.

"What am I going to do in future? Well, in future . . ." – he smiled and, embarrassed once more, began to rub his knee with his hand, but then made himself raise his head and look at her – straight in the eyes.

She was gazing at him attentively and earnestly, as if she wanted to know all about him, she was looking at him with all the enchantment of her eyes, her thick eyelashes, the life of her eyebrows, the trembling dimple on her cheeks – he almost brushed against her sloping shoulder, modestly covered by the high chiffon of her blue dress, they were sitting so close on either side of the junior-class desk . . .

"If that's the way it is," she said, with her eyes now turned away from him, as if with an effort, – "then why are you working as a teacher, not as a priest?"

Yes, that was a question that went to the heart of the matter. His conscience awoke and returned to reality. She was right, – why was he still here, at this narrow desk? So, although he was gazing at her again, he said firmly and decisively "I shall soon be leaving. I'm not going to go on teaching; one of these days my fate will be decided by the Rector of the Monastery. So, round about the feast of the Virgin of Tikhvin or a little later, I'll become one of the black* clergy . . ."

Something unexpected, like summer lightning just about to give way to heavy rain and a powerful roll of thunder, lit up in Nina's eyes.

* The "black clergy" are monks, as opposed to the "white clergy" – married parish priests.

"A monk? You? How awful!"

Following this, they both started to laugh, in a friendly, child-like way, which immediately put an end to all embarrassment and timidity between them; he, of course was laughing, not at his projected plan, but at her naive, uncomprehending horror . . . Nina was soon called back into the hall by Katya, who shouted to her from the corridor. Her partner was left sitting, as if chained to the spare desk, pushed into a corner, opposite two blackboards. He did not expect her to come back to the empty classroom; no-one came in, everybody was dancing. She had fluttered out of there like a beautiful bird, but he himself felt as if something were keeping him there. Why was he sitting there? This was stupid. He should get up and go home. After all, no-one knew him or was looking for him, nobody noticed him when he was not teaching a class. But he kept on sitting there . . . Not only did he go on sitting there, as if tied to the chair, but he even let his imagination roam, against his will: "if she were to come back again, then . . ." "So what would happen, if she came back?" – He sharply interrupted his thoughts and freed himself from the confines of the narrow desk; he got up, but just then the door flew open and Nina, breathless from dancing the mazurka, ran into the classroom . . . He stood before her in the half-light like one of the tornados in the picture "Sandstorm in the desert".

"Are you still here?" – her voice sounded a little troubled, "Still here, in an empty classroom, why? Did I drop a silver pencil here?"

For a long time they searched for the pencil under the desks and benches, but it turned out to be in her pocket. And they sat down again at a desk, as if by agreement. In the corridor someone was calling "Bodaleva, where are you? Bodaleva?" "Keep quiet," she whispered to him, "Let them look. I adore hiding. I love people to search for me."

Only at the end of the party, when the lights were being dimmed in the hall and the unsleeping white night was succeeded by the dawn, did Nina go out to the dancers, to smooth over her absence in the final mazurka.

Her partner in conversation, on coming home, did not go to bed. He sat down at once to his books. The courtyard was already beginning to wake up, steps sounded on the stairs and asphalt pavement. Soon he heard the first bell ringing for the early Mass – it was Sunday.

In his room, everything was just as it had been the day before: a book with a marker in it lay open at the same page, inviting him to continue his interrupted reading. Continued! ... It was easy to say that ... Dipping into the Works of St. Basil the Great, when his head was in a whirl, full of absurdities ... bursting with diverse thoughts, the like of which he had never experienced before. Only a few hours ago, he had been sitting here over his books, a quiet novice, – and now? Lord, what was this, what had entered his soul? Had it been sent from above or was it a temptation? He tormented himself thus, his hands pressed to his high forehead. At last, worn out, powerless, he fell on his knees in a corner, where a high stand, adapted from a reading-desk, stood, fitted with rosaries, a large psalter and a wax candle in a candlestick. After prayer, he became calmer and lay down for half an hour, but slept on through the early and late services, until his mother and sister returned from church.

Someone knocked at his door: "What's up with you, Pavlusha, are you still alive?"

"Alive? He's just been enjoying himself for once at the high school party. Well, thank God for that!" – his mother said from her soul.

However, Pavel's troubled soul did not echo that "thank God". The voice and face of Nina, her enchanting rapid speech, dogged his footsteps from that day on. In one evening he felt he had come to know her better than in those years of all-round teaching. She was as sincere as a child, without the coquetry inherent in pretty girls, ... everything in her was so bright, so clear, so upright; she would not lie or deceive anyone. She could hurt someone in a temper, she could get angry, fly into a rage, but she would never lie or behave in a sly, dishonest way...

What a companion she could be to him, if... And what about God? – he interrupted his flow of thought. What had happened to God? He had already spent so many years in secret and faithful fellowship with the Eternal Spirit. Where had that fellowship gone? He tried to search for it within himself, but it was strange how everything that had filled his life, that had concerned his soul, had completely vanished and had been replaced by the image of Nina and by thoughts of her. His mind was full of her and her alone. Once again he seemed to be sitting with her in the empty classroom, not taking his eyes off her, while in her he saw all the joy and rapture of the world, the wonderful purpose of life – so close to him. And she sat next to him at the narrow desk, twirling the silver pencil in her hands and telling him about – what? Why, the short story of her eighteen-year-old life: the pranks of her childhood. Her lessons. Games in her friend's huge garden. The question on Russian philology in her exam. How her mother and grandmother had been so afraid for her, when in 1905 she had pinned a red ribbon to her chest and had marched through the streets of Vasilevsky Island with her friends. "Hostile tempests raged above them," but they had marched on and on, until the young people's march had been dispersed by mounted police. After she had returned home, tired, shaken and weeping, her despotic father had locked her up and kept her on bread and water, in spite of the fact that she was already grown up ... Because of this episode, she felt herself a stranger in her own family; already there were certain friends whom she could not invite to her house. That brought the story to an end, or so it seemed. And he reacted to her account like a priest hearing a first confession for the first time. He absorbed it into himself, he stored it up for life in his spacious consciousness, already so isolated from many things. He remembered – and always would remember – how she had said to him, when they parted that evening:" Do I seem a chatterbox to you? But believe me, I never told anyone before, never . . . only you . . . but why?" He could say nothing in reply to this, staring at her in confusion, stupidly, as he admitted to himself, and then, disturbed and shaken, he had followed her out of the empty classroom.

A great feast-day was approaching; he resolved to fast and calmed himself by meditating on the Sacraments. All week he prepared himself, with this thought in his heart: "Make clear my path before me!" His former world pressed on his soul. He stood throughout the Mass at the back of the church and, together with two other fasters preparing for the sacrament, he was moving towards the altar, when he happened to raise his eyes – the third or fourth person going up to take Communion in front of him was Nina Bodaleva, even more beautiful than she had been at the party, with a white silk scarf framing her face and pearl earrings in her rosy ears. He stopped dead, tightly crossing his arms across his breast.

The "tornado in the desert" did not last long, nor did his confusion; he soon stopped wrestling with his emotions. During the summer holidays, everything became clear between Nina and himself; only one road in life was open to him – in company with her, and with her alone.

However, he himself admitted that, from childhood, he had been too closely attracted to a different road, which he was now leaving. Neither love, nor their meetings, nor Nina's happy eyes, radiating joy, could wipe out his memories of different joys, of spiritual states. Again and again he invoked the past, but in vain: those joys were growing dim and seemed unreal, illusory; they were dying, like an ikon lamp being blown out by a powerful draught from an open window . . . what then was saving him from destruction? What was making the lamp of his spirit waver, but keeping it from going out altogether?

A new sound made itself heard within him. It was no longer

that of his former songs of praise, his fearless petitions in prayer, his hot tears of thankfulness – no indeed! Day and night this sound troubled him, like Hamsun's bell, with its terrible, sad words – "I have married a wife and therefore I cannot come" . . . "I pray thee, have me excused" . . . But as before, he spent quiet nights alone. Through these his former way of life was re-established. His disturbed and strained emotions deepened, became unified and once again flew upwards. Finally, one August morning, he rose from his bed, at peace with himself, convinced that he must make a decision and almost cheerful. After reading through his morning devotions, he set off to visit the Rector of the Monastery. He had been putting off this talk with him, not only out of fear of the monk's accusing words, but also because of his own indecision and confusion of thought. How could he go before the bishop in this state, as he now was – in love, full of longing, no longer sure of the ground beneath his feet? How well he now understood the words "Happy is he that condemneth not himself in that thing which he alloweth." Well, all right, he would say "Forgive me, my lord, I have chosen a different way of life." The severe bishop would of course repri-mand him, reproaching him in the words which he constantly seemed to hear. However, it was not merely a matter of rebuke and accusation. His inner conflict, the torment of his unfulfilled vow, his doubts, which were still poisoning his life and the joy of love, would not leave him and would follow him out of the monastery gates.

A few weary minutes later, he had calmed down and felt comforted, as if an invisible hand had tenderly relieved him of all his hesitation and his pangs of conscience. He was in the Bishop-Rector's room. The cell-attendant had been dismissed. A lamp was glowing quietly before the severe features of the Vernicle Ikon of the Savior, of the ancient Deesis* . . . St. Nicholas looked

* The Deesis is a set of three ikons: Christ, the Virgin Mary and St. John the Baptist.

down on them forbearingly, his tall bishop's mitre shining . . .
And the Blessed Serafim, an extremely fine monastic work of art
in which he was stretched out on a rock, as if alive, praying for
the sinful world, repelling the forces of the enemy by his great
deeds as a recluse. The fir-trees, the rock, the sky and the saintly
father himself were embroidered in tiny glass beads. The little
polished bowl of the ikon-lamp threw its wavering rays of light
onto the wonderful design and the scarcely-visible pendants of
filigree silver.

In this welcoming room, not so very long ago, the first-year
student had expressed his sacred wish to the same priest-monk . . .
and his words had been accepted by the other, from the heart.
Once again he was on his knees before his spiritual guide, speaking
in confidence, agitated to the point of tears, honest and upright, gabbling like a child, but exasperated with himself as an
adult. . .

And suddenly, he was at ease . . . a great stone had rolled away
from his heart. A fatherly hand lay on his head and was gently
stroking his hair: "What have you got to be ashamed of, child?
The Lord knows you. He blessed the marriage in Cana of Galilee
and bestowed His joy on those who married according to His
Word. You are not departing from Him, but coming to Him
in this way. The rank of priest, which you have resolved to take
on, is a great thing. Who knows if the way of a monk would
have suited you? Perhaps you would have fallen away and broken
the strictest of vows? Were you not too quick to take such a
decision, not knowing life and its temptations? Your meeting
with a good girl has been sent to strengthen you in the faith, not
to destroy it. But remember this, brother, the only thing you
need: become a priest, not according to the letter, not in outward appearance, but in the inner man, so that neither your wife
nor your carnal nature, nor any other thing will be able to separate
you from the One who loved you, even accepting death on a
cross for your sake . . ."

Removing his elderly hand from the bowed head, the rector added, in parting:

"Go in peace. Get married and become a priest. Be a good priest, modest, obedient, strong in prayer, servant of all, poor in spirit, merciful, a peace-maker. Thus you will be a monk always! And if you become such a priest, as far as you can, the Lord will give you back all that you gave up in getting married – the monastic life, I mean. He will give you seclusion, and a hermitage, and deeds of fasting; only believe that, whether we live or pass on, we always belong to God, who sanctions whatever is good for us. Whatever happens, we are for ever pilgrims and monks. We are travellers to the land of Canaan . . . to our true homeland, our promised land. Go in peace!"

He did not just go, he flew, as if on wings, to meet his bride. What had happened to those crushing words: "I pray you, have me excused?" Was he making excuses for himself? Never! Peace flowed into his soul like living water, a peace authorized and blessed by God, a joyful, smiling peace – and he accepted it, laughing and crying from happiness, like a child.

Nina was waiting for him; she opened the door herself, but was taken aback by his excited, triumphant appearance. Already she had partly learned to guess her fiancé's state of mind and, although she had not wholly understood his difficult struggle, she had nevertheless suffered at times, on seeing that he was hiding something that was tormenting him from her searching glance.

"Listen, Nina! I'm going to sadden and annoy you, but I must make clear my decision to you!" – She glanced at him and even went pale, so unusually firm did his voice sound. – "As you see, I turned out to be of no use as a monk, but I cannot leave the spiritual path altogether. I tormented myself for a long time, thinking of your fate . . . and of you in general. Nina, what we are and what we become is decided from above, quite apart from our own notions and guesses. My decision came on me all of a sudden and freed me immediately from much torment. You know, I have decided to leave teaching completely. Nina, my dear, think, you still have time to leave me and meet somebody else, to marry someone with the same inclinations. I don't want to constrict you or hold you back in any way. But this is what I've decided – I shall not marry unless it is as a priest. Well, there you are – I've told you everything. Think it over and make your own decision. I love you madly, but I can only unite myself to you in marriage on this condition . . ."

She did not seem to be in a hurry to answer him; she just stared at him, without moving. Her eyes held no trace of dissatisfaction or censure, but she raised her pale brow, her face aged for a moment by a deep wrinkle running between her eyebrows. She was silent for a long time, bending her head even lower, then suddenly, she turned and ran from the guest-room where they were sitting into her own room. He was filled with compassion, trembling with anticipation. What pain he had already caused her! If she had never met him – a man so unattractive, so isolated from the affairs of the world – how deservedly happy she would have been with someone else – someone who could have given her everything she desired by nature, because of her beauty. He was asking her to play, not merely a passive, but an active role in sharing a way of life that at the moment she found barely comprehensible and unclear in its dimensions. He himself, called from childhood to a higher vocation, the service of another world, had learnt early to distinguish the nearness and reality of that other order of things; he had already reached the point of self-renunciation, and now he was in the process of uniting himself in marriage – and to whom? To a young, beautiful girl, a student of the Women's Courses at the University, his own pupil. True, she was a religious believer and would never laugh at things he considered sacred, but she had only just discovered the world of impulsive and alluring passions. Life was calling to her in all its ringing, clamouring spring voices. These poured out like the chirping song of birds in the Maytime greenery.

The door to her room remained half-open. He had never yet entered it and knocked timidly. There was no reply. He crossed the threshold – where could Nina be? For a moment he was perplexed, but then he noticed that a curtain, behind which some dresses were hanging, was swaying from someone's movements. "Nina!" A sobbing voice answered at once, angrily: "What do you want?" Was it he who stepped towards the curtain? Or did she draw back the curtain herself? What happened in that second? A silky, dark-red lock of hair was pressed against his palms, his breath touched a hot, wet cheek. Never, not once so far had he dared to embrace her so closely and fervently. Their tears flowed. For the first time since he had known her, she – so bright and self-confident, always happy – was weeping helplessly in front of him. "Nina!" These were, after all, his tears and his difficulties, which he had been passing on to her since their first day together. They stood for a long time, united in this unexpected, unlooked-for way; suddenly, she stepped back and slipped out of the circle of his arms, "You're holy, a saint, – I can't. You're too good for me. I'm a bad, ordinary girl, I only love you in my own way, no more. . ."

"But, dearest, you must understand that's what I need . . . No one could wish for anything more. What sort of saint am I? I've left the monastic life. I've decided to marry. . ."

She was already wiping away her last tears; she looked at him craftily, a smile growing on her lips.

"You've got a beard like a monk's. Your eyes are just like a monk's. Bright eyes, like coals in a fire . . . And what am I?"

He put his arms round her again and pulled her closer to himself.

"What are you? – You're my beauty, my joy! You're everything to me . . . But we're talking nonsense, my dear, we're not getting to the point. Are you with me, or are you going to leave me? Speak out sharply and decisively, wound me to the heart,

but I must know. I don't demand anything from you, I don't
expect you to be a saint or to force yourself to do anything, not
at all. Be Nina. Blossom like a flower, sing like a bird, shine out
like a star. And live with me, brightening my days . . ."

Still she kept on thinking about something and worrying,
wrinkling her eyebrows. Then, suddenly, she let fly a whole
volley of doubts: she couldn't and didn't know how to be a
"little mother" or to play the role of "priest's wife" in his life.
She wanted to finish her studies. She liked children and wouldn't
mind becoming a teacher. But then, – well, let him think her
light-minded, but she had to defend her point of view – what
about the theatre? She loved the theatre, the opera, plays, so
much . . . And then there was the ballet? Would he really never
accompany her to the theatre or to visit friends, but just stay at
home all the time? And everywhere she would be sitting about
alone, not with him, but with strangers . . . After all, he wouldn't
be coming with her in his . . . in that new garment of his? And
then they might suddenly give him a parish in some village, and
they would both have to move to the countryside. She couldn't
live for long in the country, especially in autumn, when the rains
began. And then there would be the village way of life – salting
food, making jam . . . She didn't know how to keep house at
all, and they couldn't take her mother with them to a village, as
she was used to town life. He immediately began to refute her
troubled arguments, point by point. They wouldn't leave town
at all. He would go to the rector, hand in a declaration, make a
request to the bishop – and they would go on living in town. He
would be given a small church here, in Petersburg itself. She
would go on studying, as she wanted to, and would finish her
studies. Once and for all he promised her full, unfettered freedom
as an individual. Never, in any circumstances, would he allow
himself to force her to do anything. He would never put pressure
on her to take any decision. He only wanted her to become his
youth and comfort. For himself he wanted only one thing – to be a

priest, so that he could devote his whole life to the priestly task, but he would not lay his spiritual burdens on anyone else's shoulders. He would bear his own labours, with God's help. If she herself wanted to participate in his life, she would be a help-meet and companion in everything, but if not, she would go her own way and he would hardly make himself into an obstacle blocking her path.

So they declared their feelings to each other. Nina beamed. What a wonderful person her Pavlik was! He was going to accompany her everywhere; they would go to the theatre – he would wear ordinary clothes; they were not moving to a village. She would finish her studies in a year's time. And how modest his own request had been: that she should not bother him to go out with her to worldly events on church feast-days. Then she would go to parties or to the theatre alone, or with a girl-friend. In a word, their relationship had been clarified and everything else followed as if decreed: the announcement of intention, the courtship, the engagement ... presents, the family ... and, finally, the wedding, which was followed a few days later by a solemn "Worthy is he."* He was ordained as a deacon and then as a priest and was assigned to an official position at the small Church of the Iberian Mother of God at the Institute ... And if the unavoidable moments of fuss and bother, the crowds of people and foretastes of married life inhibited his will somewhat, did love itself not spread out its great, powerful wings above his shoulders?

After that ... as he remembered in the sleepless nights of his imprisonment ... his moments of happiness were interrupted by long periods of discord and some kind of uneasy boredom. Why was this? Now life itself was strictly calling him to account – but he was not afraid of its judgement. He had time to remember and to analyse his memories. His thoughts turned first of all to

* "Worthy is he": this is part of the ordination service for the priesthood, when the candidate is acclaimed as "ἄξιοξ" (worthy).

the bright, impressionable days when there were no "buts." Are differences of opinion excluded from marriage? Do quarrels not make reconciliation all the sweeter? There were, after all, times when peace had reigned between them. Had Nina not been a joy in his life, a migratory bird of brief earthly happiness? He had lived with her for almost twenty years of his life as a priest. Why then was he asking himself this anguished question: "had he been happy with her?"? And how could he answer it? If happiness implied peace of mind, he had never been at peace.

If happiness was a harmonious duet of two voices, then their voices were always at variance.

Finally, if happiness meant a life-long union, then both he and had remained single.

However, if happiness meant intoxication, exhilaration, ecstasy, – then yes, he had been happy with her.

And if happiness included only moments of mutual communion, there had been such short moments: illusory and beautiful visitations. During the brief minutes of such visitations, he had rejoiced in the sun, the spring, the golden autumn, her elegant new dress, and in the fact that she was there beside him.

These inroads of happiness were superseded by worries, and at first these mainly concerned his wife. Was Nina happy with him?

She led a permanently busy life, but a life different from his own. Her life resolved around her work and the inspiration she derived from it, while his life consisted of crowded pastoral activity, which he had to undertake but accepted in spirit; in fact he used to get so involved in it that sometimes he became alarmed when he thought of his wife – where was Nina and what was she doing? Then he had to drag himself away from people somehow and hurry home to her, but after only one year it became more difficult for him to drag himself away. Her voice developed a sting: "What happened to you?" "Where have you been?" "Forgot everything else in the world again, did you?"

She looked after him solicitously and in her care for him she showed her qualities not only as a wife, but also as a mother – she had a maternal instinct towards him, as God had not given them any children. When he was ill, she kept away from him all those who might annoy or disturb him and, as far as she could, she guarded him during the hours he spent working at home.

They why should such questions come into his mind now, at the end of his road in life, troubling his soul? Why was he clutching painfully at his prematurely balding head, thinking of her?

She did not become a sisterly wife to him . . . But then, he could not have expected anything else from her, once he had invited her to come into his life as a songbird, a flower adorning his existence. It was precisely this kind of wonderful flower that she grew into. Wherever the young couple appeared, Nina won universal admiration, while he stood in the shadow. He was even glad of this. Especially in the early days of their life together, he reacted with painful sensitivity to his new relations and acquaintances. He had renounced worldly pleasures too sincerely in the past to be able calmly to accept the new way of life. He got used to it gradually and recognized his new position in the world, as a husband with a young bride. However he could not fully accept such a role or feel himself happy and contented in it. It was as if he were being forced to become someone different from what he ought to be, and he walked as if bewitched by her voice, but his secret inner self did not consent to this behaviour.

Those first days were unforgettably lit up in his memory. They had been like children – and he had become a child at the age of thirty-two – creating a terrible racket at times; she would knock over a chair, grab the cushion and begin to rock it like a child, while he would be touched by these motherly movements of hers. Suddenly the lamp went out from the draught caused by her arm swinging; he lit the wick again at once, but she pulled him towards her by the sleeve, there was another awkward movement and the light went out again. "Let me go, Nina, this is silly!" He tried to light it again but a rosy, warm cheek was rubbing against his own, one of her wavy curls was softly stroking his ear – and his hand fell. How could he forget that time, their wonderful spring?

Other things, however, also remained in his memory. A January of snow-storms in the third year of their life together. She had seated herself besides the window with her exercise books and had gone as quiet as a little mouse. Now he too was free to withdraw himself from her existence into the depths of his own soul. The Philokalia lay before him, and he retreated wholly into that world which he had grown accustomed to inhabiting since his childhood: "The abbot Joseph was living in silence in the desert of Lower Egypt ... One day the abbot Lot visited him and said to him: "Father, according as I am able, I keep my little rule of prayer and I observe a moderate fast. I strive to observe purity, avoiding sinful thoughts. What more should I do?"

The elder rose to pray and stretched out his hands to heaven, and his fingers became like ten lamps of fire. And he said to the abbot Lot "If you wish to – be totally changed into fire.""

The priest Pavel read this, and his heart, the heart of a former novice monk, burned within him, like the ten fiery lamps of the abbot Joseph. He lost sight of everything except that wonderful holy legend. Silently, in the nearest corner of the room, his tall figure approached the icon-stand. He fell on his knees, reciting the prayers before sleeping, his tears fell on to his new cassock; how long this lasted only Nina knew. He remembered how her sobs had unexpectedly filled the room. He turned round – the exercise books were lying on the floor and she was crouched down in her chair, weeping bitterly. He went up to her, alarmed, wondering what had happened. What was the matter with her? Her tearful voice trembled with indignation: "You've forgotten about me!"

He now understood, more clearly than ever before, what a great, half-stifled emotion, now gone for ever, they had experienced in their lives. He had loved her not only as a wife, but with the special, unique love of an affectionate father for his grown-up daughter, for she was some fourteen years younger than him. He could not deny that the years he had spent with his wilful beauty of a wife had led him along a thorny path, but nevertheless they had lived together for almost twenty years. He had learnt to give in. Earlier he had made these concessions indulgently, hardly considering them to be his fault, but now every compromise wounded his conscience. Sunday . . . two seats in a friend's box at the opera . . . they were invited. "I won't go without you," she said to him. "I'm not coming without him," she told her friends on the telephone. On Sunday! Even if it was Tchaikovsky, Glinka or Rubenstein, he was still a former monk inwardly and was now a priest . . . What music could satisfy his soul today, after he had performed the liturgy? But he went along. She was young, she wanted to go 'everywhere with him'; her promise not to infringe the feast-days was forgotten. He changed and went with her to the theatre. And so his surrender began, at first in small things, then in greater ones, finally in everything, in all things. . .

So the years went by. After the small church at the Institute, he was given a large parish. Already a mitred priest, he was now serving as a full-time arch-priest. He had grown a little fatter and suffered from shortness of breath. He was a popular pastor. All kinds of people came to his church: young people, children, the old. He had many spiritual children and one of these was his own niece Alya, the daughter of his sister Masha, that same sister with whom as a child he had once gone off to lead a life of prayer.

In the years just after the October upheaval, the church went through a period of especial renewal and upsurge. It seemed to be extending itself and laying the foundations for long years of peace and spiritual growth. No-one imagined there would be any change in the near future. Parish life blossomed. On the one hand, fellowships were being organized; on the other hand, talented preachers were appearing, attracting the religious masses of the people, those searching for a meaning and purpose in life. Children's Christmas trees, house prayer meetings, lectures and discussions were constantly springing up in that amazing period of time. It was as if someone had untied all knots and freed religious thought from its bonds. The names of the best professors of theology adorned the recently re-opened study-courses. The Western Catholic and Protestant communities did not lag behind. Everywhere there was a flowering of freedom of religious expression, freedom of assembly; fellowships blossomed, congregational involvement grew.

The archpriest Pavel's family life also opened out joyfully. Young people gathered at his house on Thursdays to read the Philokalia together, to discuss the works of Bishop Feofan and listen to lectures. And when he was leading the meeting, it seemed to Nina that she was once again his pupil, that they were once again standing together on the staircase landing at the high school. Gradually she began to take an interest in listening to the youth meetings and even sometimes took part; once she even read a lecture which turned out to be one of the best. . .

"Nina, take Alya under your wing; she's dying to perform rash exploits," said Father Pavel, joking with his niece. Alechka didn't like jokes, not even her uncle's, but she adored her uncle. "Why exploits?" The girl's dark eyebrows drew together – "I'm saying it should be all or nothing! Either we should go on to the end or stay on the spot!" Everyone at the table then fell silent and only he, Pavel, recognizing again Alya's profound zeal and purity, spoke thoughtfully to her: "That's true, Alya . . ."

In those years, he never imagined that a few years later his charming Nina, would find it as easy to join the anti-religious movement as she had to give a lecture on Feofan the Recluse and Symeon the New Theologian . . . But that was what happened:

as freely and actively as she had prepared sermons together with
her husband in the first years of their marriage, she now began
to write articles for a journal, edited a new anthology of authors,
together with two other teachers, and at the same time organised
a 'Godless' corner in her school, presenting herself to the children
as a new being, fighting against the Creator.

Now Nina had her own circle of friends and he had his. The
Thursday youth meetings were ended – they could not go on.
Nina did not come to the church where he worked – she couldn't.
And her husband ceased to accompany her anywhere, even in
ordinary clothes, – he couldn't. At school she was criticised ever
more firmly and severely because of his position as an arch-priest.
Meanwhile, the school was growing ever more important to
her, with her new acquaintances and way of life. She found all
the more obscure the radiance of former years, the lamplight of
their first years of marriage, when she had prepared Sunday
school talks together with her admired new father. He remembered the printed draft copies of those small grey books – the
publication of his *Mysticism of Symeon the New Theologian*. His
work was in print! He was one of the company of priest philo-
sophers, writers and poets, a company unnoticed by and unknown to the world. The grey books passed rapidly from hand
to hand among religious young people. He wrote a great deal,
in secret, at night – when Nina was asleep, resting from her
labours among her pupils.

How, in fact, had their last disagreement begun? They had no
children, and perhaps it was he himself who had nurtured in her
a love for her pupils and children in general, who had taught her
to redirect her maternal feelings 'towards these little ones,'
towards the children of her homeland, the people of the future,
the new generation. Had he not fostered such views in her? He
believed that these children, brought up in godlessness, would
find new ways of coming to know God, ways both original and
wise. The true life, unseen but real, would make itself known to

them in signs and indications, by a comparison of cause and effect, through the flow of their seemingly real and obvious life.

Her husband's conciliatory attitude annoyed Nina. She argued weightily and convincingly with everyone, heatedly and even irritably trying to prove to them that the schools could not and must not be other than they were ... What do you mean by saying "We submit to the spirit of the times"? What do you mean by "We approach many things in a different way"? What kind of "different" approach can you have? What kind of "mysteries" are you pitting against reality?" – Nina asked agitatedly, when they could finally find some time alone together, although they were both tired. "For you, the new school is some sort of new cross to bear, a problem, which you must reconcile yourself to somehow, which you have to understand as something different from what it really is. For me, the school of our times is the living truth: there can be no other way for children to be educated after the revolution. Other ways are obsolete." "Even the Eternal God?", he retorted, "is the Creator of the whole world obsolete as well?" She tried to reply, but some new, as yet incomprehensible emotion prevented her. Finally, overcoming her agitation, she sprang to her feet and began to walk about the room:

"We are now the creators, Pavel! Now it's our turn to create and build. We're building a new world, a beautiful world, for all mankind. Everyone will support it; it will destroy outworn customs, ossified narrow-mindedness . . ."

"So you're going away? If you no longer accept His aid? Is that what you mean, Nina?"

"I don't know what I mean; perhaps I really am going away now. But you – you're a progressive man, a philosopher and you can't distinguish the laws of dynamic movement, which govern the whole world . . ." He gave a bitter laugh. "Say anything you like, but don't call me "progressive". I'm now an outcast from society, a heretic, but above all I am a priest. I even find it strange that you should get so upset about my opinions. You're the one who has to create this new life, not I. I don't intend to depart one iota from my chosen path or from my faith in the workings of Providence. I can quite understand that you can't accept such a point of view, that it's against your inner convictions, because of circumstances, because of the legal requirements in that school of yours – well, all right! But what I can't believe is that you are denying it all completely, that you're echoing Peter's words "I know not the Man" – no, that I can't believe! I know you in your heart . . . I hope that it will guide you when you waver or hestitate, to know truth from falsehood."

He stroked her soft, wavy, thick hair, with its barely noticeable silver threads.

"You're a sincere person, like Nathaniel, in whom there was no guile."

Life was breaking apart; victims were in demand. A decision was being taken on the routine matter of expelling the clergy from their living quarters. Priests were among the first to have their rights substantially limited. What were their wives guilty of, if they simply accepted at once that they could not stand this? He loved her as much as before, but more deeply and painfully. He respected her sincerity and uprightness. He excused her sharpness and excitability, seeing only her pure heart. Finally, he believed that she still loved him as before and would go on loving him. However, he would never take off his cassock of his own free will. He would never renounce his calling, even if the cathedral in which he served was closed, like many other churches which had ceased to function. Nevertheless, he decided to go to the Registrar's Office without her knowledge. Before taking this step he had thought it over a great deal . . . how she would be better off if she were freed from his laughable figure, unwanted by modern society. If she were free, she could follow a path of her own choosing . . . with anyone she wanted. He had never prevented anyone from doing anything, least of all her.

At the Registrar's Office, a young girl sitting behind a table in the divorce section asked him for his reasons. The question was laughable, in a childish way, when addressed to the middle-aged man attentively watching her. He answered her quite simply, in a childlike way.

"My wife is a young woman, a teacher. She has to live and work. I don't want to hinder her, either because of my appearance or because of my job."

The divorce document soon arrived and was put on her table. She came back from work. At first she protested. She even wept. "What have you done? Why? I've never reproached you. Who asked you to? How silly all this is!"

However, after he had given her his short, quite calm and weighty explanation, she understood that he had acted rightly towards her, that his decision had indeed been necessary and she began to agree with his thinking. After all, what was wrong with it? To begin with, nineteen years ago they had been united by the church, not by the Registrar's Office. And then, all priests' wives who had to work in schools were getting divorced from their husbands. Socially she had to become quite free from his way of life, so in the end she had no objections to what he had decided to do. He had merely put into practice what she had often unconsciously thought of doing, but had not dared to admit to herself. At the end of the day, the divorce document had been accepted by both of them, amiably and good-humouredly. Life went on as if nothing had happened. . .

The late night service was over. He returned home and unhurriedly took off his overcoat in the hall, before going into his room. On Saturdays she used to be waiting for him with a cup of hot tea. She was not home yet. He went into the kitchen and lit the gas-fire himself. When the water had boiled, he went back along the corridor to his own room. Sitting down at the table, he gazed into the empty corner in front of him. Not so very long ago, it had been lit up by a lamp in front of an ancient carved icon-case, its faded surface reflecting the little flame. All the icons had been removed to his mother's room, some were now in the kitchen, others hidden in a trunk. Pioneer schoolgirls came here with their exercise books, and Nina was also visited here by her colleagues. It had been a matter of course. After all, she was divorced from him now!

She came home late, with the last tram. She ran into the room like the girl she had once been, red-cheeked from the frost, with her former cheerfulness, always ready to joke or laugh. . .

"Where's my divorced, abandoned husband?"

He got up, smiling, and put down the book he had been reading It was by St. John Damascene, on angels. Yes, his eye had just paused on a section about angels: "they are light, fast-moving spirits, with a God-given ability to fly over great distances; they are not all-knowing, but although their knowledge is limited to a certain extent, they nevertheless have the gift of obeying and loving their Creator . . ." – that was what he had just read.

"Where's my dear husband, my treasure? Were you bored? How I was longing to get back to you, the meeting went on so long. . .!"

What kind of divorce was this? Which of them was deceiving and deluding the other at such moments? Was he not still standing on the high school stairs, a teacher in official dress, waiting for her, his bride?

This was one small, fleeting moment of closeness and tenderness in their relationship; then everything went on as before – more and more often he was alone. He would return from the late mass, from a liturgical service or other duties; he would sit by himself, propping his head up on his hands, and think over and over again: "she has her own life and I follow a different path of my own . . . We're divorced . . . Oh, fading vision of past happiness, human happiness, depart from me. Die. . . Thy will, O God, be done – Thine alone. . ."

Love ... perhaps it still existed, was still warm, now fading, now flaring up again with its former fire, but then – there were his books! How many he possessed! What precious personal memories they held! How he loved his books – they had their own unique life, expressive and creative, known to him alone. There was St. John Damascene, and St. John Chrysostom, and then the heavy volumes of the Philokalia, bound in dark leather. He felt close to St. Tikhon of Zadonsk*, whose extremely ancient language made the heart revive and tremble. Then there was the Blessed Dmitry, that great writer of Peter the Great's time. The Lives of the Martyrs were set out in strict order on the shelves. Pushed in here and there or piled on top of the large, venerable works of religious thought were tiny pamphlets or little books, with naive illustrations, in large and small print. These were either accounts of the forest hermitages, or stories of the miracles performed by St. Nicholas or the Archangel Michael, or a short life of the Blessed Sergi ... and all these little books and stories had been read by him, ... he knew them all and could not do without them. They were like a lovely border of scented violets surrounding a bed of magnificent stemmed roses. And finally, there were his first teachers – Symeon the New Theologian and the hermit Feofan. The latter he particularly loved and valued for his clarity of language, comprehensible to everyone, for his closeness to life and his love for the smallest created things. How he had stormed Heaven! How he had soared to the heights!

Now the whole library had been taken out into the corridor, behind a curtain. When he needed a book, he had to get past a pile of suitcases belonging to the apartment in order to reach the niche, hidden by a curtain, and search for the book by the light

* St. Tikhon of Zedonsk: the 18th century Russian Orthodox bishop, ascetic and writer. The Blessed Sergi: St. Sergi of Radonezh (1314–1392), founder of the Trinity – St. Sergi Monastery at Zagorsk, the centre of Russian monasticism.

of a tiny wax candle. And then he had to make sure he didn't forget it in the room and took it back out into the corridor. If she found the book, as she had a few days ago, and began to get upset at its lack of factual precision, there would be trouble again – not that he would be troubled in spirit but he would be made conscious of his own superfluousness in an uncomplicated world – and he would have to take it out again and put it behind the curtain. For she now had to write new books, in a different spirit; the once familiar little volumes and booklets only annoyed her.

Now she often worked late into the night and sometimes, unexpectedly, she would nervously say to her husband:

"Listen, Pavel, do help me . . . Are you my friend or not?"

He would try to be firm, giving the excuse that he knew nothing of the subject matter.

"But you can edit it, put in the punctuation marks – or can't you do even that? You've always helped me – and now what? Do you think I'm doing something bad? Am I stealing, or murdering? I'm working for the enlightenment of youth . . . It's not my fault that my husband doesn't share in my work . . . I never thought he would get so narrow-minded."

Yes, without doubt she was that disciple, in whom there was no guile. The Lord saw such people sitting under the fig-tree. And then he would get up and start checking and correcting her work, the new anthology of authors she was producing together with the two other teachers. They worked side by side, as in the past they had worked on his sermon books.

Now, in his imprisonment, he painfully reviewed the last years of that way of life, from which he had been violently torn away. Those years had not been fruitless, but they had made him suffer much and he had become absorbed in his own world. In spite of the document from the Registrar's Office, his wife was still criticised for hiding the fact that she was living with a priest. Nina Vasilievna was entrusted with the job of teaching the

people – and all eyes were on her. Now she was no longer embarrassed by the divorce, as she had been at first, – she now hid
her husband from the eyes of strangers as if he were a criminal.
Often in the evenings, she was visited by pupils and teachers.
As soon as the bell rang, he would get up and go into the kitchen.
Now and then the sound of laughter and young voices would
carry through to him. He, who loved young people so much,
was deprived of the right to be in their company. He found it
unnatural to divide people strictly into good and bad, believers or
unbelievers, because, as he said, everyone believes, but many
people do not as yet see clearly what they should believe. Or in
whom? Or how? He only knew that he was forbidden to sit in
that room or talk to them about anything, even on the most
simple, uncomplicated subject. To his wife he spoke of himself as
'your cassocked monster'; such a 'monster', a bogy used to
frighten people, could hardly appear before these hostile adolescents. And so he sat in the half-light below a high, dim lamp,
with a book or sermon in his hand; at other times, he day-
dreamed, waiting for them to go. Such exile to the kitchen had
become a matter of habit. Once their lodger, the woman in the
room adjoining the kitchen, noticed the priest dozing off over
his book and invited him in. Her child was asleep, sprawled out
on the bed. In this unfamiliar room he sensed comfort and
family love. The mother quickly prepared some tea and offered
the priest a biscuit. He felt a warmth springing up within him –
everything seemed to be just as it should be. The young widow
spoke confidingly of her life, as if at confession. In this small
room, he saw a corner of real life, now already inaccessible to him.
This simple woman was cheerfully and courageously preserving
her little world, the lamp was burning, her little boy was sleeping
under the glow cast on the cross and the icon. The pastor's
loneliness disappeared and was replaced by warmth and kindness.
However, from that day on, he began to think more and more
often about his divorce from Nina, ascribing a special significance

to the document. A premonition of some approaching calamity never left him. "What am I – some superstitious old woman? What did I do when I got that divorce document? What could I add or take away from the cup we must drink together? Nothing!"

After the death of his parents, Archpriest Pavel had very few relatives left – only his sister Marya, with whom he had once tried to become a pilgrim; she had been widowed early and was living with her only daughter Alexandra, that same Alya who dreamed of great deeds and had written lectures on Feofan, when meetings had still been possible at her uncle's flat. Father Pavel also had a brother somewhat younger than himself: Arseny, an occulist. "Oh, that Arseny!" – Pavel used to sigh. All his life, Arseny had joked and played the fool, like a real jester; however, he was a provincial doctor, he was religious and high-minded, like everyone in their family, but he was no family man and was incapable of leading an ordinary life. He had his speciality, his expertise in the field of eyes – all well and good. But at home he was capable of drinking out of the same saucer as the cat, not washing the dishes for days or wiping his nose on a torn-off bit of cloth and it took a great effort for him to have a bath. Women loved Arseny for his foolery and his sharp tongue. He inspired pity in many of them, who went as far as consenting to live with such a madman. But he never lasted long in the conjugal state, for some reason, – he would go back to a bachelor existence, making appearances on the fringes of Father Pavel's family, dining at his flat a few times, extracting a little money and disappearing once more. Nina did not like him much. Pavel loved and pitied Arseny in a brotherly way. In addition, his loftily inclined mind tried to explain his eccentric brother's behaviour as that of a holy fool. The most simple matters, even utter trifles, which any ordinary person could deal with, were abandoned and left undone by Arseny, although at first he would make an attempt at them.

'Arseny, after all, we can't live merely by the "desire of our eye" and nothing else!' – Pavel would object. But in reply Arseny would point his finger at his own chest and utter the well-known text: "the light of the body is the eye."

As for Alechka, Masha's daughter, she developed a close relationship to Father Pavel and his wife in the course of growing up – they lived nearby, and Father Pavel and Nina came to love her like a daughter, not having any children of their own.

Alya was 18 years old, studying at the technical college, while in her free time she went to church or wrote in her exercise-book diaries. At one end she wrote her lecture notes, at the other her own thoughts, while the cover of the exercise-book was edged by an ornamental border of stars, little squares and flowers, mingled with texts, such as 'Knowledge and Faith', 'What is the meaning of Life?' and so on. And Alya liked to indulge in self-analysis. "I shall end my diary when I cease to exist!" – she told her mother, to whom she would sometimes, but always sincerely, reveal her thoughts. As in many such diaries, the first words formed a question: "What is my opinion of myself now?" This was followed by a number of exalted thoughts concerning her solitary nature and alienation from other people, from whom she expected nothing and whom she did not trust . . . Later on, these thoughts grew simpler and more profound: "I want to express the truth and serve it. I love everyone and would like to do good to all of them". And finally, in one of the exercise-books, entitled *My spiritual life*, Alya wrote: "I have consciously begun to believe. Lord, show me the way and I shall follow it, for my soul is Your captive."

Alya loved her mother dearly, obeying her in everything, but she confided fully only in her uncle. She adored him with the devotion of a young and pure soul, which had not yet known passion or experienced its tortures and sufferings. This love, of which she became conscious at the age of eleven, when she was already fully a church member, never left her and led her everywhere, as if by the hand; wherever possible, it led her away from earthly sorrow and directed all that was best in her to even better and higher aims. The fortunate spiritual child of a richly gifted shepherd of souls, she had known no confessions other than those she had made at his lectern*. There was no hesitation or little wound in her soul that she had not revealed to him, her 'father'. He knew the 'inner' Alya thoroughly; he knew her as well, and saw her as clearly and perceptively, as once he had seen his Nina, for a moment and for ever, when in the empty classroom she had told him the story of her young life and he, enchanted by her honesty and simplicity, had said to himself: "like Nathaniel, in whom there was no guile."

However, Alya was not Nina. Early in her life, she had shown an inclination for the spiritual, and life did not attract her with its promises and far-off horizons, as it attracted Nina. From her earliest years, her uncle's books and views became her books and views, and she tried to take possession of "the unknown homeland". Father Pavel did not find it difficult to guide such a soul and to develop her rich potentialities. However, despite her high-minded way of thinking, the girl had an excessively intense, almost too emotional, nature – like her late father. At one point, she would take it into her head to give everything away and to go away impetuously from her acquaintances and people generally; or again, she would begin to deprive herself of necessities, because she felt this was important . . . The closure of churches and convents made it impossible for her to become a novice early in life, and in any case, her uncle wisely held back her first enthusiasm, influencing her to take a middle way.

The Saturday late night service in the second week of Lent had just ended. Alya made her way to the lectern, at which Father Pavel had just begun to hear confessions. Those who were fasting were gathered to the left of the choir. He was standing

* Confession in the Orthodox Church is made at a lectern, not in a confessional box.

there, looking severe in his austere, black mourning-stole with
its silver crosses, his head bowed. He said to Alya, as he had to
the others, "Please come closer".

Alya went up to him and began to whisper. The girl's white
beret was touching his ear.

"Yes, but what do you find so awful in that? Tell me."

The priest's head bent even lower over the Gospels, while
Alya's words grew ever more heated.

"But, my dear, what harm do you see in such a reasonable
step? Why make accusations against us because of this necessary
divorce? Thanks to what happened, your aunt Nina has been
freed from the reproaches made against her. I myself did it and
I don't repent of it."

"You did it, father dear, and in so doing, you took a sin upon
your soul ... But I don't have the right .. Forgive me ..."

"Speak, tell me everything ... You and I are before God now,
Alya."

"Uncle, you forgot – What God has joined together, let not
man put asunder."

He even smiled. "But how have she and I been put asunder?
Goodness me! We are just as we were..."

He even felt quite embarrassed. He lowered his eyes, his face
fell: ... "We are just as we were, together."

"My dear, dear father! How is it that you don't understand
– you, of all people – that the slightest slur cast on dissolution
of marriage or any other matter, even the most insignificant, as
if it concerned only human law or formality, cannot go unnoticed or uncondemned in that other world. We are not children.
I don't accuse anyone, how could I? Whom should I condemn?
You? Aunt Nina? I'm just sorry, but it's the beginning of the end,
What kind of end? I don't know. The end of what? I don't know
that either. But when someone takes a step towards parting, it
will happen in the end. I don't believe there's any supernatural
power in the bit of paper issued by the Bureau of Marriages, but

there's no deed of ours which does not have consequences in the spiritual sphere ... Please understand that ... But then, who should know that, if not you? Forgive me. I shouldn't have said it."

His answer was silence ... And then he went on:

"Is there anything else troubling you, in your own soul? Tell me. Go on, don't be embarrassed, confess it ..."

A moment later he sighed, placing his hand across the stole, onto her white beret, her bowed head.

Out in the street, soft flakes of snow were billowing mildly. Leaning on his beloved staff, he made his way home through the snow-sprinkled streets.

He was going in when his wife came out.

"Where are you off to so late, my dear?"

"To the Lavrentevs'. Surely you haven't forgotten? There's an educational outing* tomorrow. We'll be working until two o'clock. Don't put the chain on the door. We'll have to prepare an explanatory lecture ..."

Quietly, without driving away his peace of mind, he entered their rooms. The smell of her scent did not disturb him. The fragrance hovered in the air, as if he had brought it with him from the church, not weighing down his heart with loneliness or turning his thoughts to the woman herself. He crossed himself before the empty corner, where for so many years a lamp had burned in front of the icon-case. How long his heart had yearned to be at peace! How well they had sung today "Now lettest Thou thy servant depart in peace"! Such peace had come into his soul, in spite of everything ... However, he – such as he was – was a hindrance to his wife. A hindrance to her work, to her whole transformed life. Once and for all, abruptly, forcefully, she had broken through the barrier dividing the old from the new,

* The educational outing may very well have been an atheist tour of churches or even a march against religion.

going as far as the 'godless' corner, even to the point of shouting the slogan 'Down with religion!'

"What is this? How did it happen? Do not lay this to her charge as apostasy", he prayed, trying to find some justification. If she was an apostate, had he himself not apostasized from the very start? Had he not been an apostate in the small details of family life, had people not reproached him more than once, many times in fact, for going to the theatre, to the cinema, for compromising with the world? It was easier for him than for Nina. He had at least remained, as before, in his cassock; he had not changed in his work, and that was why he was what he was. She was like a cart-horse, dragging her load in life behind her, her cart piled high with the cares laid on her by other people . . . and he was one of those cares on her load, helping to weigh her down, in his cassock and cross.

And Nina once again grew in his estimation. She developed and grew into a great image representing the wonderful, essential brightness of a mind illuminated from above. It was, after all, because of him and his welfare that she was performing such deeds as a teacher. The explanation had come to him, and once more their life together assumed an iridescent aura of justification and understanding.

At the end of the third week in Lent, they brought him a cross.

During services the electricity often went dim and when they were handing him the cross, the light went out altogether. It became quiet and watchful in the church. The amethysts on the cross he had been presented with shone on his breast in the darkness, even more brightly by the light of the tiny ikon lamp than when the electric light was on. He thanked the parishioners for the symbol of the best heavenly gift and, at the end of the service, he spoke a few words to the people about the cross.

He spoke of the sweetness of suffering, of that joy which is given only by the cross and through the cross. The storm died down. He no longer saw the house, his wife, his worries. The vast expanse of life lay before him, like a salty desert. Everything in it had dried up, as if of unbearable thirst. A narrow pathway led upwards, winding through mountain crags – at the summit shone a cross. If only he could reach it! At the top of the mountain there were many more houses than the one he had left below, for love of the cross. Behind the cross gleamed the habitations of the humble and meek; there, the Lord of Love Himself awaited the travellers. He stretched out His hands to them. Heavenly flowers blossomed on His forehead instead of the thorns and everything culminated in this wonderful vision. Pain disappeared, thirst was no more, the burning sands and unbearable heat of the desert were left behind, his feet no longer burned from the salt-encrusted earth, his parched lips had forgotten about water – he only longed to reach the summit of the hill!

It was dark in the church; an almost deaf old man was listening right next to the lectern, cupping his hand behind his ear to form a trumpet, while tears flowed briskly, one after the other, from his eyes . . . At the back of the lectern a wax candle was burning in a socket. The preacher's voice broke at intervals, while in the crowd stifled weeping was heard here and there. The sermon came to an end. Amen!

And he went up to the northern doors of the altar, holding to his breast his gift, still glowing with amethysts.

The warm breath of spring was blowing quietly through the birch trees, and they were covered with a scarcely perceptible emerald down at the very beginning of Holy Week, as Easter was late that year.

In many churches the bells had been taken down and the great services of Holy Week were going on in the midst of ordinary daily noises, without any calls to prayer. He hurried to the hourly services on Ash Wednesday. Standing before the Gospels in their mourning covers, he gave himself up completely to that life that had been lived so long ago. In its deep springs he immersed himself in love and, full of love, read to the people of love.

He took his turn joyfully and felt, when he was on the point of leaving the church, that he was expecting something. He himself could not imagine what. He was too preoccupied to recognize his own state of mind, even spiritually, but something seemed to whisper to him "There is a light coming." At home he gulped down some tea and lay down tired, with pains in his midriff and swollen legs. Half-dreaming he heard his wife reading the anthology with her friend.

In the second week after Easter, he was returning from a service – a requiem for an old priest from out of the parish . . . and not far from home he bumped into his wife.

A warm but strong breeze was sailing through the spring evening, and bits of paper were flying upwards and whirling along the street . . . there had been no rain for a long time. A tiny square, quiet and secluded, attracted their attention on the way. They sat down on a bench, as they had long ago, took each other by the hand and he forgot everything in her company – the fact that he was in his cassock, that he was going to a service, that they might be seen. Obviously she too had forgotten this.

All was as before, and the shortcomings and reservations which had arisen between them were hidden by the green canopy of the birch-trees. Spring was bursting out around them and they felt spiritually resigned, pure and sanctified as they once had been.

"I haven't told you yet," his wife said suddenly, "that I was summoned for interrogation. On account of you . . . They asked me if you knew Professor X? I said you knew him. What else? You and he lectured together on the same courses. But perhaps I shouldn't have said it?"

"But what else could you do?" – he replied. They both fell silent. The question of his acquaintanceship with the professor did not bother him at all. Sparrows were twittering loudly. A little girl in a red dress was running after her nurse, crying capriciously and stamping her feet. "Now I shall know what Easter is!" – he wanted to say, but he restrained himself, owing to his habit of not talking to her in spiritual language. He only felt his eyes misting over and looked away. They kept quiet for a while. Suddenly, she moved abruptly away from him. "Keep sitting there for a while – here comes a pupil of mine, we must pretend to be strangers for now." She walked quickly towards her pupil; he remained sitting, hunched up, on the bench under the tree.

In the distance a tram hooted and rolled past, ringing its bell excitedly. The mosaic on a mosque was lit up in turquoise and gold; evening was coming on, the scent of poplar and birch filtering ever more strongly through the damp air.

"Let's go home, Pavel," his wife said, returning, "It's so damp! We so rarely manage to spend an evening together like human beings. You'll read to me a bit, won't you?"

He had wanted to occupy himself with a different kind of reading today, but being full of tenderness for her and willingness to do what she wished, he replied immediately: "Anything you want, my dear."

She took him by the arm, thus annulling the unpleasantness that had occurred through their involuntary parting in the presence of other people.

At the front door, they both took out their keys together, at which she laughed and put aside his hand to open it with hers, but her key was pushed back from within by some resisting force – someone had anticipated their entrance.

Before them stood an immaculately dressed, clean shaven young man, with a military bearing in spite of his civilian dress. The caretaker of the building was standing in the doorway of their room.

"Come in, citizens," they heard themselves being invited, in a suitably cordial manner, "We're disturbing you, but it can't be helped ... You – your name, please ..." – he checked their documents at once and drew up a chair. "You will sit here and not move – that's the procedure. We must finish looking over your books."

The curtain was pulled back, books already lay scattered on the floor. Two officials were leafing rapidly through Damascene and Feofan ... The lodger was gazing in pained horror at the whole apartment from the kitchen.

From then on, the usual procedure was followed. He was asked to follow them, taking with him a bundle containing a pillow and all the bare necessities, as they could not state precisely how long his ... absence ... would last ...

They were so polite to him that they even suggested he should have a bite of something before leaving. He remembered that Nina's hands were trembling. The two of them sat down at the table and – under the vigilant gaze of the strangers' eyes – they drank one or two glasses of warm tea each ... Was it only for the sake of appearances? Or as a mark of obedience? Or was it so that they could remain together a little longer?

He had secretly tormented himself for so long because of the division and discord in his spiritual life that his arrest almost failed to frighten him. He saw the sense of what had happened clearly; the illuminating thought occurred to him, that "this is it, this is the solution to everything ..."

The car drove him across two bridges and through the streets he knew to that building, whose doors slammed behind him for an indefinite period of time.

PART TWO

Chapter 1

A tearful fog had covered the whole street, swimming before the eyes and making it difficult to walk. About half an hour ago, Nina Vasilievna had seen her husband again after a separation of one and a half years. She had been allowed to visit him at the end of September before his exile from the city to Siberia. The short moment of time which had flown by 'there' had shaken her to the core. Permission to see and speak to a prisoner was granted under the following conditions: one visitor to one prisoner, alone except for the guard standing at the door, in a tiny room with a high window, but they had immediately been told to keep a certain distance between them – this was what had upset Nina, almost reducing her to tears, although she had controlled herself with a supreme effort. And now everything she had managed to see and sense during their meeting until her departure from the place, had broken forth and was flowing out in hot tears. She walked as if in a dream past the massive granite walls; as if in a hazy nightmare, she got into a tram by the bridge, wiping her eyes but feeling her heart and head still wrung by sobs, by the question – what was she to do now? How was she going to act towards him? When she was allowed to visit him, Nina had not imagined, of course, that she would see the former Pavel; she had even kept telling herself that he would no longer be the tall, stout man he had been, but the shadow that had appeared before her in the doorway of that room, coughing incessantly, trying to smile with a completely toothless mouth and finally managing an open-mouthed grin, and then his pitiful swollen face, his pallor, the tear-tracks under his swollen eyelids! – It wasn't him.

But how could it not be him? It was the same Pavel, but completely different, a new person, and she had to think of him in a new, different way . . .

On emerging from 'there,' the first instinct of her heart had been to go after him, to leave everything – the room, the school, her ordinary life, to take her mother to live with her sister, to sell up everything in the city and, swallowing her pride, to settle with Pavel where he was beginning a new life, to devote herself wholly to improving his health. Everywhere, even in the most distant villages, there were schools and educational institutions, and if not, then there were nurseries, or hospitals, especially since she had worked as a nurse in 1914–15, like many others. In the last resort, she could work in a village shop, and she was still strong enough to take on simple work on a collective farm, although she was not used to it . . . Hands and brains were necessary everywhere and would serve her in building up a new life.

So she made her plans, calming down somewhat, on the way to the school. By advance agreement with the headmaster and the senior teacher, she had postponed her arrival until 4 p.m. It was the second day of a conference . . . There were three days left to the beginning of term.

She hardly had time to come in and take her place before determined attempts were made once more to offer her extra teaching hours.

Nina Vasilievna roused herself and began to reject the offer heatedly, declaring that for many reasons she could not agree to such a suggestion, that she already had a considerable load of work. When the matter was settled and the extra hour was assigned to a younger teacher, in other words, when everything had gone Nina's way, she was as pleased as if she had actually decided to stay at the school. Always active and ready to speak, today she sat down out of the way and thought about her projected departure. When should she give in her resignation? It was too late. If her meeting with Pavel had taken place even two weeks earlier, it would have been a different matter, but now, when the classes and lessons had been assigned, when the time-table was ready? Who would allow her to go, two or three days before the first of September? And who would then help Pavel by sending him parcels and money? Nina was honest enough to be unable to understand her retreat. She went on reproaching herself for being poor-spirited and cowardly, while stubbornly drawing up in her mind a statement containing all the direct and indirect reasons for her departure. Going out of the school at 6 o'clock in the evening, she bumped into the senior teacher, who handed her some new text-books, tied up with thick string, asked her to look them over and give a quick opinion on 'this anthology here' and 'this arithmetic book.' Nina thrust the books into her case and went out into the street, with her head aching and her thoughts in a complete muddle. Of course the books didn't prevent her from doing anything else, but at home she no longer felt capable of writing a declaration of resignation. Tomorrow not only would she have to avoid being late, as she had been today, but if she were to carry on she would have to concentrate on the course of the day and the work connected with it . . . after all, it was the final day of the conference! She lay down on the divan and remained lying there for a long time, asking herself again: "What shall I do? How should I behave?"

Later that evening, after calming down and resting for a while, Nina told her mother about her meeting with Pavel. She felt better for the sympathy she received, but the collapse of her impulse to go and join him became ever clearer in her mind. It did not augur well for her decision that she had promptly concealed from her mother her heedless, hasty impulse to travel into the unknown. She realised quite clearly that she could not do this – for the time being. And what did this subtle qualification mean? Someone would have to go. She had been told that he was being exiled to the Western distribution centre – to Novosibirsk. He was ill, weak, spiritually shaken . . . What kind of work could he do when he was released? He could hardly become a loader of barges on the Ob river. Nor could he build anything, like a combine harvester. He would need somebody to be near him and help him, until he grew strong again. But who? Who could be trusted with such a task? Who was capable of meeting him and helping him? Troubled by the multitude of thoughts that came into her head, Nina – the very soul of honesty – understood quite well that, in talking of helpers, she had already excluded herself. With every question addressed to her mother, with every phrase that came to her lips, she stepped back, as it were, from her former plan of action. That plan had not justified itself. It had been still-born. It had flashed before her for a few hours of self-willed daring and then disappeared, like a youthful dream. In front of her was present-day reality: the botany book in its colourful cover, the anthology – fresh from the printers, with its pleasant, tasty smell of freshly printed letters and glue, like all new books; her own name headed the list of editors. These things, these new little books, summed up the main way in which she must help Pavel. . .

"Arseny!" – her mother's voice suddenly broke the silence. "His brother. His own brother and a doctor. What could be better? If he wants to, let him settle there. What does he have to lose? He has no land, no children to cry for him. Inform him right away, tomorrow. Let him go out to him. Send him a telegram at once, in the morning."

At the name "Arseny," Nina at once came to life. How simple – Arseny! He would now have a real task in life. Why had she not thought of him immediately?

Night fell. They both went to bed. Nina did not sleep until morning. In the powerful grip of tensed-up insomnia, she re-lived in one night her whole life with the silent, prematurely-balding scholar, who had always been absorbed in secret thoughts of his own, which he had not shared with her. For the first time, her

heart went out to him in overpowering compassion. She began
to consider which of his warmer socks and mittens to send him.
What was the main thing he needed, that she could put in the
suitcase? Undoubtedly, a fountain pen, his beloved inkwell,
the morocco writing-pad . . . what else? After a single review of
his effects and belongings, things he needed and was accustomed
to, she felt much better and more cheerful in spirit. She was already
providing the active help needed, by ensuring that he would
receive all his own belongings, homely familiar objects which
would cheer him up, and she even felt a semblance of happiness.
At five o'clock in the morning she fell asleep; her mother woke
her just in time to get to school.

Chapter 2

The roomy family suitcase, which had stood for years on the old shelves in the entrance-hall, was taken down, dusted and cleaned out. There was a smell of moth-balls from the fur-coat and the sleeveless sheepskin coat. Russian high boots, soft felt boots and a warm sweater piled up on the divan. There was no time to lose – Nina worked fast, for she had been told on the day of her visit that his group would leave one day soon. It took five or six days to reach the Western distribution centre – Novosibirsk. What was she to do with the heavy fur-coat? Should she send it at once to where he was now? But what if they already been sent off? Or perhaps it would not be allowed? And if he was allowed to have it, how would he drag it along on his weak shoulders? In the end, she sewed the fur-coat, together with the felt books and the sheepskin coat, into an old plaid-cloak, and filled the suitcase with warm underclothes and all sorts of house-hold effects. She also put into it his personal belongings, writing materials, books and such plates and dishes he would need. As she filled up the suitcase and its compartment and stuffed the corners with all the small, soft things, Nina kept remembering items that would come in useful and be of great value 'there.' While packing his things, she imagined for a moment that he was somewhere nearby, separated from her for a short time, that there had been no divorce, that they were young again, that he would return and then he and she would begin to live a friendly life together, without conflict or rebuffs. She imagined how, when he received the things, he would joyfully look them over and even smile. More and more she wanted to fill up all the spaces and cavities with something homely and pleasing, so that he would feel – as she imagined – moved, contented and at peace. Finally she put in a few little boxes of calcium tablets, aspirin and codeine – there was no end of such little boxes! At last, the suitcase was ready to be locked and sent off. Satisfied and tired, Nina sat down on the divan, closed her eyes and thought about the best way to send the warm clothes – what if the weather changed? – and about the necessity of putting in a piece of soap and a tallow candle.

At this very moment, Arseny Petrovich arrived. He worked in the suburbs, about 40 versts from Leningrad, and had come in answer to her telegram. He walked in, blinking in the clear light of the autumn sun, and was preparing to adopt his usual joking manner, but Nina's anxious look sobered him. He sat down opposite her, on the rocking-chair, and asked where his brother was being sent, and when.

"My dear!" – his face took on the expression of a devout church reader, – "All things work together for good with us, and our Pavel, of course, with his sentiments . . ." Nina got up, frowning . . . "In a word, my dear, "Blessed are they which are persecuted for righteousness' sake" . . ."

At this point, Nina thumped the arm of the divan with her fist: "Arseny, if you say one word more from the Scriptures, I don't know what I'll do . . . murder you on the spot, probably. Stick to practical matters, how we can both help matters along, and as quickly as possible!"

"Dearest girl! Nathaniel, in whom there is no guile, am I not talking of practical matters?"

"No, you're not, to begin with, and only Pavel could compare me to Nathaniel; he wasn't scoffing at me, but you're not Pavel and don't you dare. I'm not a little girl and you're not a missionary. I can't stand humbugs, especially in the guise of doctors. If you know your own job, stick to it, that'll be good enough for me, – and as for heavenly matters, I got enough of that from Pavel."

Arseny Petrovich heard her out without taking offence – it

must be said, to his credit, that he was not easily offended.
He merely moved back a little and meekly asked "What shall I
do first? Is everything ready? Where are the bundles?"

She glanced at the bulging suitcase . . .

"That's what I thought . . . but is everything there? Perhaps
there's something else he needs?"

As if by agreement, both of them began to pile everything
back out on to the divan and the table. When the suitcase had been
completely emptied out, he muttered as if in passing:

"Of course, the most important thing's not here, my angel . . ."

"What can it be?"

"Three or four things, really . . . But I'm afraid that you
might . . . murder me . . . again, or . . ."   . .

"Stop joking, I beg of you. I'm not Ivan the Terrible . . . What
are the things Pavel lacks? Tell me."

"My angel, you haven't put in his stole, his cuffs or his missal . . .
And then there should be a head-dress, even if it's the most
faded one . . ."

"What would he need that for, out there? His right to take
services has been cancelled."

"As to legal rights, you are correct, but not in terms of his
calling. If he retains his priestly office, who knows what may
happen? Remember the poem "We live in a distant land, a land
without churches or priests, where great hunters and fishermen
live in poverty" . . . He is not forbidden in any way to have
such things with him. After all, these are his tools of production
– so to speak. He will always be a priest, in the fullest sense,
wherever he finds himself."

Her eyes now filled with tears, "Arseny, you're so right!
You've made me feel quite ashamed! I won't murder you, I'll
give you a kiss for your advice. How did I not think of it myself?
Well, anyway, we'll put it all in here, I'll fetch the things at once,
and then there's this little New Testament, and his missal . . ."

Together they packed the suitcase once more, locked it, put

a cover round it, tied it up and that same evening they took both pieces of baggage to the luggage reception office, addressing them to Novosibirsk, W. Distribution Centre, Detention Block, and sending them by slow passenger train. In two weeks the baggage would be there, they calculated. The weather was still warm at present. It would reach him before the frosts began.

Arseny Petrovich, who had immediately agreed to make use of his holidays to go and see his brother, also promised to spend two or three additional weeks there at his own expense. That very day they borrowed the money for the ticket and his expenses. According to Nina's calculations, it would go like this: of course, Arseny would get there before his brother; he would wait for him there, taking care of the luggage which would have arrived; then he would travel with Pavel to his appointed place of exile . . . So, that would mean two weeks stay with his brother in the village or town he was assigned to, preceded by one week for the journey out there, and one week to reach the place of exile, plus another two weeks in reserve, to get back home . . . Unknown Siberia seemed to them like a homeland, waiting to welcome not an exiled priest, but a tired traveller.

Chapter 3

The same evening, tired and worried, Nina Vasilievna went straight from the station to visit the Voinovs – her sister-in-law and Father Pavel's niece. She was troubled in spirit. Her main worry was Arseny, who was unreliable but had nevertheless immediately decided to take to the road. Maria Petrovna heard her out attentively and at once stated her frank opinion: as she was well acquainted with Arsik's character, she felt he could let them down at the last moment. At this Alya, who had meanwhile been quietly ironing sheets, flared up. "But why should you think so, why? Uncle Arsya will do whatever he promised. Why should you think badly of the man?" – she exclaimed.

"Be quiet, Alya!" – said her mother sternly. "If you don't know anything, just keep quiet . . . But, if he does refuse to go in the end, Ninochka, who else could go? You're busy at the school and, anyway, now you're . . ."

Mary Petrovna broke off . . . Nina's divorce from her brother Pavel had greatly distressed her at the time. And now, if she had not restrained herself she would have asked: "What's it to you? When did you think of pitying him?" She would have unburdened herself of all she had stored up in her soul, but Alya's presence and the tears in Nina's eyes held her back. She merely repeated "Yes, indeed, . . . Who would go then? Who?"

With the same fervour she had felt on the day she had decided to follow her husband, Nina spoke out nervily and with some touchiness: "Of course, Maria Petrovna, you can condemn me – and you have a right to – for not going myself, for thinking it all over and asking myself who would then help Pavel with things like money and parcels. Let the whole world judge me, but to lose my position, to abandon 22 years of seniority just like that, to travel to the outer borders of Siberia with no certainty of being employed . . . and would there be any point? Would I be able to take care of him? . . . Marya Petrovna, if you had just seen Pavel yourself, what he looks like now! He's just a shadow!"

Her words penetrated Marya Petrovna's secret thoughts, like blows. As one who deeply loved her brother, she now began to understand Nina's new state of mind. Something utterly sincere and simple, recognized for the first time through contact with human unhappiness, could be heard in the familiar, quick voice. The voice broke off, Nina got up, went to the window and, tearing off a dry geranium stem, said through the tears that were stifling her, "If I could blot out . . . the last eight years . . . I think I would . . . all of it . . ." Her voice faded away. She was weeping. Marya Petrovna, hunched over the table, also wiped away tears. Alya, having finished with the ironing, was writing something in her note-book. They were all silent. Suddenly, the young girl's radiant, bell-like voice broke into the silence of the room.

"If no-one else goes – I'll go to him. Just so you know!"

"That's all we need! Don't talk nonsense!" – her mother shouted at her.

"Keep on going to your chemistry, go on learning and mixing powders. After all, you're within about three minutes of becoming a pharmacist now!" – said Nina, turning towards her momentarily.

"Well, my training won't be wasted, I've graduated from the technical college . . . I won't be old for a long time yet . . .," said Alya jokingly, yet not quite joking. But just then, a thought occurred to Nina: "If Arseny won't go, this could be a way out of the situation. Alya could take his things and give them to him . . . perhaps she would be allowed to visit him and could take him letters, messages and presents. She'd have a trip to Siberia and back . . . And when she gets back, she'd immediately get a job through the District Labour Exchange. Most of all, when Pavel reaches the Western distribution centre, she could be with him for a while, and maybe she could stand surety for him, as he's so ill." So all kinds of plans formed in her troubled brain. A young girl with an eager, sensitive heart – it was not surprising she had reacted as she did!

It all happened as Marya Petrovna had foreseen. The ticket to Novosibirsk was bought four days before the date of departure, but two days before he was due to set off, Arseny Petrovich arrived at Nina Vasilievna's looking extremely confused and hanging his head: "I can't go, not if you kill me."

Nina had already said so much and experienced so many doubts about his resolve that the news did not come as a shock to her, but nervous and angry as she was, she could not say a word at first, then broke down and cried – in this way she vented her anger at Arseny. He stood there, looking depressed, and repeated:

"I have weighty reasons, my dear, I beg you to listen to these unusual obstacles, I implore you not to be angry. You will understand that it doesn't depend on me; hear me out, then beat me."

Such wordiness was not to Nina's taste, but all the same, she allowed him to tell his story, keeping herself at a distance from his embarrassed figure, while he hesitatingly explained the reasons for his refusal, pausing many times.

"I went to my polyclinic, dearest friend, – I told them this and that, I had a holiday owing to me and I was going to take a few extra days at my own expense. They didn't object. The holiday was arranged, then. I wrote an application, the decision was made, no-one had anything against my taking a holiday – everything was arranged the same day, when I came to see you three days ago, my angel."

"All right, go on, I'm listening."

"Well, later, my dear Nathaniel, I mean angel, events unfolded. Man proposes, but God . . ." Nina made a movement of her hand and shrugged her shoulders . . . "I'm not playing the fool, I'm not joking, I've calmed down, my precious, don't scold me, please . . ."

"So what obstacles could there be? You responded in all sincerity, or so it seemed to me, so where was the obstacle? Your holiday was allowed, so what happened?"

"Well, the unforeseen happened. That night the senior doctor at the polyclinic fell ill—·a heart-attack or something. He was taken to hospital at once. Who was to replace him? There was an immediate conference. And who, my dear, my child, did they pick to replace him? I was married against my will. It was me they picked. The whole collective chose . . . me."

"How could that be? What about your holiday?"

"Holidays, my child, are not taken into account in such cases. After all, I had planned to take it later. I don't have tuberculosis or anything, so I don't have to get to a sanatorium right away . . . I didn't tell them anything about Siberia, I made it more acceptable and said I was going to the Urals. And then it was a collective decision, by colleagues . . ."

"Arseny, you really are a lazy character . . . I don't understand you and I don't intend to try. Your first duty is to help your brother, but you've left it to others to help him. Aren't there any other doctors? Why must it be you? I can't imagine why they would pick you. Of what use are you? I can just see how you'll manage things! What a wonderful administrator you'll be! It's enough to make a cat laugh! What reason could they have had for appointing such a good-for-nothing?"

"My dear, it's only for two or three weeks altogether. For such a short time, even a good-for-nothing will do . . ."

"Yes, to mess things up . . . You've got a ticket in your hand, your sick brother is travelling thousands of miles away – and you couldn't find an excuse for them?"

"My angel, how could I make the position clear to them? It's absurd . . . As it was, I told them from the beginning that I was going to the Urals. And then all at once, I was appointed and no one remembered the Urals any more. You know what else occurred to me? That there's nothing simple in life. How much money would I have spent on my journey? And you've borrowed another three hundred. But now I'll earn twice as much, and we'll send him a really solid parcel. We can resell the ticket at once – today. We can go to the station right away, to the ticket office. But I'll tell you frankly, my dear, when they told me at work I'd been appointed to deputise for someone, I felt quite relieved."

Nina drew herself up to her full height, giving her brother-in-law a queenly, angry glance.

"Give me back the ticket!"

"I'll . . . I'll sell it, my dear, don't worry, I'll do it at once . . ." However, he took the ticket out of his note-book, gave it to her and silently left the room. Nina lay down, buried her face in a pillow and gave herself up to vexation and anger.

Chapter 4

The dull 70-watt light-bulb under its plain, round, green shade, such a familiar sight in all institutions, schoolrooms, hospitals and government offices, shed its soft, homely light over the large table, on which stood a tiny cupboard; small jars with painted stoppers were placed on its open shelves. On the other side, the lamplight fell on a multitude of paper squares folded ready for stuffing, on the little amber-coloured scales, swaying up and down on their thin strings, until they achieved an equal balance. Keen young eyes checked its accuracy and then sprinkled powder after powder onto the papers. The lamp lit up all sides of the table and all activities there. After the powders had been stuffed into the papers, the sticking on of labels began, then the weight of the drugs was re-checked, under the supervision of the chemist's assistant. Round the table sat four trainee medical assistants, who had left technical college in the spring; one of them – Alya Voinova – was mixing the powders. Her thoughts were completely concentrated on the dose of codeine . . . she was thinking of nothing else. The weight did not balance; once more the voice of the chemist's assistant became agitated as it had just been about the luminal: "Check your weights, don't give me any heart attacks; you were calling out 0.1, 0.1, and now all of a sudden it's 0.2! Where did this 0.2 come from? I'm asking you, where did it spring from? Are you weighing potatoes, cucumbers or drugs? I ask you – are you in the market place or in a chemist's laboratory?"

"0.015," whispered Alya. Where had those weights got to again? "I'm always losing them . . . Soda, 0.2! That's it! Soon it'll all be done! Soon I'll be able to go home!"

"Comrade Voinova!" – a voice was heard from the doorway – "Come out into the chemist's shop!"

At the door stood Nina, with the news of Arseny Petrovich's refusal to travel to the Western distribution centre and asking for her help in selling the ticket at the station – here was the ticket! Everything whirled round in Alya's head at the sight of the beige-coloured card, wrapped in a seat-reservation slip. It held everything for her – travelling to join her 'father', meeting him, helping him, obtaining his blessing, being close to him, if only for short intervals in his heroic life. She was ready to run, to fly to him, to snatch at the wonderful, unexpected chance of this journey. To run away from here, from this monotonous, grey, everyday existence, to be of use there in obtaining his things, and who knows in what else! There was only a day left, plus a few hours, before the train's departure! She would have to arrange everything – leave her training job, finish all she had left undone, declare that she was leaving right away – and then she would be on her way!

On hearing the two words "I'll go" from Alya, Nina embraced her, kissed her vehemently and began to make plans together with her.

Alya found it easy to get permission for special leave on account of a relative's illness. She was not in government service, but in training as a pharmacist, and had graduated with good qualifications from technical college in the spring. Another trainee pharmacist was working together with Alya and remained to deputise for her. So her decision to make the journey seemed to have met with the approval of Providence. Nina Vasilievna immediately began to give the girl some idea of her real task: helping her uncle Pavel to prepare for his departure to his place of exile, not to mention finding him at the distribution centre; then she was to collect the luggage, which was going by slow train and might already be on its way to Novosibirsk, and when she was in possession of it all, she would accompany uncle Pavel to his train, or perhaps it would be a boat. At this point all her surmises and acquired information as to where, how and when the niece would meet her uncle came to an end. Nina thought that, as he had been sent to the Western distribution centre, when he got there, he would surely be released at once. Or would he still be under investigation? Then Alya could stand surety for him.

Alya's decision came as no surprise to her mother. A mother's heart sees ahead, and Arseny's consent had seemed suspicious to her from the start; so Marya Petrovna at once decided that no-one except Alya could carry out the task properly and honestly. If only her zealous and sensitive little girl did not take on anything beyond her power or ability, she thought. She was so hot-tempered! She would have to try and obtain an extra hundred roubles, to equip Alya for the journey. Marya Petrovna largely conquered her motherly feelings. She did not argue with Alya, did not try to get her to change her mind, or beg her to stay; she persuaded herself that everything to do with this journey was taking place in accordance with some unchangeable spiritual laws. She only asked her daughter – if she had indeed decided on this courageous step and was risking missing an educational year – to be careful and restrained in all circumstances on the journey. Like her sister-in-law, she made out a mental plan of Alya's actions in Siberia, dividing it into weeks, and added up as accurately as at the chemist's the meagre amount which would have to be spent on the journey. According to her calculations, Alya should have returned by the middle of October. A month and a week would, of course, be enough for her! So she did not put in her winter coat. Neither Alya nor her mother considered the possibility of any delay in Siberia; on the contrary, they calculated that all variations of the journey, the meeting, collecting the luggage, escorting her brother, added up to a very satisfactory total – 37 days. All the same, her mother was anxious and, while she was packing the suitcase, shed more than one tear into it.

Alya kissed her hands, saying that God would help them in everything and that all was according to His will. Marya Petrovna knew this quite well, but nevertheless, her heart was still full of misgivings about Alya's distant, risky journey.

Chapter 5

NOVOSIBIRSK

Novosibirsk, which Alya reached at the beginning of September, struck her immediately by the multitudes of people at the station, the crowds like white dust – on the platform and the streets. . . . She had the address of acquaintances, but if they did not take her in, she might be able to go to the House of Collective Farmers or to a cheap hotel; however, this prospect did not attract the girl – she had to conserve her money. She set off at once for the address given, which was far from the centre, almost on the edge of the town; on the way she called in at the House of Collective Farmers and at a hotel, but there were no rooms in either of them, everything was full up. She suddenly experienced an unpleasant sensation of loneliness in the unknown town. She was told that Novosibirsk was full to overflowing with exiles and workers who had come looking for new jobs and good wages. Alya remembered the station. It had looked like a gipsy camp of sorts; the new arrivals and people queuing for tickets sat on the floor in the station hallways and the luggage storerooms, sitting next to each other on their bundles, or simply lying on the floor. Children were crying monotonously. And even outside the station, right next to it, along the deep ditches bordering the streets and beside the wooden pavements, people who had no shelter for the night were sitting leaning against the walls of houses. It was lucky that September in Siberia had sent them nothing but warm days and evenings reminiscent of the tropics. The sky was full of stars, the air was warm. Alya walked on, carrying the plaid bag and suitcase, thinking only of how she must search the prisons for

Uncle Pavel tomorrow ... and praying that the Lord would give her refuge and shelter for the night in Novosibirsk.

The friend who was supposed to put Alya up had been exiled here a year ago and had fortunately settled in on the edge of the town, in a worker's flat, but besides herself and her huge, beloved cat, there were four other people living there, the family of a steel-foundry foreman; Alya was greeted by them not so much with hostility or grumbling, as with pure amazement – where could they put her? It was already a tight squeeze.

"We're not doing well," the mistress of the house at once began to complain to Alya, "It's not only that we're no longer the owners of this little house, citizeness, we're just tenants – but sit down for a while, give me your suitcase," and she made Alya sit down on a shaky stool. "We're watched so closely! You've been sent to this address, to see Valentina Kirillovna, but how can can your Auntie Valya help you? She herself only has a temporary registration permit, she's ill, she was exiled here in connection with the case of the red professors – perhaps you've heard of it?" She mentioned some names – Alya nodded. – "Well, yes, that's not really the point, but now we've got into certain difficulties. My eldest, Vovka, he's only 14, should have finished the seven-year school by now – but one day he suddenly announces at school: "I'm a Nazi" He was arrested, because his friends immediately informed on us, and now they're harrassing and tormenting us ... And you say you've also come here about an exiled person? But what can come of it?"

A tall, grey-haired woman appeared in the doorway, followed with a spring by a Siberian cat displaying a fluffy, positively foxy tail.

"This is the one you sent the letter to, our Auntie Valya," said the mistress of the house good-naturedly. "As for me – I'm Vassa Yakovlevna. What about you? What's your name?"

"Me? I'm Alya, Just that, please ... Nobody calls me by my patronymic as yet."

"All right, Alechka. What are we going to do with you?"

"I only need a roof for the night," said Alya. "For about a week or two. I'll sleep on the floor, or on a bench, it's all the same to me. In the daytime I'll be out, on my own affairs. I'll buy some milk and a bun at the market. And that'll be enough for me! Just a roof over my head!"

Alya was given a place on the floor, on a hay-mattress, in the room of the red professor, Auntie Valya, who adopted a somewhat apathetic attitude to the new guest. She glanced rapidly through the letter asking her to put Alya up and said to her: "All right. Make yourself at home. You won't tease the cat, will you?" The professor's head and hands were shaking. Her subsequent behaviour showed quite clearly that, apart from the cat with the foxy tail, she held nothing dear and was simply not interested in anything else. And when Alya, over a cup of tea at the end of her journey, spoke warmly and trustingly to her and Vassa Yakovlevna about the reason for her arrival, the professor noted languidly, not really thinking about it but as if glancing over it: "It will be difficult for you to find him here . . ." – and began to feed her cat by hand.

Vassa Yakovlevna was a decisive and energetic woman; she told Alya that her neighbour had been 'driven to this point' and that was why she was 'like that', that you couldn't get one word out of her, but that she was harmless and just a bit "crazy." For a long time that evening, when Alya had settled down on the hay-mattress, with its pleasant smell of wormwood, Vassa responded to Alya's candid story by telling her about her own case, her husband's work, her sorrow over Vovka – "he's such a fool, it's no use trying to instruct him! What does he understand?" Alya kept nodding sympathetically, but was really dozing off, tired out after her five-day journey, – in answer to Vassa Yakovlevna, she mumbled incoherent, sleepy replies and woke up only in the morning, when a continental sun was playfully flashing its beams through the whitewashed windows and the good-natured Vassa

Yakovlevna was asking her, "Did you get bitten by those dratted bugs that crawl out from behind the stove?"

She had to go into action at once – by beginning her search. The day was overflowing with sunshine, its rays spattering against the old street pavements and the walls of houses, which were whitewashed as in the Ukraine; Alya felt that it was on just such a golden day that she would meet her Uncle Pavel. It couldn't be otherwise! Such sunshine, the slight gust of wind, the roads beginning to get dusty again after being soaked with rain, which they had not known for a long time. She renounced a bus with disdain and walked, both in order to economise even in small matters, and also to release the pent-up emotions in her heart. People pointed out the way to her – first she would get to the town centre, and there, starting from the main road, she would take two turnings to the left and there would be a high fence; behind it was the Detention Block of the Western Distribution Centre . . . Alya walked on as if on wings – she could hardly feel her legs . . . perhaps she really was flying?

The centre of the town astounded her by its size – not long ago this had been the fishing village of "Nikolaev." She was surprised most of all by the sudden change from unpaved streets to asphalt, smart windows, gilded signs and, most of all, the many-storeyed houses. These high buildings were in sharp contrast to the part of the old town she had just left behind, with its two-planked bridges, wooden one-storey houses – rarely two storeyed, its small gardens, graced by two or three rowan-trees, bird-cherries and poplars, where behind white muslin curtains balsam and many-petalled geraniums bloomed in comfort. Surely there would be at least one hotel here! What an elegant, imposing building! What bars on the doors, what a fine doorman, still young, but full of his own importance, standing on guard! He seemed to be saying severely "No room here!".

"Bank," read Alya . . . "Savings bank. Telegraph Office, Ah, this is where I should be going, on the right of Lenin Street, a long road, on the corner of the 'Gastronome'. Going round the corner, she glanced fleetingly at some posters of a pale pink piglet, and glossy, brown sausages – since yesterday she had not eaten on the journey; she had not been able to dine at Vassa Yakove-levna's, and there was nothing to dine on anyway, the red pro-fessor only had enough for herself and her cat, and in order to live here for a week, Alya could spend only 5 roubles a day – or so she calculated. Her mother had thought that she would be able to get cheap meals here or boil potatoes for herself. Both were uncertain and difficult. Especially as far as boiling food went – on Vassa Yakovelevna's pitiful oil-stoves, Aunt Valya's paraffin lamp with its black mica peeling off, or on the kitchen-stove, which was lit when circumstances allowed – about twice a week, for washing-day and warming up the meals brought over from her husband's factory. These were the fleeting thoughts going through Alya's mind on her way to the Detention Block after her glance at the display-window of the Gastronome – but they could not dispel the wings speeding her on to the prison.

There she experienced her first disappointment. The window of the enquiries office opened. The girl's eager, inquiring gaze fell on the masculine-looking figure of a woman in a khaki uniform, with tin-coloured buttons and a tight belt round the waist, which made her bust crease into deep folds. When she heard the surname asked for, her reply was a stern, watchful glance, followed by an equally calm and indifferent answer – "There's no-one here of that name." Alya moved away, making room for someone else at the window.

A few minutes later the window closed. She remembered that she had omitted to inquire about other prisons. However, the other prison visitors enlightened her: there were two other prisons in the town – one a reformatory for young criminals, the other a small prison for persons being resettled. They told her the way, the direction to follow ... Alya's mood of confusion and disappointment did not last long; after drinking a little water from a tin cup chained to a barrel, she set off again, easily and cheerfully walking the route pointed out to her, and arrived at the criminals prison. Of course he wouldn't be here, but she must ask all the same.

The criminal prison was not far from the centre, however strange that seemed. It had formerly been a garage. The windows were barred. Behind them, adolescent faces could be seen. It was not at all like the redistribution centre, but somehow simpler and more open. The enquiries office was beyond the porch-doors ... once more she received the answer "No-one of that name." Alya had not expected anything else. It was ridiculous to search for him among criminals. She went out and walked round the building, heading for the resettlement prison. Shouts from the side windows followed her. She turned her head – they were young boys, adolescents! And the whole unruly band of them were shouting after her: "Hey, auntie, who'd you come to see?" "We're hungry! Give us one of your eyes to make soup with" – yelled the adolescents. Quickening her pace, Alya thought: "Poor things, they're hungry! And so must he be! Faster, faster, ... I must find him ..."

At the resettlement prison, even at the reception desk it was crowded, stifling and smelt of strong tobacco. The man on duty was asleep on a straw mattress in the corner, in a quite homely manner. At the window she was told, as if mechanically, that there was no such person there, but those waiting became interested in the girl who had arrived to look for her relative in the prisons.

"Go to the redistribution centre every day – if he's not there today, he will be tomorrow. But there's no point in keeping on coming here. They're all collective farmers here." They merely shrugged their shoulders on hearing that "he was exiled from Leningrad two and a half weeks ago," "If that's so, he should already have been here. Without a doubt."

At this, Alya left. On reaching the market-place, she drank a glass of milk and bought two cream-cheese buns. This meagre meal fortified her somewhat, but did not cheer her up. She returned home at about 4 o'clock in the afternoon, but without buying anything else at the market. The prices were terrible – how was she to live in such an expensive town? It would be different if she had a stove; then she could have survived on potatoes alone . . . on bread . . . Musing in this way, Alya limped back to her lodging, to the narrow little street, which tailed off into waste ground, but nevertheless bore the proud title of "Leninist Communist Youth Avenue." She sat down on the stool in the kitchen and was about to let herself relax . . . when suddenly, she heard the sound of shouting coming from outside, together with something that sounded like a large, wet cloth being slapped hard against a stone. What was going on?

"Damned creature!" – Vassa Yakovlevna was shouting at the top of her powerful voice – "Hold him, hold him, Vanya! Katyusha, help him! We'll have to wash him again! He's been bathing in mud, the good-for-nothing! Hell take him!"

When Alya ran out into the little courtyard, the following picture met her eyes: Vassa's children – nine-year-old Vanya and twelve-year-old Katya – who had both just come back from school, had pinned down a squealing, hellishly dirty piglet in a corner of the yard, fettering its feet, pushing it over onto its side and still scarcely managing to hold it down.

"Hold him, children!" – shouted their mother. "I'm going to wash the cloth and brush! I'll show you, you monster!" At this point, Alya forgot all the troubles of the morning and rushed to help. The whole tangle merged into a general effort – Vanya held the piglet down, Katya pushed from behind, while Vassa Yakovlevna and Alya helped to hold him, washing and scrubbing the madly squeaking animal, dipping the rag and the thinning brush in a tub of water.

"Get your hands away, let me do it myself," shouted Alya, crawling along with the cloth beside the hands, which were both helping and hindering her, "Like this! Now for his belly, and his tail! How dirty he is! That's all now. Turn him over. But don't splash me! Vanya, hold him more tightly. Lower down, Katya, lower. Oh dear, he's on top of the thistles there. Is that enough? That'll do. He's clean, isn't he?"

"We ought to wash his legs," remarked Vanya reasonably, "and his hooves, they're really dirty."

"Hold him tightly, everybody, I'll go for some clean water," – and Vassa Yakovlevna rose from her knees.

After the bath and the final detailed scrub-down, the piglet was once more its usual pale pink self. They gave it some food and drove it into the shed, onto the straw, determined not to let it out to feed among the gutters, if only for one evening. They rinsed the rags, swept the path and washed out the tub. The racket and general exertion had dispersed Alya's depression and had even raised her spirits. The family sat down to supper. They invited Alya as well, but she politely declined.

"You gave us such a lot of help," said Vassa Yakovlevna, ladling out some pea soup for her and putting down a piece of bread in front of her, "Every week he takes a roll in the dirt, even if you try to keep him locked up. Now we've secured him for a while, at least. Vanya, go and see if he's cooled off. Has he eaten everything we gave him?"

Vanya went off, came back and announced to his mother: "He's asleep. He overturned the bucket. He's almost human now."

Chapter 6

Instead of staying only one week, as she had intended, Alya spent a second week in Novosibirsk. She saved her money as much as she could, cutting down on her food, and tormented herself by going to the prison every day. However, there was still no sign of Uncle Pavel. Every day she gave his name, after waiting in line at the window, and went away with the answer "No one of that name here." Back at Vassa Yakovlevna's house, Alya helped her as much as she could – she washed the floors in the evening, washed a few clothes for Aunt Valya, darned her socks ... The impassive old lady sat for days at the window, without any work, as if she no longer belonged to the living. The money Alya paid for her bed and accommodation also seemed to be of little interest to her. The cat's upkeep did worry her somewhat, but even so it was not she who went shopping for it. Both the cat's fish and meat and Aunt Valya's own food were brought home either by the children, or by Vassa Yakovlevna herself, who often also prepared meals for her, taking pity on the half-deaf, mentally disturbed old woman. Occasionally Aunt Valya would read a page of *Pravda*, or run her eye over it, sometimes she would stroke the cat, or wash out a cup or a plate of soup for herself – but that was all. Her apathy irritated Alya, and now and again she would suggest to the old lady that she should go out for a walk, or leave the cat in peace, sluggish and tired of her caresses as it was. The red professor did not become angry at such remarks, but neither did she emerge from her impassivity. She would give Alya a sideways glance from behind her spectacles and tell her, as if the words came unwillingly and with difficulty, "I've already walked all I'm going to."

"But it's such a beautiful day! You should take advantage of it," Alya persisted.

"Well, you take advantage of it . . . Go out and walk . . . It's your own affair."

After every such argument, Alya thought sadly of her uncle. If she, Aunt Valya, had become like this after spending only half a year inside, what would the father look like? An unbearable melancholy overcame her. The days came and went in unending labour, not for him, but for strangers who had given her shelter and accommodation. In return for her services, she received a plate of soup, or supper, and was more or less nourished. Towards the end of the second week after her arrival, the fine weather began to wane. Even while the days and evenings remained captivating, as warm as in the South, even hot, the mornings heralded the coming winter – the wormwood in the ditches had a silver sheen and the ruts in the roads were hard with frost. The clear morning dawns were very frosty – there was no time for autumn rains in Siberia! The mist-covered, rosy-lilac Ob seemed to be freezing up in its steely, morning immobility: Alya's patience was running out; it was at breaking-point. The father had still not arrived in Novosibirsk. When she walked to the prison in the mornings, she still hoped that he would have arrived, but, walking through the town centre, she realized there would be something absurd in his being here, near the splendid restaurant and hotel, near the gigantic factory. Even the outlying streets, with their hard plank fences and solidly-built little houses, were somehow unsuited to him. Where should she go to find him? And where would they live? Alya thanked God that she was not sitting on her suitcase and plaid bag in a weed-filled ditch, like some people. She had gone through all the prisons; every morning she was told "no one of that name here." And instead of supporting and caring for her dear uncle, she was feeding an invalid old woman, scorching out bugs to ensure a peaceful night for herself and the others, washing floors and, finally, in the evenings, going out into the fresh air, into the open, thinking of only one thing – "Where can he be?" If he had fallen ill and been taken off the train, he would be in hospital, if not in Omsk, then somewhere else, but where? And she knew nothing of his whereabouts. Her frustrated longing to take real action, her dreams of meeting him rattled round her head, as if in a restricted cage. Perhaps the Western redistribution centre was a mistake, a mirage of some kind? Maybe he had travelled further? There was one church left in the town, but its fate hung on a thread. Alechka headed for it, on people's recommendation of the good, "very holy" priest, Father Alexander. If she still managed to meet Father Pavel here in Novosibirsk, surely his fellow-priest would take him in. She stood before an attractive little house, hung with ivy and wild vines. A glass porch opened on to the churchyard. The flagstones in the small yard, the trailing greenery, the little path to the gate, thickly overgrown with mint, plantain and chicory, reminded her of provincial Russia. What kind of unknown country was this, where she had ended up? What kind of town was it? Skyscrapers in the centre, the wide Ob with its barges and ships, and courtyards like this.

How good it would be for him to rest here, if only for one week! She went up the steps, and groped for the bell for a long time, pushing her hand in among the green, winding plants, but was unable to find it. She knocked. Someone looked out of the window and boldly opened the door. Alya was confronted by a tall, red-haired man, who looked like a Cossack and reminded her of the deacon Akhilla at the Cathedral; and it was indeed the deacon of the small local church, with its low, rounded porch steps and its narrow, Gothic windows. It was the size of a large chapel, rising above the cosy courtyard of the priest's house and the small barn, filled to overflowing with firewood.

The deacon's large, freckled hand pulled the bell handle out of the greenery on the end of a wire.

"We hide it well, our father's wife is very ill, at the point of

death," he explained to Alechka. "Otherwise people keep ringing
it all the time. If you want Father Alexander, please ring twice,
but ring once for me, sinner that I am. We live in different parts
of the house, it's a big place; our sick mother's* in his quarters, in
his study. There's no hope for her . . . Allow me, I'll take you
to him . . ."

"Will I disturb the father? Perhaps I should come back some
other time?" asked Alya.

"He sees anybody and everybody, at any hour of the day,"
responded the deacon. "He's that sort of man . . . You'll see for
yourself!" – and he knocked twice at a door with a silk hanging
drawn across it.

On seeing Father Alexander, who got up quickly from the
divan, where he had been lying or rather sitting hunched up
with his feet on a chair, Alya not only felt that she had certainly
seen that face somewhere, but was quite sure of it; she knew she
had known him for a long time and for some reason had delayed
so long living in the town and not coming to visit him. Without
hesitating, she told him immediately about the situation she
found herself in, her search for Father Pavel in Novosibirsk, her
vain expectation of his arrival. She asked for his advice – what
was she to do? How could she go home, not knowing where he
was? However, at the first sympathetic questions of the rector
about Father Pavel's case and the length of his imprisonment in
Leningrad, Alya suddenly couldn't stand it any more. Worn out
by her fruitless search, her walks between prisons, her misgivings
about her uncle, she broke down and cried bitterly. Her tears
seemed to be searching for an outlet; they flowed in torrents.
She wanted to restrain herself, to pull herself together – this was
no way to behave – but the dam had burst . . .

"You must forgive me, father. I can't bear it any more . . . I
have to cry."

* The priest's wife is often referred to by Orthodox Russians as "mother," as
the priest is their "father."

"Cry, my dear, cry!" – was his reply. "How can you not cry? Such a business! It's quite understandable that you should cry."

At these simple words, her sorrowful soul felt a breath of holiness, of heaven. The whole supernatural, heavenly, celestial world, with his help, was summed up in that permission to weep. She had not heard here the usual words "Don't lose heart, pull yourself together, it's a sin to despair" – he had said to her "Cry." And she cried from the heart, without embarrassment, freeing and relieving herself of her spiritual burden.

Father Alexander was thinking deeply about something, wiping his forehead with a handkerchief.

"Now we'll think about it all, you and I," he went on. "I'm afraid that you probably won't be able to settle here, even if you find him. My lodgings are large, we used to have two priests living here, and the local deacon, all with their wives, and three children as well. There's lots of room, I could let you have some good rooms, but what kind of people are we now? People without hope. If not today, then tomorrow I'll be taken off to the same place as everyone else. I expect it every night. Our day's past – that's all. My old woman's in a bad way, perhaps I'll have to leave her in the care of other people in the last days of her life. And who will those people be? The deacon won't be spared either, the rooms won't be allowed to stay empty. They won't take people like her at the hospital. Yes, in truth, "the one shall be taken and the other left." Only something has occurred to me about Father Pavel – perhaps he's been sent to the Eastern distribution centre, to Irkutsk? I haven't heard of any priests being sent through the Western distribution centre. From the Eastern centre they're sent directly to the villages where they've been assigned. The Angara and its banks is their land now, but where would they go from Novosibirsk? Up the Ob? But the Ob is already crowded and built up; an incalculable number of exiles and workers are working on its banks. And what you were told in Leningrad about the Western distribution centre doesn't mean

anything. They made out the convoy papers wrongly – that's all.
My best advice to you is – do you know anyone in Irkutsk? You
do? Well, that's fine! You must send a telegram there at once,
asking if he's there. Let them work it out at the detention centre
and you'll soon get an answer . . . What about his belongings – are
they coming by slow train? That's a problem!"

"Yes . . . it is a problem . . . Sending it by slow train was
really a mistake," sighed Alechka.

"A mistake?" – repeated Father Alexander. "Perhaps it wasn't
a mistake in the eyes of Providence. Perhaps we need the delay,
perhaps it's to test our patience. If we live, we'll find out. So
then, we've decided: we'll wait for the answer to your enquiry.
If he's there, come and see me at once, and if I'm still at liberty
and not with them, I'll take your receipt for the luggage; I've
got a reliable friend, an honest worker. Immediately, the same
day, – you don't know what the next day may bring – I'll give
him the receipt for the things, with a letter of authority from you,
and he'll send it all to your place of settlement. But if I'm taken –
I won't be able to help you, only through prayer."

"This worker you know – is he an exile too?"

"There's hardly anyone here who isn't an exile. There are two
kinds of people in Novosibirsk: engineers for building industrial
enterprises, caretakers of skyscrapers – merchants, all sorts of
activists, foremen, Jewish bigwigs who control the business here.
And then there are those who work for them, almost all exiles
and a few long-term residents who are not exiles."

The same evening, after her visit to Father Alexander, Alya
sent a telegram to her relative in Irkutsk, a god-daughter of her
father's. The reply came the following evening, at five o'clock:
her relative had managed to get to the enquiries office of the
Irkutsk detention centre and informed Alya: "He's here. Bring
some butter. Liza."

The difficulty of obtaining a ticket, as people waited for weeks
to get them at the railway stations and town depots, was over-

come by Father Alexander through his friend, who took the receipt for the luggage and promised to sent it on at once to the address she gave him, for a small monetary compensation. Alya did not know how to thank Father Alexander. She saw him for the last time in the small church, before her departure for Irkutsk. The late night service before the Feast of the Nativity of the Mother of God was in progress. The fate of the church was to be decided within days, but at present the two lamps were burning softly, brightly and luminously; during the canon, Alya went up to Father Alexander. When she looked at him, she did not at first recognize him. He stood before her, so triumphantly ceremonial, so austere. His mitre glistened, his chasuble glowed and his whole handsome face reflected light and joy. Anointing her forehead generously, he whispered: "Have a safe journey! Pray for us!"

Her wilting wings unfolded again to their full breadth, in preparation for flight. Alya hurried home, not staying to the end of the service, – she had to pack her things and say goodbye to all her friends, – and then she set off for the station: the train to Irkutsk was leaving at about 11 o'clock in the evening.

Chapter 7

IRKUTSK

Once again she was standing on the platform in an unknown town. The two-day journey had exhausted Alya and she felt giddy. On emerging from the carriage, she looked all around, fearing she would not recognize her relative, Liza, in the crowd. She had last seen her five years ago, as an adolescent. It turned out that Liza – eight years older than Alya – was also afraid that she would walk past the little girl who had been so good at throwing the coloured ball, back at the country house in Pskov, where Liza had lived with them. Now the girl in the blue scarf began to stare at the woman wearing the black lace kershief on her head, who was standing at the entrance to the luggage compartment and was also scrutinizing each passer-by closely. Finally, both of them cried out simultaneously: "Alya! Is it you? Liza! Is it you?"; they moved towards each other, Liza tried to take Alya's suitcase, while she refused to give it up, and both of them hurried towards the exit.

Alya had formed a clear picture of Liza in her imagination, from Liza's letters to her mother. Very lively and detailed (she wrote in the same way as she spoke), these letters described – as if in snapshots – her life, her housekeeping and her needs. She wrote too about her ill, invalid husband, about the prices in the market, her hens, her own skill at making ends meet. Not without humour, always good-natured and anxious about others, these pages were read aloud to the family. Liza wrote in this manner to her godfather's wife, because he had been good to her, had loved his god-daughter like a daughter and had been interested in her life. Not long before his death, he himself had found her a suitor, from the upper ranks of the civil service in Pskov, and had helped with the dowry. When Alya's father died, Liza's letters began more often to be addressed to her; a certain friendship by letter grew up between them, but all the same Alya had never imagined, when reading Liza's bright, lively correspondence, that she would see her distant god-sister so soon or that she would be walking hand-in-hand with her along the winding railway station road towards the Angara bridge . . . It was a bright autumn day. The river greeted Alya, with its steel-grey expanse and thundering sound.

"See, what a beauty we have, as good as the Neva!" – boasted Liza, "I tell you, this is really some river! Look at it throbbing, throbbing like a living heart! And it's so wide! Look at the width of it! At this point, I think it must be wider than the Neva. And it's deep! A bottomless abyss! The whirlpools – you're dead if you fall into them! It doesn't freeze from the upper reaches down like your rivers, but from the river-mouth up, unlike Russian rivers.*"

However, Alya, was interested in other things.

"Where's the prison here, then? Tell me, have you seen him? Yourself? How?"

Liza pointed out to Alya a ridge of hills not far away. An offshoot of the Baikal mountain range was still visible in outline, in the rosy distance. The dim contours of the hills in the sky, in the light of the morning sun which was crowning the tooth-like crags with gold . . .

"There? It's over there?" – asked Alya anxiously.

"Well, of course it's there, where else would it be? I left all my guests on my namesday,** I was having a party, I rushed over there when I got your telegram. I bought him a loaf of white bread

---

* Rivers in European Russia freeze first in the upper reaches, where they are more shallow, but in Siberia most rivers flow northwards into the Arctic Ocean and therefore freeze first in the lower reaches.

** Every Orthodox Christian has a namesday – the feast day of his patron saint. A namesday is celebrated like a birthday.

and some sweets ... they gave those to him ... He's been here, they said, for about two weeks now. And you were searching for him back there? They'll soon be sending them on. I wasn't allowed to see him. Probably just as well. "Who are you? Where from?" I said to them "I'm nothing to him ... His niece now, she'll be coming soon." As for me, I was out of there like a shot. I was frightened, my dove. Once you land in there – you won't come back. You'll have to go there, I'll even take you the first time, that way – across the river Ushakovka. It's just a little river, a dried-up little puddle ... But those hills, Alya, just look at our hills!"

"Lizochka, thank you for everything, thank you!"

Alya could not say more. Her uncle, her treasure – he was over there, here, in the rosy rays of the sunlight, among the misty, scarcely-visible tooth-like crags of the Baikal ridge. But he was in a prison, a gaol. How could it be? How did it make sense?

"The prison's really something, my dear!" – said Liza. "They've done it up in pink paint, just like the colour of romantic love – it looks like a proper castle – if you don't know. And if you look up from the prison, Alya, at the rampart, the hills, the Buryat tombs ... the view from there is like a picture!"

She looked perceptively at Alya, who was silent, thinking of her own affairs.

"You're so worried about your uncle, Alechka! But how is he related to my godfather, Father Fyodor? I don't seem to remember this Father Pavel. Is he a good man? Well yes, I know, they're all good, aren't they?"

"This river," said Alya, "it's like something out of a story. And everything here – it's not real, not solid fact, but something that's always been and will be, which will never disappear, but it can't be pinned down; even the prison is like an illusion, a dream."

"Well, some dream! You say it's a dream? When our neighbour, the engineer Pogodin, was dragged off – the screaming, the howling there was! We were dead beat. His wife was lying there in a faint. You say it's an illusion? They sent for me. And I'm always responsible, Alya, for everyone . . . Why is it always me, no-one but me? Go there, do this . . . And people just take what you give them, but only while you're necessary to them. Now you've come, and on such a matter! Don't get offended, I'm talking like a relation. You responded, you came. But who will thank you? Well? You say you didn't come for the sake of thanks? Well, all right, you came anyway, Liza's very glad to see you. Would you like to go to see a film? Or don't you want to?" – Alya kept quiet.

"All right, we'll take him a parcel, Liza comforted her. "You'll be at peace in your heart . . . I like to grumble – that's the sort I am, but I'll do what I can. I want to be an egoist, but it never works out that way. But it should, How can we feed ourselves otherwise? There's a shortage of potatoes, and the marinated fish is going off. My Vanya lies there, his heart at its last gasp. And you'll see, Alya, how it is with me, your heart'll break, all the values will burst . . . I don't even need to be ill, No help for it. I have to do everything myself. On such a small pension . . ."

Such an introduction to Liza's life was neither cheerful nor reassuring. She was going to be a charge on someone. Alya's money was running out – if only it lasted out for a few parcels. . .

Liza lived in a small shanty dwelling, a little house with two rooms, divided by a corridor, with a cellar, as in almost all Siberian houses. In the hall, Alya sensed at once that there had been no time to tidy up . . . and her first glance did not meet the domestic order and homeliness she had imagined from reading Liza's letters.

Coming to meet his wife and their guest, moving with difficulty in his felt slippers down the wide, slippery steps, was a small, middle-aged but already grey-haired man with a bluish nose and cheeks mottled pink and dark blue. He immediately nodded to Alya and smiled.

"Vanya, why haven't you carried out the slops?" – Liza fell

upon him – "When you heat up food for yourself, your heart doesn't bother you, but when it's time to carry out the slop-bucket, then he's got a bad heart . . . Pour it into the bucket and take it out."

"I'm just going to," the small man meekly began to say, but young, strong hands were already attending to the matter.

"Show me where to carry it – right or left?"

"He's just being humble in front of you," explained Liza, when Alya returned. "If you weren't here, he'd be muttering "Do you think I'm an unpaid flunkey, or may be you should have had twelve little boys?" Oh, Lord, if you knew the way I live!" – she added, but her hands, used to doing everything, were at work, sweeping, lighting, the stove – half an hour later, they were all drinking coffee, and Ivan Alexandrovich had turnip essence poured into his cup. Alya's sympathy immediately went out to her sick, quiet and reticent uncle Vanya. He tried to carry his share of the work, even unsuccessfully, even if it bothered his wife, but he found it hard. Liza spent her whole time complaining about life, about the egoism of other people, while Alya began to feel bored and uncomfortable, worse than she had in Novosibirsk, where she had lived simply and freely with complete strangers. She realized at once that she would be a nuisance to people, especially now that her meagre means were daily diminishing, but the idea of giving joy to her uncle, of serving and supporting him, forestalled all difficulties. After all, she was not alone here; beside her was a good soul, who had known her as a child and could now see her in such distress and trouble. She was a grumbler, and would obviously go on grumbling, about her lack of money, her husband's illness, uncle Pavel – whom she did not know but whom she had gone to help, in spite of the fact that she had decided to be an egoist . . . starting from tomorrow!. And all the same, having persuaded Alya to lie down and rest from the journey for a couple of hours, she was already running to the market, to buy what was needed for the first parcel to be handed over. On coming home, she immediately lighted the stove and put in fresh dough for meat-pies – "We must hurry today, Alechka, later we'll hand over a proper parcel! If only we're in time to get it to him!" So she encouraged her guest. Parcels were accepted at various guard-posts, including the 12th, where Father Pavel was, where they were taking parcels until 3 o'clock that day. They allowed a comparatively wide selection of foodstuffs, without detailing what was forbidden. Every day from one o'clock and even earlier, people hurried here with their baskets and bundles. The bent wooden bridge across the shallow Ushakovka creaked audibly under their feet; white dust whirled across their path, getting in their eyes, – an unpleasant but inevitable phenomenon in hot weather. Because they were late, they had to press on fast.

When Liza and Alya reached the prison, some women were already crowding round the entrance where parcels were being handed in. They were arguing boldly and insistently with the guard on duty. "Let me through, my dear," – "Where's yours for? The second section?" – "No parcels today, look at the notice ... Tomorrow, from one o'clock ... Fourth section? Wait until 4 o'clock, 4 to 6 o'clock. Go back to the bridge, don't stand round here. Those for sections 10 and 12, step up now ... You're late, citizens!" – he said to Liza "If you'd been a bit later, I wouldn't have let you in. You should come earlier."

Alya's fingers were trembling on top of the napkin covering her woven basket. She had forgotten the journey and her weariness – if only she could hand in her parcel and ask about visiting. It was too late for that today – visits were allowed up to two o'clock in the afternoon. She glanced warily at Liza – she was also carrying a small bundle, while her face showed her readiness for battle with any guard.

"We've got a parcel for the hospital," began Liza, "For engineer Pogodin. I bring him parcels from his wife every day. She can't come herself – she's ready to die of sorrow. But a fool

like me can always be talked into it – "take this!" and I take it,
like the idiot I am."

The guard shrugged his shoulders slightly.

"That's your own business, citizeness . . ."

"Not at all my business. I'm no godparent to his children. And
I'd like to stay away from here . . ."

In the end, they were allowed in at the second door, where the
guard sitting behind a table was marking off those who had
received parcels on lists of surnames. Liza asked after Pogodin's
health – she was asked to wait – "the medical assistant will soon
be here, he'll check your foodstuffs."

"You see, Alechka," whispered Liza, putting down her bundle
on a bench, and rummaged in it. "The main thing is to get
inside. Well, you and I are inside. Pogodin is an important man,
even if he's inside now. We'll soon be hearing all about him. And
tomorrow – we'll get inside earlier – in the same way! You'll see
your uncle, Alechka! Pray to God."

Two people came in at once: the medical assistant, in a new
overall of unwashed cotton with large pockets, and the pale
prisoner in charge of distributing parcels. The medical man
lazily put an accustomed hand in Liza's bundle: "What have you
got here?"

"We didn't know what to bring," chattered Liza, "There's a
bit of dried salmon-fish, and two onions. A bread-bun, a cucum-
ber – oh, yes, and this meat-pie."

"If it's all ready, can I take it?" – interrupted the "pale fellow."
"And this basket – is that for him as well?"

"Oh, yes, this one . . . if you're so good as to offer . . ." – and
she deftly pushed a three-rouble note into his hand.

"Could you tell us at the same time where to find him? And
would you allow his niece from Leningrad to visit him tomorrow?" At these words, Liza turned to the guard on duty
behind the table, giving Father Pavel's name.

"We're not giving out permission for visits today, if you don't know his section. Come tomorrow."

"You don't receive anyone here tomorrow. Decide today."

He ran his eye down the list:

"We don't have any priests here."

But Liza would not give up: "Excuse me, citizen, I know it's like that sometimes – it seems as if he's not here, but then it turns out that he's here after all. It's not a week since I heard he was here – he was in the 12th section."

"Why didn't you say so then? So he was in the 12th section! – and you kept quiet about it . . . Well, now he's been transferred to section 10 . . . Hand over the parcel – we're closing. You should come earlier with your parcels . . ."

The pale orderly, who was a prisoner in the same section as Father Pavel, did not utter a word during this conversation. He had been well trained. He was not the one who handed out permission for visits. He took both parcels and disappeared behind the door.

Chapter 8

Once more Father Pavel held a carefully packed basket in his trembling hands. Where had it come from? Who was caring for him? Who could have come here? In spite of all reasonable conclusions, rejecting false thoughts, in spite of everything – it could not be – "Nina," he thought quickly. However, when he glanced through the list of contents, in a corner of the paper he discovered the words: "trying to obtain a visit, Alya." So that's who it was, here in the town, with him . . . He was shaken by his mixed reaction, his divided feelings – it was she, his loving, rebellious, self-willed Alya! How had she thought of it? Who was she staying with? He was moved and worried, but glad – and yet not glad. Weakly and irritably he considered her arrival. She had left her job and her mother and had rushed here . . . What for? He would be sent away, if not tomorrow then within a few days. How had she had such resolve? Such a journey! He could not react to Alya's arrival with joy or peace of mind. An incoherent, uncaring protest arose within him, battling against all that tried to drag him back to that life from which he had gradually retreated. Anything that called him back to that region of dead and dulled emotions harrowed his nerves and deprived him of minimal peace of soul or body, a body which was getting used to lying on a bench and to his almost permanently somnolent state . . . Still considering the parcel he had received, he thought both of Nina, who had not been able to come, and of Alya, who had journeyed here so unexpectedly and, as he felt, so irrationally. Finally he turned to the wall and went to sleep, pulling up the prickly blanket around his shoulders.

In the evenings it grew quiet in the cell. Some people were

snoozing, others playing draughts. The daytime noises had vanished, as if by agreement, and section 10 was silent. They were daily expecting information on the exiles' destination. They spoke of the Angara, on which navigation would cease within days, and of the hard journey to Tulun-Bratsk, and then fell silent once more – only the thud of draughts and isolated remarks could be heard.

Father Pavel did not feel any better. His weighed-down legs hindered his last movement, his shortness of breath and his cough made it difficult for him to eat the smallest morsel, to swallow a mouthful of water. He could not help thinking of this final difficult journey ... indeed, how would they be taken to Tulun, particularly on foot, as some gossip alleged? If only they could get to their destination faster, to some Siberian village – to lie down there and rest and not to move at all. He considered giving away everything which Nina sent him to the people with whom he was to settle – for their hospitality in taking in a man as weak as himself. For himself, he needed only the Gospel, the cross, his stole and head-dress – he knew from her letter that these things were on their way ... To match his mood, some-one in the cell began to sing in a pleasant tenor voice, some-one else immediately took up the tune from the opposite corner and the age-old, gloomy song rang out:

"Ding-dong, ding-dong, listen to the sound of the shackles!
Ding-dong, ding-dong, we're off to distant Siberia ..."

They sang for a long time, with whistled accompaniment, sometimes drawing out the tune until it was almost inaudible, sometimes unexpectedly making it louder. The day was fading. Father Pavel quietly rose from his bunk. He divided the loaf, the meat-pies and the sweets and sugar into portions corresponding to the number of people in the cell. He had already given away the milk, butter and oranges during the afternoon, as soon as he got them, to criminals who had no families and also to the pale orderly ... The bits of bread, meat-pie and sweets lay evenly on

the newspaper, as if they were on a tray. He went round everyone, asking them not to offend him by refusing to taste his gift.
He looked so benevolent, in the old cassock without a cross on
his breast, his eyes expressed so much consideration and love and
his hands were extended in such a friendly manner to everyone
with his small treat, that no one laughed at him as they took
their portions one after the other, while the accountant, gasping
asthmatically, said uneasily, "You should eat it yourself, you
can't feed all of us . . . look how you're wasting away . . ."

Chapter 9

The prisoners in sections 12 and 10 were waiting for their parcels and visits. Dinner-time was approaching. Some conversation came to Father Pavel's ears, or rather, he drowsily tried to hear what was being said, to catch some fragmentary phrases. Someone was relating the prison news – so-and-so had been moved from one section to another, the criminal Mokeyev had overeaten or had poisoned himself and had been taken to hospital . . . To the sound of human speech, he drifted into deep slumber, just a few minutes at a time, as he often did of late, in these oppressive days before the last stage of his journey. He had always been somewhat plump, but now he was thin in the extreme, only his legs tormented him with their abnormally swollen appearance. But even here, in the company of 'real people,' quite unlike himself, something strange had happened. His appearance did not provoke fear or indifference, but one face after another reflected a sort of mild timidity. When he made his unwilling feet walk round his section cell to his bunk, avoiding those in his way, or gasping for breath, swept the flea-ridden floor with a wormwood brush, someone's hand would take the brush from him with rough pity while he, unexpectedly relieved, would gaze at his helper thankfully; then he would sit down on his bunk and break into wearisome, tearing coughs, worn out and sweating.

"Priest – have something hot to drink, here's a biscuit for you." It was the pale prisoner, carrying parcels. He would quite often make friendly overtures to his neighbour, then – half-defiant, half-embarrassed – he would address his cell-mates: "Brothers, do you think I'm giving it to him for nothing? Well, he's an important man, you know. He can get a soul out of hell into heaven! That's what I need! And how!" They all laughed, he himself laughed more merrily than the rest, but his eyes did not laugh – they remained uneasy and sad.

Someone was standing on the threshold, shouting out Father Pavel's name. His dream broke off; his neighbour was already tugging him by his shoulder. He lifted his head with difficulty, propped himself up on his right elbow and sat up in the bunk, letting his legs hang over the edge.

A voice shouted angrily through the door:

"How many times do I have to call you? Get on downstairs! Visit for you." – Once again he called his surname, adding severely "Hurry up."

Breathing hard from bending down, he concentrated on doing up his shoelaces, which had been threaded into the holes of his old slippers, cut to his size. The laces slipped out of his trembling fingers like worms. Luckily the pale prisoner again came to his aid. Finally, Father Pavel went out into the corridor. He went along it, descended the stairs and at last reached the hall, where a few chairs were set out.

Father Pavel's deathly pale hand lay on his chest, feeling the beat of his heart – when would it stop at last? But the guard took him down another passage, turned a key in a door and let him past, saying "Take the second window." This was the visiting room, a wide hall with three windows, divided into compartments without bars or glass partitions. The window allowed one to see a person coming from the door fully, to his full height, and to just below the waist when he sat down in the visitor's seat. Two windows were already occupied by waiting prisoners. Visits here were allowed for half an hour; the visitors had not yet been allowed in and Father Pavel, taking his place at a window, also fixed his gaze on the entrance. The key rattled in the lock, the door opened wide, letting in people carrying bundles and baskets and a young girl in a blue headscarf, with a huge basket in her hand – like a bright vision – rushed towards the second window.

At first, no words would come. They stood almost touching, so close that Alya could hear his heart beating and could touch his hand. But she merely gazed at him, whispering through tears:

"Father! My dear father!"

"How did you get here?" – he managed to say at last, hoarsely, with a dry throat. "Such a distance . . . and you decided . . ."

She would have recognized him at any time, anywhere. Even if he did not look like himself, in different clothes. Here, on the street? It wouldn't have made any difference. His brow, his beard, his features . . . it was he, and yet – he was different. He was thinner, his shoulder blades and collar-bone outlines were more prominent, and his face seemed quite new and strange to her – pale yellow all over, his lips and the bridge of his nose had a blue tinge; his eyes – formerly bright – were now dull and bloodshot, – and why was he coughing all the time?

Still admitting reality only faintly, but rushing into the new situation headlong, as young people do, Alya asked him anxiously:

"Why are you coughing so? Have you caught a cold?"

He lifted his dulled eyes to look her in the face, then transferred his gaze, it seemed to her, to a large fly crawling along the partition and, as if dismissing the subject, like someone not wanting to give away secrets, he let fall some words, like a person who lets something drop out of his hands unexpectedly:

"I'm tired to death, Alechka."

The journey, illness, lack of food – was her reaction, and she hastily asked him, without understanding properly what he had said:

"What is it from, Uncle Pavel? Was the journey hard?"

He seemed to come to himself.

"No, it's just like that, Alya . . . Don't worry. It's all over now. Now I've only got to reach my destination."

"Everyone sends you their respects and greetings," Alya hurried to say, "They all remember and love you and pray for you" – she went through the names, transmitted their words of sympathy and their good wishes, but he seemed to be taking it all in rather hazily. He was listening to her, even trying to smile, but she realised she was not saying the right thing, in the right way . . .

For an instant, his defences broke down. From his eyes, as if squeezed out, the two first tears ran down, followed by more, hurrying down in streams. He tried to find his handkerchief, which he had forgotten in the cell; Alya gave him hers, he took it but he stood as if numb, holding the handkerchief, not making use of it.

"Nina?" – he stammered out . . . "Mother? Are they all right?"

She hastily reassured him, held out a packet of letters and, understanding his new position more and more, she realised that she would have to do the talking, to make things easy – the minutes were going by, there was no time to waste . . ."

"Father dear," she moved towards him, holding back her tears, "I have here . . . a package . . . of medicines . . . You're coughing so, you've cought cold . . . you look through it all, everything's written on the medicines . . . Aunt Nina and I got it all together, and here's another letter from her that I was to give you 'personally'. Put it somewhere safe, in your breast-pocket, yes, in that pocket! Well, what else do I have? – Here's some jam and buns – don't forget them! Here's some condensed milk, cheese . . . eggs, home-made pies . . . Here are some en-velopes and stamps for you . . ." The basket was in her hands, on the other side of the partition, – time was running out. The guards at the doors were not looking. Alya held out her hands to him and whispered "Bless me." Immediately, with no fear of those around him, he blessed her. She covered the hand he had given her with kisses, lifted her eyes once more to look at him and suddenly, as if he had pushed her away, she stepped back from the window. He had not even noticed . . . But it was not his paleness, nor his human exhaustion that made her step back. The face she had known from early childhood rose before her in the full force of its suffering and anguish. The blue veins stood on his temples, trembling as they had a minute ago: the awful picture before her was not clear enough for reasoned thought, but obvious and vivid to her sorrowing heart. Behind the partition stood, not Uncle Pavel, but Another Man, younger than him. The centuries vanished, all was as it once had been. Had the rough rope really been tied round his pale hand? The sweat running down from his temples, the tears streaming from his eyes – were they not really trickles of blood? Were the lips of this Man not whispering to her of Love, of the Cross, of Heaven? This lasted for only a few seconds . . . and once more it was Father Pavel coughing behind the partition, her dear Father, her uncle . . . And Alya, forgetting herself, went on hurriedly, feverishly:

"I'm going with you. I won't leave you or forsake you. If there's no-one else to help, so be it . . . but I must. Where you go, I'm going. To a village or into the taiga . . . I've decided, I'm going!"

"What are you saying, Alya, are you mad?"

"But why, why? I've said I'm coming and that's decided. Don't you want me to, aren't you glad I'll be with you?"

"How can you, Alya, of course I'm glad. But . . . the distance . . . the journey . . ."

He was very worried, but Alya's words had temporarily given him back the power to speak more connectedly and precisely.

"After all . . . you must have heard about it . . . the paths are so narrow that in one place, people have to walk in single file, under precipices. They say we'll be taken on horseback, one by one . . . on shackled horses . . . Or in long waggons, like coffins, I heard recently . . . A hundred miles from Bratsk it's a wilderness, the taiga. What do you want to do there? And what about your work? And your mother? Don't say any more, I won't listen to such nonsense."

But Alya was completely carried away, as if on wings.

"Those abysses are nothing. And the precipices as well. They're just trying to scare you. The climate's good there, better than ours. You'll get better and stronger. I'll work, cook and wash for you, read aloud to you . . . I'll get a job. When you serve out your term, we'll go back home together. Perhaps there'll be an amnesty?"

"My sentence is for life, Alya." His voice faded again. "What have you dreamed up? It's madness!"

"I'm not going at once," Alya said decisively, "I'll wait for your things to arrive at Aunt Liza's. As soon as your baggage comes, I'll be off after you."

"The river," he said, dismissively, "The river will be frozen."

"Let it freeze. I'll go by land."

"Alya! The frosts . . . Siberia . . . I don't know how I'll get there myself . . . My legs are dead weights . . . And how can you leave your mother?"

Quite shaken by her resolution, he still did not believe she had really decided; he looked at her – his lips trembled . . .

A bell sounded, like the buzz of a giant insect.

"The visit's over: time to leave, citizens."

"Just two more minutes, only two," begged Alya.

"Not even one allowed, citizeness."

Again she turned to him – "Bless me."

"Only not your planned journey, Alya . . ."

He gave her his blessing once more.

"I'll come again," whispered Alya. "I'll apply again. When are you leaving?"

"Thank you, I don't know . . . in a few days, they say . . ."

"And as soon as your things come, I'll follow you at once . . ."

"All right, my child, all right, we'll see . . ."

"We won't see, that's what will happen . . ."

"Citizens, it's time to go."

He had already moved back from the window. Alya saw how hard it was for him to walk, with the bag in his hands. Now he had disappeared behind the door. The key turned in the lock – it was over. How many varied emotions the heart could bear. She was laughing and crying. Liza was waiting for her at the entrance, surrounded by a few other women who had come from visiting their relatives. Liza's voice was severe and insistent.

"Watch out, Alya, if you cry, I'll push you into the Angara" this sounded childish, but at these words Alya recovered her composure, and began confusedly to try and acquaint Liza with her plans. Liza began to protest. while the stern Siberian women, their scarves wound round their heads, in spite of the heat, listened to Alya's stammered words and Liza's remonstrances; one middle-aged woman nodded sympathetically to Alya:

"You might well have missed him, mightn't you? You can see he's awfully ill, just skin and bone, and his eyes . . . We've all come to help them, but apart from the parcels, what can you do? The journey, you know, it's unbelievable!"

The Siberian spread out her hands, speaking of the winter, the snowstorms, of how people froze to death on the roads – and terrible unknown Asia threatened death to her brave enterprise.

But in that young heart, a song of joy arose, a song of the freedom that was near, a song of her journey into the unknown.

Chapter 10

The only things in favour of putting Alya's unexpectedly conceived plan into effect were her youth and her fervent determination. Everything else immediately seemed to come out against it. The difficulties of the family she was living with were spoiling her daily attempts to economise and balance accounts strictly. It was decided she would merely lend them some money, but their poverty and need for medicines for the sick man were obvious.

However Alya tried to economise on her keep in Novosibirsk, the parcels she had prepared here had not been cheap. Alya had a good appetite and eagerly ate what was put before her – a marinated herring, potato pies, – but she could not escape anywhere from the talk, the complaints and even the oblique laments about her unwise journey. If the luggage had arrived, she would at once have relieved them of her presence and would have started off on her journey. But now Father Pavel had no socks, no sheepskin coat, no mittens ... if only the weather would hold out until he reached his destination ... However, in spite of everything, nothing clouded or shook her decision, even if it was taken in haste, although from the first people tried to disabuse her of the idea by realistic and sober argument. The first of them was Liza.

"You'll freeze to death," she wept ... "Your mother will die of grief. You won't be able to find a job there. He should be accompanied by his wife, not by anyone else. If you lose your job, you'll ruin your life. You'll be a burden to him and everyone else."

All such words and arguments were easy to reject by means of the text: 'A man's foes shall be of his own household.' These words sank ever deeper into her consciousness and made her decide to act faster. Besides going to inquire after the luggage, she went to the steamer landing-place. There she was told that steamer traffic up the Angara would soon stop, that the last voyage to Bratsk would hardly be later than 10 October . . . and it was now the end of September. "But why?" – she protested. It was such find weather. Such heat – it was like the tropics! And she looked agitatedly at the rigged-out steamer, ready for departure to Bratsk tomorrow. Surely it couldn't be the last or next to last one?

However the frank young Buryat captain held to his own opinion. Today it was like Africa, tomorrow it would be Siberia again . . . Today it was hot, tomorrow there would be a snow-storm. "The rapids near Bratsk . . . if winter comes on you suddenly there – it's really something! And here winter often comes in October, round about the 10th or 15th. That's why we're trying to get on with it a bit earlier. Don't want to lose a ship."

At this, Alya left the wharf. It would be wonderful if her uncle could get on to the steamer, even if it was the last one. But what about herself? Well, what was there to worry about? She was young and strong. She would reach the place where he was, whether it was by train or by steamer. She could get skis, a stick. She would cross the hills, pass through the villages, on foot, crawling, or on horseback . . . She had heard that she could get there for 60 roubles, going part of the way on foot, partly on horseback.

She gave rein to her imagination. There were the little houses, half covered with snowdrifts, with lights shining out from inside. The hills rose up in front of her, with their narrow and barely distinguishable footpaths. Before her was the blue expanse of fir and pine forests, where squirrels leapt from branch to branch, and finally the road grew more level and widened, timber groves rose high around her. All difficulties were behind her – Alya had reached her goal . . . the village . . . From here she would write to her mother tomorrow, that she had arrived, that all was well, that Uncle Pavel . . . but where was he? How would she find him? How would it be? A high new fence. The house of a well-off peasant. She would go into the hut. The owners of the house would tell her the father was asleep. She would wait patiently, warming herself by the fire. At last – the door would open, he would be standing on the threshold, rested, cheerful and smiling at his Alya. "You've come at last" – he would say to her "Are you frozen? You'll soon warm up . . ."

Chapter 11

Before the prisoner transport was sent off, Alya easily and freely obtained permission to visit Father Pavel again. This visit was less joyful and opened Alya's eyes even more to his condition. She was shocked by his tense, nervous appearance; he seemed not to be all there.

"Is he glad I'm here or not?" – she thought. He did not say a word about her proposed journey. "Has it been decided between us after all, or has he no hopes of me?" – she wondered, glancing at his thin face, listening to his cough and his broken words. The atmosphere of their first meeting still echoed but now it was fading. The first time she had not managed to tell him about his brother or Nina's school work, but she had hardly begun, when he interrupted her, not sharply, but decisively and severely:

"All that's in the past now. It's God's will."

Just before the visit came to an end, Alya apprehensively told him that his things had not yet arrived . . . but she hoped soon . . . and then . . .

"The Lord will help us in all things," was his reply, "If God wills it, we'll get there while it's still warm. If only it's not on foot. I'd fall down . . . my legs . . . But they're going to give me some boots . . . The people here promised they would."

Today's parcel contained home-made pies of two varieties – with bird-cherry and potato stuffing, eggs, apples, onions, white rusks and sweets. In the last few days, two more letters had arrived from Nina. . .

"Anisyushka!" – he suddenly remembered a holy fool at Novodevichy monastery . . . and, taking one of the white rusks out of its wrapping, he stared at it . . . "What strange people they are! It's come true . . ."

"What's come true, father?"

"All of it . . . She said to me once 'Eat, priest, eat, without knife or fork . . . When you go down the river . . . you'll be glad to eat rusks . . .' And it's come true."

He blessed Alya again.

"Thank you for everything, God bless you," he said, "If, in spite of everything, however unlikely it is, you manage to get there – get hold of some consecrated bread and holy water. There'll be none there, I'm sure, and nobody else will have any. The village church is closed – I found out. I don't know if we'll be stopping in Bratsk. And say some good prayers for me. For my sins, my lack of piety . . ."

She wanted to whisper something, to put into words her concern and love for him – but she couldn't. He lightly laid his hand on her head, she caught hold of it and pressed it to her lips – a moment later, he had disappeared behind the door.

A strong, but warm, breeze blew Alya along as she was going back over the Ushakovo bridge. A young, clean shaven man, in a dark-brown travelling cap, walked past her. He went ahead of her, stopped by the railings, as if he was gazing into the water, let Alya go past, but then began to follow her again, sometimes almost catching her up, sometimes falling back; this went on until she had almost reached home. This annoyed her, as she realized what was happening. She should have expected something like this to happen from the moment she reached Novosibirsk. She confronted him boldly and sternly.

"Is anything the matter, citizen? Why are you following me like this?"

He was not put off.

"You're such a nice-looking girl. Why don't we . . . get to know each other . . . Would you like to go to a film? I'm right in thinking you're a stranger in town, aren't I?"

"Decent people don't introduce themselves like this. If you want to know the number of the house where I live, that's it – Number 18. I'm not hiding anything. And anyway, you'd find it yourself without being told, if you needed to."

"Clever girl, aren't you?"

"And I can put two and two together . . . I'm right, am I not? Goodbye."

"Goodbye."

Alya did not say anything to Liza about this conversation. Liza was frightened enough already. But they could harass her, Alya, whenever they wanted to, of course. If only, if only . . . Oh, bother that luggage . . ."

In Liza's little house, life went on as if undisturbed by Alya's arrival. The daily household tasks, the preparation of the cellar for winter, the insulation of the windows, looking after the hens, rooting up the cabbages, drying salmon-fish – all these domestic matters, that had to be dealt with in a hurry, were seen by this troubled soul as disturbances of her own peace of mind, so high-minded and sensitive did she feel herself to be. Alya understood that she would have to do her part and share in everything with the family that had given her shelter; she did help in everything that came to hand, but all the same, the hens, the fish and the potatoes with cabbage seemed to her like obstacles in the way of her own affairs and exertions, or like completely superfluous and unnecessary intrusions into that inner world in which she lived and worked. She dreamed of the victory which would crown her efforts: a tired and sick man was impatiently awaiting her and fearing he would never see her. Meanwhile, she could not even obtain a warm hat for him, and she and Liza would go to the market and return weighed down by cheaply-bought, roughly-ground flour and strings of onions, otherwise in a week or two they would have frozen hard and would be no good, – and there was a lot that Liza wanted to preserve by buying it up before the frosts began. In the evenings, the flour was sifted through a large sieve onto newspaper laid on the floor, then poured back into bags, fine and without impurities, and stored – only not in the cellar, but in the large chest, bound round with tin bands, which stood in Liza's kitchen; this also served as her bedroom in winter. They spent two days cutting up white cabbage in a large trough and made two big barrels of sauerkraut.

Even the ailing Ivan Alexandrovich participated in cutting up the cabbages – he removed the leaves, cleaning out worms, and cut out the stalks; Alya chopped them up together with Liza and found an outlet for her troubled soul by starting to imagine that she was cutting up the cabbage there, in the village, for Uncle Pavel. She felt that the work progressed better when she mentally transferred her activities there. The piles of cabbage in the barrel were lightly salted at intervals and sprinkled with caraway seeds. They also made one barrel of pickled carrots. Liza kept praising Alya for her diligence, thinking all the while that she would soon give up this nonsense, that when Alya received letters from her mother and aunt, she would come to her senses and go back home. Ivan Alexandrovich grew weaker towards evening, complaining of headaches and pain in his heart; both of them peered out of the window – Liza forecast a snowstorm, calling her husband a barometer.

The doctor would come, listen to him and write out a prescription. The sick man would mutter capriciously:

"It's the same powder again. I don't need it . . . I can't."

Liza declared brightly: "I feed him on parsley, doctor, to bring down the swelling.

After the doctor left, they felt more cheerful, and Liza went to close the shutters. Alya could not reconcile herself to this daily shutting out of light and air. What was the point of such artificial darkness? How painfully the bolts grated when sliding in! And poor Uncle Vanya would find it even harder to breathe. Could they not leave just a quarter of the window open, just a little chink?

"No, we can't," explained Liza, "Mother Siberia, you know! The climate's so severe here! Lord preserve us!"

Ivan Alexandrovich would lift his head from the pillow and add his own explanations about the taiga, the beautiful town and much else besides. Alya listened to it all and, thinking of the Siberian village, decided that she and Uncle Pavel would not close the shutters, but would gaze out of the little window of their peasant hut at the conifer forest, the snow-covered limbs of fir and cedar trees, the swarms of stars in the sky.

"Yes, Mother Siberia," repeated the sick man, "And what about our Irkutsk? It's always on a military footing: although they try to keep it policed, there are such a lot of criminal elements in the town, so many that you wouldn't believe it . . . Irkutsk, Alechka, is one big prison. Remember that song 'the Alexander central gaol'. Well, here in Ushakovka, we've got the Nikolai central gaol. Raids on peaceful residents – it's so common, there's no point in talking about it. Raids by gangs of thieves, ordinary exiles, runaways, mutineers. It's always been like that and that's what it's like now. So how can we not close the shutters? All right, it's stuffy for me, but I admit – 5 o'clock, they have to be closed!"

They fell silent . . . He took one of his short breaths and began to cough.

"You'd better stop chattering, old man," Liza broke in. "Now it's my turn to speak . . . Have you seen our market, Alechka? You saw the Siberian gypsies there, those stalwart men. What do they do for a living? They wander about all over Siberia, their exclusive territory. They're horse-thieves and robbers. They were trying to find gold here, they say there was some near Baikal somewhere. Those who found it got rich, and those who didn't were ruined and became vagabonds. In that same taiga . . ."

"That's where Uncle Pavel is, as well as them!" – Alya remembered sorrowfully. "What's it all for? Some sort of thieves, vagabonds, and that's why we have to close the shutters . . ."

"You must close the shutters," Liza intercepted her thoughts, "Siberians aren't bothered by it at all. But we're newcomers, and newcomers always find it disagreeable to put up the shutters."

Ivan Alexandrovich gave a start at this.

"Yes, that's how it is with me. As soon as I hear the bolts grating, it all begins. It's as if something was sucking at me from inside. Of course, scientifically, medically speaking, it's my bad heart. But I say – an Asian doesn't feel as we Russians do, who landed up here during the civil war. Distance brings on sadness. You don't feel so homesick for your own country anywhere as much as you do in Siberia. And there's nowhere else, where it seems as close as it does from Siberian windows. I would give anything to see my own town again: I'll have to die in Asia, seemingly, but in my heart, my brain, there's still a hint of gold. Hanging by a thread . . . And that thread is hope . . . The thought of my homeland . . . If only I could see it, just with one eye."

"Quiet now, old man, that's enough . . ."

Alya looked affectionately at Ivan Alexandrovich. He had shown her sympathy, without affection. He had entered into the spirit of her mission and her reasons for living there. Liza also did all she could to help her, feeding her, worrying that she was not assisting and welcoming her as well as she would have liked, going with her to the prison and waiting for her there. She gave Alya advice about life, scolding her for her wilfulness. However, at the same time, she tried, insistently and feverishly, to change Alya's mind about going off into the countryside. She secretly wrote a letter to Marya Petrovna, asking her to dissuade her daughter from her plan. And, what was worse, she complained from morning to night about their poverty, and ill health, threatening that she would die of a heart-attack, begging Alya to write to her aunt Nina to send more money for parcels and living expenses – everything was dear out here; they, the Bogdanovs, had no money to keep her, Alya, if times got hard.

Of course, Alya wrote nothing of the kind in her letters; instead she threw herself wholeheartedly into Liza's uncomplicated but tedious daily tasks; she fed and drove out the chickens, swept the yard, carried out the slop-bucket as well as she could, freeing Liza from much of her work, but all the same, Ivan Alexandrovich continued to endure his illness, the complaints, their poverty and Alya's visit, while Liza went on moaning about the good times she had known in the town where she spent her youth, about her ruined health and people's ingratitude.

"Go on, look at him," she would whisper to Alya, looking at her dozing husband, "he'll outlive me! He drags on and on . . . this is the third year . . . and I could die right now! All of a sudden! He's got a bad heart and so have I. And why? People should be egoists, and I don't know how to. Egoists live well. And I suffer all the time. It's all these prisoners I've got landed with. One asks you to bring him a parcel, another . . . And on top of that you arrived! How is it I've not been 'put inside' in Ushakovka yet? Now's the time for me to become an egoist! I won't do anything for anybody any more, I won't lift my little finger!"

"Wait a bit, do something first," – the sick man opened his eyes," Do what I tell you, and then go ahead and become an egoist."

Liza looked at him guardedly.

"Right," said her husband, battling with his shortness of breath, "go and open the cupboard where we keep our warm things, that one. Take Sergei's sheepskin coat – with the red sheepskin collar – out of mothballs. It's old, but it's warm, a real stove! Shake it out and hang it in the corridor. And give it to Alechka for Uncle Pavel. For his journey."

"But what's up with you?" Liza stammered, "Have you gone out of your mind, old man?"

"No, I've not gone mad. I said give it to her, so do as I say. There's going to be a snowstorm – if not today, then tomorrow.

And they're going to be sent off on Friday, I've heard they always drive them off to their destinations on Fridays."

"What about Sergei? It belongs to him."

"He won't even remember it. I'm his father, am I not? I gave him the coat myself. He hasn't worn it for two years now. He's got a new one. I'm not giving away our last possession. In Siberia you can't live without a sheepskin coat."

"What a coat!" – Liza said with feeling, as she went to the cupboard. "Old but warm!" I could do with it myself, when winter comes."

"Liza!" – Ivan Alexandrovich raised his finger, "you listen to me! These are people, you understand – such people as this Father Pavel, and others . . . so you'd better keep quiet and give it away. If you have a coat, and you give it away, you'll receive in return a hundredfold."

"Well, no," Liza said, rustling the newspapers in the cupboard. "Such a warm coat – with a red fur collar, won't be seen again, I'll never get one like it. However, since you've told me to, I'll do it. But from tomorrow, whether you like it or not, Vanya, – I'm going to be an egoist."

They handed in the sheepskin coat, together with a warm scarf and mittens from the same cupboard, only just in time. The day after giving in the parcel, Alya heard that the transport of exiles bound for Bratsk district had left in the morning from the wharf, on the last steamer from Irkutsk to Bratsk.

At the Bogdanovs', everyone rejoiced that Father Pavel was making the journey by river. Liza said that they had St. Innokenty to thank for this grace: not only had he got the warm coat, but the winter had not yet begun, and he was travelling by boat, not on foot, as far as Tulun, although the 100 verst journey from Bratsk to Ust-Vikhorevo was still a hard one, or so people said. "Thank God," said Liza, embracing Alya. They had managed to get the parcel to him! "You know what, my dear," she said, turning to her husband, "I don't regret the sheepskin coat any more! It's as if someone had rolled a stone away from my heart, but last night, when I was trying to get to sleep, I kept seeing the coat hanging in front of me, nothing but the sheepskin coat. Now you've only got to collect the luggage and then . . ." She did not have time to finish what she was going to say "and then you can go back home" – at that moment she felt the girl's eyes on her – such sad eyes, but severe in spite of their melancholy. She took pity on her and said instead:

"And then you'll have such a weight off your mind . . . isn't that so, Alechka?"

After receiving the news of the steamer's departure, Alya headed for two places – the station, to see if the luggage had come yet, and the cathedral, the only church in the town. Alya went to the early service every day, so as not to waste time for Liza and Ivan Alexandrovich. Alya followed her dear father in her thoughts, along the Angara to Bratsk. She saw the wheel of the paddle-steamer cutting through the fierce waves; together with him she reached Bratsk and helped him to alight at the jetty. After Bratsk, her thoughts clouded over, his journey farther on was veiled from her sight. It was time to wait for letters. Day followed day.

It was still a bright, clear autumn; only in the mornings did frost whiten the road and the roofs of houses. In about the middle of October, two letters arrived – from her mother and Aunt Nina, which reduced her to bitter tears. Not only were these pages not in harmony or in accordance with Alya's feelings and emotions; they were like cuts, blows or bites – like wounds in her heart. What was it all about? After all, she wanted – not for her own sake, but for theirs, for them – to save a sick man, who was as close to them as to her. If she could not save his life, she could lighten his sufferings. "I'm tired to death, Alya," she seemed to hear him say again. In the first letter her mother, always firm and strong in the faith, reproached her daughter for completely forgetting everything dear and holy to her, forgetting it all for the sake of a senseless adventure. "My brother, your uncle Pavel, has no need of anyone to go to the village with him, except Nina, but she cannot go with him." He did not need either Alya herself, or her 'hysterical notions'; he only needed parcels, which would be sent from time to time, but if her daughter wished to perish in Asia, let her do so. Alya did not recognize her mother in this letter. She remembered the moment of her departure for Siberia, one and a half months ago, when Marya Petrovna, wiping away her tears, had blessed her for the journey, the aim of which was to deliver the luggage and to be with Uncle Pavel if he needed her. And then she had tearfully asked her to greet and kiss her brother Pavel on her behalf.

"Can this be you, mother?" – cried Alya bitterly, "Can this be the same little Masha, who once went off on pilgrimage with her nine-year old brother? Your parents made you return home then, but nobody knew how hard it would be for a child's heart to renew that broken dream!"

Alya's mouth took on a bitter curve from the wormwood thus poured into her soul and, without having recovered from the first letter, she read the second.

"Alya!" – wrote her beloved aunt Nina, "I have no more money to spare for your expenses with regard to Pavel's affairs. I gave you all I could afford and will send you some more for your return fare. Are you economising? Are people not exploiting you? In your letter you explain yourself to me lovingly, but I know that you love Pavel more than anyone else in the world. So don't say, untruthfully, that you've decided to travel to the village out of love for us – personally I don't accept your sacrifice. Nor do I sympathize with it. If you want to do this for him, for Pavel, do it, but don't mix me up in it. I shall of course continue to support him; as I am bound to do. But remember, I have no money to spare, and try to cut down on expenses. It would be difficult for you to travel to the village. I doubt if you would find employment there. So – I can send you the return fare, but I shall support him alone financially ..." This was followed by instructions about a warm hat, about some other things, and then, without even her usual "love and kisses," aunt Nina ended the letter with her initial and surname, in an unintelligible scribble.

"So I haven't been economising!" – Alya was appalled. "I bought two buns, and now I'm living on Liza's salmon-fish. I've saved every penny, not even taking a bus where I didn't have to·! And here, I'm living for free with poor people, and even if they mutter a bit about my coming, it's only from unhappiness, from infirmity, and they've even helped by giving him the warm coat. Who'll help me now? What shall I do? Go back? But perhaps this is the enemy fighting against me, to stop me getting to the village and making the pastor's life easier? Could I not get a job until the luggage comes? Even if it's only as a cleaner in the chemist's shop?"

Alya lay on the trunk in Liza's kitchen, hunched up into a ball. She was running her hands through her hair and her hairpins had fallen out. The read letters lay scattered on the floor by the stove. It was in this state that Liza found her. Seeing the envelopes, she immediately realized what was the matter and her conscience began to ache, like a bad tooth. She picked up one of the letters, the one from Nina, and read it slowly. Alya did not move. She merely started nervously at the touch of Liza's hand.

"Don't jump like that! People are all worthless ..." began Liza in her usual manner, "Forgive me, Alechka, but I read your letter. From his wife, your uncle Pavel's. The letter was lying there, you were crying, so I read it and you can scold me for it. And my advice is – spit on it and tear it up! Look at what she writes – "don't mix me up in it." So is she his wife or isn't she? It's one or the other – either she's jealous of you, well, that's possible, and understandable, or she's taken up with someone new, some teacher there ... Don't protest, Alechka. You don't understand, you're young, and aunt Nina's a beautiful woman and she's been married for so many years, – you, my child, have only just been exposed to love, but there's no sense in it, you've been attracted to misfortune, and you want to love . . . If Father Pavel were young or a bachelor . . ." At this point, Alya sat up, like one risen from the dead, and put her hand to stop Liza. "Alechka, don't be angry! I'm speaking directly . . . Love between people always begins from high ideals. There's no-one to explain it to you properly, my child. You're so innocent!"

"Liza! Come to your senses! He is a priest, after all! He carried me in his arms when I was a child! Don't insult what's sacred! Are you against me too?"

"I'm for you, my dear, not against you. Some day you'll understand . . . Priests are people, and the enemy is strong. Your things are still not here, they just don't come. Who knows, perhaps that's as it should be, so that . . ."

"So that I won't go to the village? What are you saying, Liza? Understand me, once and for all. He's waiting for me, I've given him hope, he's ill – and you, all of you are against me!"

"But you'll see that no-one's against you, Alya! We all only want his good. I'll be the first to pack some buns and fish for your journey. It's only that, if you see what I mean, if things turn out so that you can go, that's how it will be, but if the opposite happens, then however you cry, nothing'll come of it. It's no one's fault. That's how it happens. You'll be standing outside a locked door, knocking with your eyes."

Alya sat there as if rooted to the spot, hanging her head low and clutching her hands, as if pondering and thinking something over. When Liza asked her if she was going to the cathedral for the all-night service, she answered, as if in a dream, "Yes, I'll go."

"Then I've got something to ask you. After the service, don't let Father Symeon go past you, wait for him. He'll leave through the church. Ask him to visit us tomorrow after the liturgy. It's Ivan Alexandrovich's birthday, he could give him Communion. And you could ask his advice about your problem – he's a wise man, preaches a sermon like St. John Chrysostom; he's experienced it all himself: two years exile, and it was touch and go whether he would get a registered post here. He had quite a lot of trouble ... He's ruined his feet. Walked 25 kilometres on foot, in the frost. That was when he was travelling back. He got rheumatism and cramp in his legs."

Alya calmed down somewhat at the thought of the cathedral, of being able to talk about her troubles to the pastor, a fellow-sufferer of Father Pavel. One after another, the names of the saints, the eternal intercessors, rose in her mind, and the first of these was the name of St. Nicholas. It renewed the warmth of her faith in intercession and aid. On entering the cathedral a few minutes before the beginning of the service, Alya hastily found an ikon of St. Nicholas. The image was in an ancient style and dark in colour, on the right side, near the northern gates. There were already a number of candles burning on the candleholder. Alya placed her own on it and, kneeling down, fixed her gaze on the ikon. The bishop without a mitre looked austerely down at her. "Father Nicholas!" – she thought in those moments, "you're like dear Father Pavel; he bears his shame, as you once did after being disgraced by Arius. Oh, what a lot I have to tell you! And how could I have left you?" Alya now recalled that during her whole journey she had only rarely turned to him in prayer, and then only briefly, in formal words, hurriedly in the mornings, when reading the troparion, but she made up for it now. Now she gazed at him as the only help in her trouble, like Justice itself in relation to her plan, as the quickest way of fulfilling her wish and completing her journey. Her soul prayed passionately. The ancient face of the saint looked down on her impassively, attentively and severely, bareheaded, with hair slightly curling on his temples and a high, prominent forehead, just like dear Father Pavel's. "No-one can help me but you!" whispered Alya, her heart burning and tears falling onto the floor one after another, mingling with tears of candle wax. "You alone know me wholly, you can do anything – I must go to him, I'm worn out and I wear out other people; people don't understand me and the luggage hasn't come; soon there'll be a snowstorm – it'll be winter; and then the letters they sent me, such cruel letters, how were they not ashamed?"

At these last words Alya, like a soft round ball, fell on her face at the foot of the candle-holder.*

"Surely, Father Nicholas, you don't disapprove of my intention? How could you be against it? Have I thought up something bad, or sinful? I'm so sorry for him! Nobody else could do it, all of them have left him, but I want to be with him . . . He's like you, a true pastor, a good man, walking in the right path . . . I can't do anything anymore, I can't, Father Nicholas! Help me! Open a way for me! Make them send the luggage sooner. So that I can go! Give peace to my spirit! Open a way for me!"

Alya spent the whole of the evening service by the ikon, praying, weeping, or merely gazing at her heavenly helper, but at the end of the service she waited, until she saw Father Symeon coming from the altar and then she went up to him.

After Ivan Alexandrovich had made his confession and received Communion, when he was sitting propped up on cushions, in expectation of tea, Liza was briskly laying the table with everything she had prepared and anything that came to hand – salmon fish-pies, potato shepherd's pie, curd-cakes with bird-cherry jam. In the cupboard she had found a little wine flavoured with lemon peel, and a jar of jam, which Alya had brought with her back in September. In the kitchen the samovar soon boiled, and everything so hurriedly assembled on the table betrayed not a trace of poverty or want; on the contrary, it radiated abundance and festivity. Only good housewives know how to serve up a meal like this.

* This is the usual attitude assumed by Orthodox Christians in making the "low bow," in which they kneel down and then bow their heads to the floor.

Father Symeon was a small man, with thoughtful grey eyes and a plain, pleasant face. His long hair curled round his shoulders. "As soon as I was released, I let it grow again," he told them frankly. There was nothing special about him, apart from his flowing hair; he did not stand out because of good looks, or ascetic appearance, or because he was plump, as Father Pavel had formerly been. However, from his first words, it was obvious that he was a man who had talent for speaking, not merely chattering, but speaking wisely, well and with originality. He spoke in rounded phrases, without searching for words, in full-blooded, clear and pure Russian. If the Novosibirsk priest, Father Alexander, had seemed a saintly man to Alya during the service on the feast of the Mother of God, in the severity of his features, lit up by the candles, in his anticipation of the unavoidable cross he must bear, then at this moment she remembered what Liza had said about Father Symeon, "speaks like John Chrysostom" – and in listening to his ordinary conversation, she immediately agreed with her. Father Symeon had returned from exile a year ago – he had been accused of spreading some sort of propaganda. He was now allowed to take services once more, without the right to preach, in the only church left open, but even now he was hoping to move on "to a less distant place," as he remarked. A visit from such a guest livened up the Bogdanovs' house as a whole. Liza was concerned, like all housewives, to regale her guest, to lay a spread on the table for him; Ivan Alexandrovich was in the unique state of nervous joy that fortifies and inspires a sick man about to receive the Sacrament; Alya was prepared, after her prayer in the cathedral yesterday, to see in Father Symeon a miraculous adviser and expected support for her case from him. He had managed to talk to her a little yesterday, while they were going home. He had not failed to observe her tear-stained eyes, or her trembling voice. She had briefly managed to explain to him her situation and her worries. He had known much suffering in recent years and, although he was not advanced in years, in fifteen years of service and three years in exile he had become a wise, respected adviser, a *starets**, because of his experience and knowledge of men, of Siberia itself, with its customs, traditions and way of life. He had already decided yesterday to talk to Alya about her plan, not on the street, however, but at home, at the Bogdanovs'. But how? How was he to begin and carry on the talk he needed to have with her, and how would that sincere and troubled soul take what he had to say? And he had already formulated the advice he would give; he had decided on it yesterday, thinking it over thoroughly in his mind as a pastor: she must go back to her relatives. He himself had once had the same problem; his only daughter had wanted, like Alya, to ease her father's fate and rush after him into the wilderness, but it had not happened in the end, and thank God for that!

They rested after tea. Always silent, Ivan Alexandrovich was full of sad longing for his homeland . . . Usually he hid what he was thinking. To weep and wail about the white-walled town of ancient churches and bells they had left, the quiet waves lapping the walls of the old fortress – that was what Liza loved to do and did . . . But today, he could talk without interruption about it. He saw it in his dreams, and seemed to see it even when awake . . .

"Father," he said, turning to Father Symeon, "I don't feel at home among the Siberians. They're not my own folk, somehow. A bunch of gloomy hunters. Always got some troubles of their own on their minds. And then, when spring comes, the wild cherry starts to blossom on the edges of the taiga, and here along the river banks, everywhere – there is so much of it here. There are big trees of it, with its tiny blossoms in the thickets and gardens, "the Siberian sparkle" they call it – it's not the same sort as in Russia. This "sparkle" doesn't have such a strong scent, but when I see it, a real longing comes over me. In our own parts

* A *starets*, is a priest, nearly always a monk whose advice is regarded as having great spiritual authority. A *starets* never holds a position of ostensible authority in the church but is recognised as having authority in himself.

they sell it in the markets in barrow-loads, make bouquets out of it, such huge white branches of it. So I feel homesick . . . I had a dream, father, not so long ago. I was in a boat, with a white sail, sailing down the Angara, it seemed, along the Angara – and suddenly, it was like a miracle, – I saw before me the church of the Saviour of Mirozh and the other churches, as they used to be – a great many they were, and the quiet peal of their bells in the evening, so I sailed up to the shore and stepped out, beside myself with happiness. And then, well, I woke up."

"All the same, dear, you've got accustomed to Siberia," said Liza interrupting, "You don't like them, you say, but you talk just like them now – "well" this and "well" that."

"It was a good life at home, I can't deny it," responded Father Symeon, cutting his curd-cake in half, "Even if we take the most simple thing – this curd-cake. All honour to our hostess, it's well-baked, well-ground, but if we were to imagine one cooked at home – what sort of stuffing would it have?"

Everyone began to argue. Liza shouted out "cherries," Alya said it would be cream cheese with cinammon. But here and now, in the market, just before the onset of winter, everyone was buying up stocks of bird-cherry jam, and it wasn't at all easy to find cream cheese! Even in daytime you had to look for it with a light! And it was expensive – a small pot for 10 roubles.

"Yes, it was good, a good life, at home!" sighed Father Symeon. "I'm from Orlov province myself. There are such restful little gardens in the central belt of Russia. I would give anything to go into a little garden like that. Especially in spring, when it's turning into summer: the apple trees and lilac in bloom – and I'd sit down on a grey, warped bench. And in front of me there'd be a roughly carved round beam of a table, with a striped linen tablecloth. Just imagine – a calm evening, the soft sound of a church bell . . . ringing for the Six Psalms perhaps . . ."

"That was what it was like when we were young," said Ivan Alexandrovich, remembering, "distant music coming from a

town garden, while you would be coming out of church – with
your own music in your soul . . ."

"Yes, indeed," Father Symeon agreed, "The church bells will
ring out again; we won't hear them, but others will."

"Still, don't you believe, father," interrupted Alya, who had
been silent until then, "don't you believe that the Church will
be restored, here on earth?"

"I don't know how to put it . . . I think it must be, even if only
for a short time. For the sake of Christ's little flock. For a few
chosen ones – as a sign of the complete triumph of heaven. But
only for a short time, as the end must obviously be coming soon.
Our homeland is not here. Our real homeland is eternal, but
many people on this earth have never heard of it. It is unknown
to them . . . When I was still a schoolboy, an adolescent, I
happened to be in Odessa visiting relatives. We went to the
botanical gardens there. It was there that I saw a bush, a little tree,
growing in a flower-bed by the roadside, with a board attached
to it, saying in Latin "Terra incognita."

That means "Homeland unknown." And that inscription
remained in my mind for a long time. I imagined that flowering
plant's unknown homeland in all sorts of ways. As people we are
all like flowers, reaching upwards to the sun. Rooted to the earth.
When I come to think of it – that was the year that I came home
and told my parents "I want to study on the spiritual side." Well,
they agreed – and I entered the seminary. See how much influence a flower has! My thoughts and conclusions troubled me,
led me to find the road to that unknown homeland. And since
then I've been on my way to it, still searching. From childhood
we read about the Promised Land in the Bible. And you know,
we always imagine Canaan as our own homeland. That is, we
give it the features of scenes and places we've seen in our childhood. Like the apple orchard in Ivan Alexandrovich's memories
of his town, or the scenery of the Crimea, for those who've
seen it, or early spring and Easter in your home village – the

bright green grass, the smell of the first green plants coming up. These scenes are always linked with memories of childhood purity, innocence and love of everything and everyone. We choose the best we have dreamt of, the highest we have known. The most consoling of our dreams and impressions of this kind, if only in part, give us some idea of "Canaan." How much more blessed and beautiful it must be than our imaginings, if our childhood purity and innocent youth in our parents' house is only a pale likeness of that Eternal Purity, that – how shall I put it? – Essence of Love, which we shall know to the full in the true land of Canaan! And dare I suggest also, that now we see that land, still unknown to us in its great and final form, in imaginary or visual images of fatherly love, beautiful gardens or early spring in our homeland? Many people, however, have been completely deprived of consoling images of childhood as symbols of paradise; they have never known love or joy . . . They have no memories of childhood purity, they have always known everything that should be hidden from childish eyes and have always seen it in the most abhorrent light! They have always been cut off from beauty. But even they, by God's grace, those who are sincere, that is, have reached towards the light, have sought it through swamps and quite unclean places, but have sought it with longing – and in general those chastised by God for the sake of their own happiness, – after all the Lord who sees in secret knows all secrets, all human aims, fates and souls . . . I feel that they will all attain Canaan, to the extent that they ought to attain and receive it . . . all are invited to the feast – all and sundry . . . Come and eat!"

He suddenly fell silent, as if he had been interrupted, and all of them were silent for a long time, as if an angel had passed by.

"I can't help thinking" Alya's voice broke the silence – "of the social outcasts of today, I mean the persecuted servants of Christ . . . They, I think, will enter Canaan and the heavenly habitations at once! My poor father!" – She lowered her head . . . They all turned in her direction. She was thinking of only one thing, and was completely taken up with it. And at once everyone's thoughts turned away from Canaan and the father's gardens to her troubles.

"Will he recover? He was so ill ..." said Alya, wiping away her tears, "How will he get to the village? Liza, don't be angry that I'm crying. Yesterday I told Father Symeon all about it. He knows everything. How strange it is, father," she turned towards the priest," that I came here with a reserve of strength, and yet I can't help the one I'm trying to reach, except by sending him parcels ... I can't follow him immediately. I haven't even managed to deliver his things to him in time."

Father Symeon gave a start at her words, which seemed to go right through him: "But please tell me, my dear child, why should you follow him at all?"

"What do you mean, why?" – Alya burst out. "After all, I'm his spiritual daughter and his niece. I lost my father, a priest, in my childhood. Father Pavel took the place of my own father, but in spirit he was closer to me.

Many children do everything for their pastors. They turn aside from their own lives and leave their father's house and their children, as the Gospel commands, to make life easier for these martyrs and to help the Church ..."

"That's ... that's all true, of course," said Father Symeon slowly, "altogether praiseworthy words, and perhaps I'm being very clumsy in wounding your most devout sentiments. But don't you think, my dear child – as I'll call you again, that such sufferers and martyrs, as you yourself have called them, need nobody's help to reach the land they are travelling to – whether it is by their own will, or under compulsion from others. The Lord Jesus Christ, though this is a bold comparison, was not helped to go to the Cross by anyone, except his executioners. It would be a different matter, if you had come to this decision because of some special call, but to live with him, making him suffer even more when he looks at you and realizes you've left your job, your mother and relatives, who are angry with you and annoyed at not having enough money to support you as well as him – and after such a journey, too! Your self-will has taken them aback ... You told me yourself that you had come only with the intention of meeting him and delivering his things to him ... to provide for him by means of parcels, but surely no mention was made of accompanying him to the village? And have you not thought, that his wife is the one who has a right to be with him? – No one else has such a 'right. You will be an absurd and pitiful figure there ..."

"I don't care if I am absurd ... or pitiful ..." Alya stammered out.

"All right. You say you "don't care" if you're pitiful; that won't bother you then, but him. It'll be a new torment for him. You won't make his lot easier by your presence but more distressing. Will you be able to find a job in a remote Siberian village, so that you'll be able to work and justify your existence, and not merely be a burden on his wife? It seems to me that she feels compassion for him, but regards him as a burden at the same time. Should you get involved in this situation? Tell me. Only by being truthful ..."

"I don't understand what you're saying!" – Alya exclaimed, weeping," He's so pitiful and ill, his legs hurt him, he's got a cough, and I promised him that I would follow him, when I saw him in the prison. He's waiting for me. Why shouldn't I go, why? In recent years, many spiritual children have helped their spiritual fathers! What's your opinion of them, tell me?"

"But why did his wife not follow him?" – interrupted Ivan Alexandrovich somewhat grumpily ... "You'd only be a reminder to him, Alya, that his wife failed to come out to his and sent you out in her place, that's all ..."

"You don't know his wife at all!" – said Alya, with restrained bitterness. "I could read you her letter to me. She didn't plan my journey here, or to the village. I, I myself offered to come to

him . . . And now – I don't understand it at all! I'm confused.
She writes to me that, if I want to do this for him, "do it but
don't mix me up in it." Yes, that's what she said. It's a terrible
letter. "Don't mix me up in it." I didn't recognize my aunt Nina
in that wicked letter. And I loved her so much."

"Is she jealous, perhaps?" said Liza, interrupting.

"Or perhaps she's got someone else?" – and Ivan Alexandrovich
crossly pulled his blanket round himself, but Father Symeon
immediately shook his head.

"Neither the one nor the other, my friends. She's not jealous,
nor has she got attached to anyone else, she just feels that you,
Alexandra Fyodorovna, my dear child, have done the wrong
thing in trying to follow her husband. You'll lose your job, and
you've abandoned your mother, whom you should have been
thinking of first . . . You're still young! A child! Not twenty
years old yet and performing such deeds! You'd make his
position easier by sincere prayer, than you would by journeying
into the wilds of Siberia. He has been sent a cross to bear, not
you . . . think of that, my dear, think it over carefully, don't be
in a hurry. Yesterday you were right to devote it all to St.
Nicholas. Who can disentangle your difficulties, if not he? But
don't let us distress you further. We've tormented ourselves
enough. However, I had to express my opinion. Yes, indeed.
You yourself asked me to, yesterday. So please, don't be offended.'

At this point the discussion came to an end. Alya got up and
left the room in tears, and Father Symeon said no more about
Alya's affairs; he concentrated on drinking his tea and praising
Liza's curd cakes.

The Siberian morning had not yet penetrated the thick shutters,
but Liza was already standing over the sleeping Alya and shaking
her by the shoulders.

"Get up, my dear, get up, it's really dreadful weather

outside! A snow storm! The hens have been completely scattered? Help me, quickly! Here's your coat! Wrap yourself up in it. We'll have to run and round them up!"

Still half-asleep, (after yesterday's tears, she had slept the more soundly), Alya pulled her boots on to her bare feet, put her sheep-skin coat on over her nightdress and ran out after Liza into the corridor, where a piercing cold she had never known was blowing in through the door, and on into the yard. It was hellish outside; the hens were difficult to catch, they were clucking and flapping about; a snowy whirlwind was blowing round her and almost knocking her off her feet, a thin layer of frost obscured her eyes, the sand beneath her feet was whirling and twisting into funnels; the poplars and the lonely bird-cherry tree in the yard were creaking mournfully. Alya was almost knocked over by a gust of wind – at first she thought she had gone blind – she couldn't see anything! All the same, she ran about despite buffeting from the wind, supporting herself against the fence or the house wall, then leaving her shelter and bravely obeying extraordinary instructions and running errands – unpegging some washing hanging out on the line, pulling the bucket out of the well, and so on. At last the hens were shut up in a cage inside, and the cock took up a position that suited him, in the centre of the hearth. Outside, the wind was howling, while people were moving along the streets, leaning on fences, some-times sitting down in the snow or on the ground to avoid falling headlong. Even these pedestrians were rare; few braved the snow-storm. The last leaves were falling off the trees and everything seemed to be freezing solid from the sharp, piercing cold.

In the cellar Liza and Alya were working hard – they stopped up chinks with rags and boards, threw mats on top of the potatoes and tried to warm up the cellar as much as possible, then they crawled upstairs to stoke up the stove and the fires; this went on until midday.

Again and again Alya came up against the peculiarities of

winter in Siberia, while Liza gave her no respite, muttering about something all the time . . .

"There you are, my dear, if it hadn't been for your affairs, would I have left such chinks, and the vegetables uncovered, till the snow came? Such a whirlwind, and I knew quite well it would be. It was just yesterday we were sitting with Father Symeon and he and my old man were going on about the homeland, but my homeland was that cellar! Leaving the house uncovered! Did you see what a crack we had to stop up? Oh Alechka, let you and me go down there one more time! I'm afraid it may freeze on the right side. It doesn't take much for the potatoes to freeze, and in that place – wasn't there a draught from the corner? Shall we slip some more mats under them, or not?"

They crawled down into the cellar again, then they warmed up the kitchen as much as they could and opened the door into the corridor for the birds. In the evening they let them take a walk round the kitchen. Because of the bad weather, Alya had not managed to go to the station to inquire about the luggage. But suddenly a thought somehow occurred to her: the luggage has come! And already she was happily pushing to the back of her mind all the difficulties she had had to endure, as young people do, and calculating that the storm would die down in two days. The things had obviously arrived. She could now set off. But how was she to pay for her journey? She had only 50 roubles left over from the parcels. She put her hope in the money she had been promised would be sent for her return fare; she could use it to travel on. Liza owed her more than a hundred, she would give it back to her or send it. In the last resort, the market would save her; she could get rid of her new shoes there, she wouldn't be wearing them out there, and some of her underwear as well.

Pacified by such thoughts, she followed Liza down into the cellar again the next day, dragging up into a corner of the kitchen five buckets of potatoes for consumption. The weather still did not abate, and snow blocked the road.

All of a sudden, taking pity on Alya's thin face and silence, Liza set about comforting her and cheering her up. Although she had always disagreed with Alya's plans, she encouraged Alya to hope, saying that an acquaintance of hers, former investigator Zubov, had promised her to lend her a hundred for her relative's journey to Bratsk region.

The same evening the long-awaited news from Father Pavel arrived. He had arrived at his place of exile. He had got there. The grey envelope, stamped by the internal censorship, trembled in their hands.

"I have reached the place assigned to me at last, after a journey of five days, very difficult and full of dangers and discomforts," read Alya, "This is my rest for ever, here will I dwell. The roads leading here are in such a state that no-one could get here until after the winter feast of St. Nicholas, as local people say. I thank you and aunt Liza for all your trouble and worry, the inconvenience you've both suffered on my behalf. May the Lord bless you, my dear child, for your love. May he arrange your journey in his own way, in accordance with his holy will." The address followed. Alya pressed the precious lines to her face and said to Liza:

"Well, that's that, even he agrees I can travel to the village."

Now, after the lengthy delay in the arrival of the luggage, Alya's road seemed to be opening up before her. The luggage, which had held up everything, had finally – through the efforts of Father Alexander – arrived in Irkutsk from Novosibirsk. It seemed that matters could not have turned out better. Alya had to decide whether to take the things home to Liza's from the station or, if she was to set out on her risky journey a few days later, to send it on ahead of her to Tulun for convenience. Liza advised her to take the things home. "It'll get to Tulun, all right" she calculated, "but later it'll have to get through such backwood

roads, such hills and precipices, that the cover'll come off the
suitcase, and how will you deal with something so heavy?
Wouldn't it be better to divide it into four or five parcels and
send it on tomorrow or the day after? And I'll keep the suitcase
for him, I'll send it on to him in the spring, he'll find some use
for it."

They decided that Alya would travel lightly, with just her own
things. When she got to the village, the parcels would already be
there.

After the snowstorm the frost intensified; for the third day
running it was over 30 degrees below zero. They got five parcels
out of the big suitcase and, after addressing and tying them up,
they put them on the sledge again and took them to two different
post offices, to avoid any delays and enquiries. When they had
sent off the parcels, Liza's mood changed in an amazing way.
She was tired out from all her experiences with Alya and now
her guest's departure seemed the best way out, and her un-
shakeable resolve to journey on even aroused her respect. At
first Liza liked to repeat to Alya Nekrasov's words: "We are
destined to have fine adventures, but it is not given to us to complete them." The luggage had not come for a long time, everything had been against her, the young soul was rushing to and
fro, longing for action. But of course, that was how it was bound
to be: "it is not given to us to complete them." Now it turned
out that Liza, so unreconciled to Alya's journey, had completely
changed her mind about her plan. That evening, after they had
sent the parcels off, when Alya's head began to ache and she
became feverish, and in the morning the doctor treating Ivan
Alexandrovich said she had follicular angina, Liza began to
nurse her devoutedly with both the prescribed medicines and
her own remedies – she made her gargle with hot sage infusions,
swallow half a teaspoon of unrefined alcohol ... and in the
evenings, a glass of vodka with salt and pepper in it. The homely
remedies seemed more effective than the ones from the chemist,

and Alya drank everything Liza gave her. Muffled up to the ears, she lay in the warmth, with her uncle's postcard reposing under her pillow, while Liza kept pushing honey or spirits into her mouth, and the angina did not seem to be in any way a serious obstacle to her journey. The illness had obviously appeared as yet another small test of her patience, that was all.

After two days, Alya's temperature dropped, her throat cleared, she found it easy to swallow again and regained her appetite. The second week in November was coming to an end. She decided to go at once, without putting it off, to the station to buy a ticket to Tulun. Liza's friend had brought the promised 100 roubles, which added up to 150 with Alya's own money. Her head wrapped up in Liza's woolly headscarf, thinking only of the journey and her meeting with him, Alya undid the ring high up on the surrounding fence, fastening it to the gate, but as she went out on to the street, she ran right into a man who was coming towards her and barring her way. Where had she seen that face? He stood in front of her, not allowing her to go a step further.

"You'll be citizeness Voinova?" – When she confirmed this, he declared in an inflexible official tone "You'll have to come back inside. With me."

She still could not tear herself away from her goal – the station, the ticket ... and stood there in front of him as if half-asleep: "I don't understand ... what do you mean?" – she began, in confusion, "I'm just going ... I don't have any time! I have to be quick ..."

"It can't be helped, citizeness Voinova." – He was still standing in front of her, stopping her from going past.

"But what do you want?" – her voice was trembling, "Why are you here? Let me pass. I can't help you."

"We'll explain it all to you immediately, at once, and then you'll understand everything ..." He stressed the word "everything," and started gradually to push Alya backwards, edging her back to the gate, like a disobedient child.

In the corridor, Liza almost collapsed in surprise. Alya sank down on a chair in utter silence. The invalid had only just woken up and was gazing attentively at the stranger. He had been in civilian clothes on the street. Throwing off his coat, he revealed a khaki military uniform, with a holster. He was of average height, with rosy cheeks and an almost boyish appearance, his head smoothly shaved down to the skull, with small, grey eyes darting from one place to another, – "crooked eyes" – as people call such a glance. Everyone in the room, both Liza and Alya, and Ivan Alexandrovich, simultaneously felt at once that they had been separated, or rather divided, from each other. They were all silent, waiting for their visitor to speak. He put a small case on the table and took out a piece of paper and a fountain-pen. "Have the goodness to read this, it's my warrant," he said, handing Liza the piece of paper.

"I can't see anything without my glasses, comrade, sir. Allow me to fetch the spectacles from the kitchen."

"Please do, don't mind me, citizeness Bogdanova. This is your house, and anyway . . . you're perfectly free . . . But as for this young lady, citizeness Voinova, I shall have to detain her at home and limit her movements, according to instructions – that's the order."

"So you're Ivan Fomich Fomin, the investigator?" – asked Liza, reading the document.

"Well, that's a bit grand – "investigator" – I'm still a small fish. I get assigned to minor investigations. But you know how big affairs can grow out of little ones. Isn't that so?" – and, laughing a little, he looked at Alya, who was sitting quietly and even seemed to be rooted to her chair; she suddenly burst out.

"You'll get nothing, little or big, out of me. My affairs are in order. If you have to interrogate me, then interrogate me as you should, according to law."

"What's this about interrogations, citizeness Voinova? We're just going to have a talk, a discussion, you and I. You'll see, I'm a simple fellow. I'll tell you about myself. I've got a wife in Minusinsk, and a son. And you must have a daddy and mummy."

"Only a mother" – Alya unwillingly let out.

"How's that – "only"? Mums are everything . . ."

Alya was silent.

"You can't buy mums in a shop! And where are you going, citizeness Bogdanova?"

Liza, in her coat and headscarf, was heading for the door. She turned round at Fomin's question.

"Where am I going? To "you know where" . . . You said yourself I was free. How am I to take that?"

Fomin smiled.

"Pardon me, I was somewhat mistaken . . ."

"Indeed!" – Liza, in her role as housewife, no longer seemed to be overawed by Fomin. "He asks where I'm going! You'll be here, won't you, for some days, but we've got nothing at home, I have to buy something . . ."

"Don't bother, citizeness Bogdanova. We have our own rations, we'll just need tea, perhaps . . ."

"I know your provisions. We know quite well . . . this is Siberia, not Russia. Out of every five people here, one's an investigator. And everyone has to eat. There's nothing in the house – a couple of salmon-fish and potatoes. Let me say a few words about the housekeeping to citizeness Voinova. See how grandly I speak of you now, Alechka! You can come into the kitchen with us, of course . . ."

"Citizeness Bogdanova, I've told you quite clearly that you're not limited in your home life in any way, you can go out any time you like, but we're keeping citizeness Voinova at home . . ."

"I'm not going to be "kept" anywhere," exclaimed Alya, "I keep myself, always have and will. I'm not an object to be "kept," or a thief or criminal to be "detained." And she turned to Liza, who had placed a hand on her trembling shoulder.

"Calm down and don't be so nervy!" – said Liza. "Comrade Fomin, we'll just be a few minutes. You make yourself at home. Once you've got the warrant in your hand, that's it. There's your couch for the night. I'll just get a pillow and a blanket for you. How many days will you be staying? Two or three?"

"Well, that'll depend entirely, you see, . . . on our little chats . . . I suppose."

"Alya, let's go into the kitchen. We won't be a minute. I won't detain her or hide her, we're just going to talk about the housekeeping . . ."

And, before Fomin could say anything, Liza pushed Alya into the corridor and began to whisper to her:

"Listen, pay attention to me, be a bit more polite to him! You can't behave like that, my dear. After all – he's the law. He's only a boy, but he's got a warrant. You have to submit to the authorities . . ."

"To what? Why should I submit? There's no point. And what's happening anyway? If I can't go out on the street, what about the ticket? And my journey?"

"You've waited a long time, and you'll have to wait a bit longer . . . You're under house arrest, Alya. It might have been worse. – We'll boil some potatoes, everyone likes those well salted!" – Liza shouted out at the top of her voice, too loudly perhaps. "I'm just on my way!" – and once more she fell to whispering in Alya's ear – "You took him three parcels at Ushakovka, and sent him the others, and you visited him twice; he must have been on their lists already, as an important case . . . Did you think no one was looking or listening, nobody's feet were following?" – And once more at the top of her voice – "I'll borrow a little from you. We'll boil up the samovar." Then she whispered again: "Tell him truthfully what you know, don't lie . . . Speak the truth to God and don't try lies on them either . . . Lord, what a hole there is in my bag, give me yours. Go in to him, go on, or it'll look as if we're whispering together. What did you say, get a litre? Right . . ." Again a whisper: "The situation's clear . . . I've had experience of it . . ."

She disappeared out of the door. Alya went and stood before Fomin, like a dummy, then sank into a chair. Ivan Alexandrovich watched all this, coughing uninterruptedly from the strong cigarette smoke.

"Could I ask you, comrade Fomin," – Alya now spoke in a tone that was neither shrill nor nervous, if not exactly friendly, "to smoke in the corridor or the kitchen. Uncle is very ill and it's not good for him to breathe tobacco smoke."

Fomin nodded his head in agreement, put out his cigarette and laid a lined piece of paper in front of himself.

"What shall we begin our friendship with?" – With this opening, he glanced at the girl's slight figure, sitting before him with her head still muffled up and her hair coming down somewhat. Alya adopted a prudent attitude, remembering what Liza had said, and tried to enter into the role of a person under house arrest.

"Our friendship," she retorted, "didn't begin today. Two weeks ago, you escorted me home from Ushakovka. Isn't that so? I recognized you at once."

He looked at her: "You have a wonderful memory, citizeness Voinova!"

"That's not surprising, I'm too young to forget even chance acquaintances. But I must admit, I had forgotten about you and had no wish to meet you again."

"Is that so? How mortifying. You were going to the station, when I stopped you."

"How did you know where I was going?" – Her voice was surprised and annoyed.

"How should I not know? That's our ABC – the first lesson. I understand he's like a father to you? You've come because of him and that's why you're living here. To make his life easier. But he . . . the one we're discussing . . . he can't be given help in this way . . . not at all." He continued in an almost lyrical tone. "There have been many, citizeness Voinova, who have tried . . . to help their dear ones . . . But how will you live later? Be honest. For instance, what will you do . . . in the village with him? There are no opportunities for either of you there. The church there is closed. And you have your work back in town, your mother and your studies. How could your mother have let you come? Or perhaps she's longing for you to come back now?"

Both of them fell silent. Fomin was writing something down. At first Alya wanted to ask "What business is it of yours?", but some sort of inner hesitation held her back. She looked down at the point of her shoe and kept quiet, as if she had become dumb.

"Your uncle," began Fomin again, "is an important political activist, an anti-Soviet person and a dangerous opponent. You know, of course, of his early friendly relationship, which lasted for years, with the professor of history . . . and the patron of the institute where he worked as a teacher. Do you know all the circumstances which led to his ending up here? Do you know or not? Tell the truth . . ."

"I don't know about anything or anybody – I don't even know what he's accused of. Personally, I don't and cannot believe in his guilt. I wasn't at the institute. I only have secondary education. He's not guilty of anything except the fact that he's a priest."

"Young people always talk like that. I very much want to believe that you yourself were not closely linked with him. But don't you know that his sentence was recently reduced from the death penalty?"

"In other words," interrupted Alya, "they admitted he was innocent?"

"No, not at all . . . They merely took pity on a sick old man, whose days are limited . . ."

"Took pity on him?" – Alya raised her eybrows, "A twenty-five year sentence, that hard journey and exile in a distant village . . . was that taking pity on him?"

"We'd better get back to the point." – And he took up his pen, to question her about her documents. He wrote for a long time, then asked her to hear him out. The testimony showed that she, Alexandra Fyodorovna Voinova, aged 19 years and 8 months, born in Vitebsk province, also the daughter of a deceased servant of a religious cult, living at – her address followed, had in 1930 completed 10 years education at Leningrad Medical College Number 1, was working now at Pharmacy No. . . . as a trainee pharmaceutist; on 8 September 1931, she had arrived in Novosibirsk, the Western distribution centre, and then, after failing to find her relative, a servant of a religious cult, there, she came here to Irkutsk, the Eastern distribution centre, in order to visit him and hand over to him his warm clothes and other belongings, which were coming by slow train, as luggage. These belongings had been sent to him by his brother and the former wife of the accused, who had been divorced from him for 8 years. At this point, Fomin put the paper down, hoping to continue after more questioning.

"Now, tell me, why did you decide not only to hand over the luggage, but to journey out to join the exile? To lose your identity and ruin your young life? Who influenced you to do this?"

"Me? Nobody influenced me. It was my own wish?"

"All right. We'll write down "at her own wish." If I were the gentleman I used to be, I would say "your sentiments do you honour," But our sentiments often choose an object unworthy of their veneration. Isn't that so? Let me ask another question: what were your plans in going first to Novosibirsk, instead of coming here? Were they connected with this same old uncle of yours?"

"What plans?" – Alya frowned. "We were told in Leningrad that he was being sent to the Western distribution centre. So I was waiting for him there, finding myself lodgings somehow and going round the prisons, but he wasn't there. I sent a telegram

here, to Mrs. Bogdanova, she found out that he was here and
I came here. She doesn't know him herself, she's never met
him."

"And how is this citizeness Bogdanova connected with you?"

"She's my late father's god-daughter."

"Why is she living here?"

"She's been here since the Civil War. Her husband – that's him,
the sick man lying there in front of you – was working in a bank
that was transferred first to Ulan-Ude, then here. And so they
remained here."

"I see . . . a fine lady! But let's get back to you . . ." continued Fomin, now in the official voice of an interrogator, "How
did you personally see your situation, after you decided not
merely to hand over his belongings to him, but also agreed to
follow him into exile? What made you change your mind?"

Alya could not hide her amazement.

"What made me change my mind? Just pity. But now you
tell me something – how did you know I changed my mind?
We talked only to each other. No one else was present."

He could not hide a grin.

"That's the ABC, citizeness Voinova, the first letters of the
alphabet. So, then, you took pity on him. We'll write that down,
too, shall we . . . "In a fit of pity . . ."

She considered for a while.

"I don't know how to explain it to you more clearly . . . At
first we, his relations, thought that he would be released almost at
once and allowed to live in Novosibirsk. I would take him under
my wing, as a sick man." Fomin laughed. "I believed, and still do,
that he was innocent and would be released right away. But
when I saw him here," – her voice trembled – "how could I not
follow him into exile? Anyone would have been moved. He was
a shadow of a man . . . something you can't express in words . . ."

He interrupted her quite sharply.

"It's obvious that you're legally and politically illiterate. A real crackpot! If you'll pardon the expression. But fancy waiting around for a half month in Novosibirsk . . . to take charge of a character like that after his release!"

He got up and unexpectedly went up to Alya, putting his hand on her shoulder, in a would-be friendly manner. She immediately twisted her shoulder down sideways, throwing off his sympathetic gesture. He backed off at once.

"Go on home to your mum. It'll be better for you."

"Why shouldn't I go to the village? Am I not free to do as I please, after he has been sentenced and exiled? Even if, which I don't admit, he were guilty of anything, I am not accused of anything, and surely I am at liberty?"

"You? You are now also under surveillance. And you will remain under surveillance, not only after your arrival in the village, but for the rest of your life. You won't be allowed out of our sight. After a short period of time, he will die. And you will return home. But nevertheless, I assure you, you will remain under surveillance. In time, if you come to your senses, work, learn and serve the motherland, you will earn the confidence of the authorities and your first mistake will be cancelled out, you will no longer be under suspicion and the surveillance will be lifted. But while you're entangled with this old uncle, with his present existence and his political past and his activities, whose criminal nature I don't doubt, you will be under surveillance."

"But listen," Alya said, getting annoyed and barely controlling herself, "surely you don't link everybody with some case or other? Don't you recognize the claims of kinship, friendship or even of simple human feeling for a seriously ill man?"

Fomin shook his shaven skull and, bending over his paper, wrote on without stopping. "We have no such feelings, citizeness Voinova, nor can we have, while such dangerous elements exist . . ."

The door to the corridor opened and the cold flowed in round Alya's feet.

"My darling hens! You dear little feathered things!" – chanted Liza in the hall. "Just a minute, I'm coming, my little friends! I forgot all about you today! I'll give you some grits this minute, my little winged ones."

She came into the room as if nothing had happened, without looking at Fomin or Alya, first going up to her sick husband, as in duty bound:

"I forgot you too today, my old dear, and I didn't feed the hens. I would have boiled you some eggs in the morning, but see what happened! Well, how are things going? Have you finished your talk? You'd better knock off, you've had enough for today. Alya, lay the table! Is she allowed to walk round the flat? As if there were no end to the corridors here! There's just the one room and the kitchen. Found a real criminal, have you?"

"A political suspect, perhaps?" – Fomin corrected her gently.

"Our Alya doesn't know the first thing about politics. I can assure you of that."

"That's bad . . ."

"Oh, stop trying to trip me up! I won't be caught. Sit down, sit down. Alya, help me, dear! Drag out whatever was left over from yesterday, the piece of pie, the salmon-fish from the cellar, put these mushrooms in the salad-bowl, slice some bread! Put the frying pan on the stove, heat up the potatoes! We'll have something to start off with, and while we're eating that, the fresh potatoes will boil . . . Where are the brandy glasses, the cut glass ones? We'll have some of the strong stuff, iced, – or did I go and get it for nothing?"

And Liza, throwing her arms out gracefully, began to sing:

"Put on, put on the samovar, that golden cup,
I'm wating for my darling, in his silken shirt."

"This is a pleasant surprise," said Fomin, smiling, "I like it when the citizens aren't afraid of us. After all, are we some kind of horrors? We're just people. And if the law says we have to do something, how can we not? That's the position."

"That's enough about the law for today! Sit down! It's time to eat!"

As if in a fairy story, in spite of Liza's assertion that "there's nothing in the house, except some salmon-fish and potatoes," everything appeared on the table: mushrooms, and a piece of pie, cucumbers from the market, and salmon-fish . . . and fresh bread. And when she put on the table the green brandy glasses of rough glass, together with half a litre of table wine, the atmosphere became quite festive.

"This is real aristocratic crystal!" – boasted Liza.

"How come? Where did you get it?" – inquired their guest.

"There in the market, like everything else, at the Chinaman's. It was a present from my son, when he was at home. Cost 3 roubles 50 kopecks each."

"Those Chinks! They should have got a real hiding for that."

"Well, what do you expect – they were glasses belonging to the aristocracy, after all."

"The aristocracy have never been near them. It's just trickery!

"These Chinese" – said Ivan Alexandrovich's hoarse voice from his corner, "those scoundrels, who sell fake aristocratic glass, and treat the sick with all sorts of weeds, they're the ones you should be after in the first place, not people who aren't guilty of anything!"

"That's enough, Vanya, the authorities themselves will discover who's guilty." Liza interrupted him, "Let's have another drink to? Your health, Ivan Fomich! We didn't have a drink on the holiday, as Alya was ill. To the 14th anniversary: To peace! To everyone's health! Have a drink with us, my old dear, I'll give you some sweet tea in one of the Harach glasses."

Five days went by, like one. Alya calmed down, sat behind locked doors, slept in her clothes, felt restricted by Fomin's presence but was rarely subjected to his short interrogations during the day, in the same manner as at first. It was like a lesson –

the teacher would come, the pupil answered and everything proceeded in the same peaceful, homely way. Ivan Alexandrovich even joked somewhat: "I'm with you as a chaperone." However, he could not interfere, lying in the farthest corner of the large room, half-deaf, and indeed the "little chats," as Fomin called them were conducted quietly. At those wearisome moments when they took on an official tone, when the fountain pen and Alya's file were taken out and it seemed to be growing into a lengthy report, Alya's face would wrinkle, as if at a smell of wormwood. However, she answered quietly and calmly. Everything was turned over and was written down – her relatives, her childhood, her friends, the college, her work at the chemist's, and most of all, her church life, from the moment Alya first knew her political relative, the servant of the religious cult. They touched on the highest patron of the institute where he had taught, but Alya had not studied there and did not know him, although his name, as head, had been known to all. It would seem there was no need of further questioning, but all the same there were still uninvestigated points to probe.

Fomin was trying to convince Alya that she must not only forget her planned journey, but that she must completely expunge from her mind even the memory of the criminal who had been spared the death penalty. Something strange and terrible took place in her during such interrogations, something living and real was evaporating from her soul; the thread of hope that she would meet her dear father was being cut. She seemed to have spent all her strength before taking the final step; her fiery longing to follow in his footsteps and serve him had died down. All her desire to be free of questions, to go for her ticket and travel to the village from Irkutsk had become a thing of the past. The reality was this: the clean-shaven young man, with his hair cut down to his smooth skull, his glance darting from place to place, who oppressed everyone in the house, especially the sick Ivan Alexandrovich. Fomin went on smoking, forgetting her request not to smoke in the room, while she had got tired of reminding him constantly; he lay on his couch, with his note book or a newspaper in his hand, whistling "Varyag"; putting his feet on the stool, applying polish to his boots with a rag, but he was everywhere, penetrating into every place, and she could never hide from him anywhere. Liza nicknamed him "Alya's room-mate," which drove the girl mad. At such moments, she would whisper despairingly to Liza "It would have been better for me to be in prison" . . . "What are you saying, don't take on so, bear up," – was the answer, "It'll soon end. I know what it's like."

Sometimes he sent Liza for cigarettes, sometimes he went for them himself, showing his trust in his prisoner.

Fomin had finished going through Alya's case long ago; he understood that there was no danger in her, but his behaviour was dictated and planned out from above; he had to toe the line and carry out his duties to the end. If water had to be brought in from the well, or if Alya merely had to go out into the corridor, Liza went with her, as if by agreement, and although Fomin had no doubt that Alya would not run away, he still did not allow her freedom of movement. They ate at about six o'clock. Liza performed culinary miracles, transforming thin tripe into something resembling liver. She sacrificed to the 'room-mate' two salmon-fish intended for Alya's provisions on her journey, cooked bean fritters and each day she brought home half a litre of alcohol, spending Alya's travel money, and her room-mate drank it out of an aristocratic green brandy glass. The aristocratic glass was a real help to them. Liza and Alya also drank quarter of a glass each. Everyone grew more cheerful, and most of all, the stranger turned for a while into an ordinary guest, quite talkative and even considerate towards the sick man.

"What, have you tired your sides out sleeping, dad?" – he would say in a sympathetic tone, "Get up, have a drink with us!"

At one of these moments, Fomin told them he had a wife and
three-year old son in Minusinsk, that he had been sent here on
temporary assignment, and that he was longing to see his family
again. Alya longed only that no news should come from the
village at present, as this man would of course open the letter.
When everyone went to bed in the evening, Alya alone did not
undress, but sat at her made-up couch of stools and benches, such
was the oppressive effect of her 'room-mate's' presence. He gave
her benevolent advice, "don't be shy" – "We're honourable
family men, you can't behave as if you were in a railway carriage
for the sixth night running." . . .

Paying no attention to such advice, Alya continued to be shy
and only at dead of night did she lie down, taking off her shoes
and lightly unfastening some buttons, while listening to her 'room-
mate's' tranquil snore and Ivan Alexandrovich's tiresome cough.

It was very early in the morning. In the corridor, the cock
had flown off the hearth and was clearing his throat. Someone
knocked at the door. Liza, her sheepskin over her shoulders,
dived into the corridor. Still dreaming, Alya heard Fomin's
name. A telegram from Minusinsk was handed to him. It had
just been received at the police station. The temporary address of
the official at the Bogdanovs was known.

Woken by Liza, Fomin leapt up at once. While they were
opening the shutters, he ran out into the yard and there opened
the telegram from his wife. The few words decided everything.
"Vitya has scarlet fever, he's in hospital, come at once."

Fomin got ready to go just as suddenly as he had come, without
wasting a minute. The train was due to depart in the afternoon,
but he had to hand in his report and register his departure. The
father in him now came to the fore. The case of some girl, who
had landed herself in Siberia, whose motives he had been assigned
to clarify, as well as the girl's character, – all this vanished,
became – as it was in fact – harmless. Vitya, with his little blue

eyes, his single words, his puffy little hands, might die, could die suddenly while his father was on his way to him! And Fomin swore, putting on his belt, pushing something into his pockets. Alya hurriedly sewed a button on to his cuff, Liza was wrapping up two biscuits and a piece of pie for him to eat on the journey, for surely he would get hungry. He protested, but took then in the end; both of them brushed his shirt for him. Finally, his footsteps left the room, he was already in the past. The shutters were wide open, the hens were clucking away in the corridors. Alya fell on Liza's neck, both of them crying and laughing; Ivan Alexandrovich sat up in bed, saying something which the two embracing each other could not hear.

"Liza, you're saved me from everything! Darling! I'll never forget you!"

But Liza was already wiping her eyes and laughing, and singing: "Put on, put on the samovar, lay out the golden cups . . ."

They counted up what was left of Alya's money after Fomin's departure. Six half-litres, and the snacks for supper, the two salmon-fish borrowed from a neighbour – the travel money had decreased almost by half. They decided to sell the shoes on the market. After all, what good would beige shoes be in the village? They were snapped up immediately, but at half price. The intimidated Alya was in constant terror that Fomin would return. Liza only laughed. "He's rushing to his son at full speed now, he's forgotten all about you! What a noxious character he was!"

Walking round the market with Liza, Alya breathed in the icy air to the full extent of her lungs – "Free, I'm free!" – she whispered. But in spite of everything, new, unhappy thoughts knocked at her heart and crept in. After Fomin, the flat smelt of cigarettes and cheap after-shave. Liza wrapped Ivan Alexandrovich up in her woolly blanket and set to ventilating the room. Quarter of an hour later, both of them started to wash the floor.

"So that not a trace of our room-mate will remain!" – said Liza, wringing out her cloth at this. "Then we'll light the fire . . .

And tomorrow morning . . . be off and get your ticket! If you're going, then go!"

While they were drinking their tea in the evening, Alya wilted and retreated into herself. Neither Liza's caresses nor her cheery jokes about their recent guest could raise her spirits. She was depressed. Where had her longing for the road gone? Was this the same Alya who had rejected all persuasion, Father Symeon's talk, Fomin's threats, who had made nought of difficulties – and firmly held to her resolve? No, she was not the same. Apathetically, she stirred her tea with a spoon. She found it hard to lift her head to look at her surroundings. Now, when the path was open before her, when no-one was dissuading her as before, when everything was on her side, she was overcome with a feeling of heaviness. The luggage had been dealt with, she was travelling lightly, and by going she was relieving people who had suffered difficulties in one way or another because of her . . . yet, unexpectedly, an incomprehensible weariness had enchained her; some kind of change had taken place in her soul. Not only did she not want to travel anywhere, even getting out of her chair was difficult. How eagerly she had awaited his belongings a few days ago! How happily she had carried round the parcels with Liza! How she had longed to go to the village. Everything had faded away completely in her unhappy soul. She scarcely replied to questions. She excused herself by saying she had a headache and swallowed a piramidon tablet. At last night fell. The shutters had been closed long ago; if she got a ticket to Tulun in the morning, she would be leaving in the evening. However, as soon as Alya closed her eyes, she started to think of her mother. Her mother had been screened from her, as if by a dividing wall, by her worries about Uncle Pavel and her efforts on his behalf. Only once, when she had received the bitter, reproachful letter from her mother, had Alya turned to her in her thoughts, but with what thoughts! Those of agitated emotion, of annoyance . . . They were divided by the wall of Alya's sudden wish to go to the village, the torments and sorrows produced by such a decision, by all the incidents of life here, in this distant provincial town. In the quiet and darkness of night, when the minutes flying silently by into eternity were interrupted by the invalid's cough and Liza's even snoring, the image of her mother came before Alya in almost tangible form. In a short dream – they were standing together in the cathedral which Alya had recently visited, in front of the ikon of St. Nicholas; her mother was standing very straight, a thin figure who seemed to be merging with the wall, on a level with the ikon; Alya was holding in her hand one of the amethysts from Father Pavel's cross and heard her mother telling her "Give the stone to the Saint" . . . Alya hesitated, but her mother came to her aid. Separating herself from the wall, she took the Book of the Gospels and its cover from the Saint, revealing his living powerful hand. With an inquiring movement of the palm upwards, the hand moved towards Alya's fist, which was clenched round the stone. And Alya unclenched her fingers . . .

"Take it, Father Nicholas," she said to him, "I'm sorry that you had to ask . . . take it . . ." The amethyst shone with a heavenly light on his palm, the hand that had taken the stone closed round it, and once more Alya saw before her the image of the Saint, his hand under the book cover and under the cover, the Gospels. Alya awoke. It was morning. The heaviness of yesterday had disappeared. She felt light hearted. The journey did not worry her. How blessedly easy it was to breathe freely, she felt in a beautiful mood, somehow beyond her own existence and will. But she had hardly dressed and gone out, when the light and shining feeling in her soul changed to alarm and tears. Liza was opening telegram – it was from Nina Vasilievna. "Mother ill, no money left, come home at once."

There are commands in life, which cannot be ignored. Perhaps there are a few people who force themselves to, who become heroes, but Alya immediately buried all thoughts of

journeying to her dear father. There was no time even to go into
what had happened in detail. The train would leave at 6 o'clock
in the evening. Naturally, a daughter could not feel as joyful as
she had that morning. But there was no longer any burden
weighing her down; it had been replaced by worry about her
mother, which now awoke in full and turned her thoughts to
home: "Come at once, mother ill." The words "no money left"
would not have held Alya back, although she was intending to
travel with only the bare necessities. But her mother? What was
the illness? What had happened to her? "Give the stone to the
Saint" she had said to her last night, in her dream, ... If only
you're alive and well, dear mother!

She had to hurry. They got the ticket at once, the same morning. Alya took an envelope and writing paper. She blotted the
letter with her tears. But never mind the blots and stains, or the
gaps – he would understand, he must understand it all! She would
receive a reply from him only when she reached Leningrad. She
asked his forgiveness for her unconsidered action. Everything had
been against her idea and her promise to follow him. She felt that
all the heavenly powers had come out against her plan. Her
mother had fallen ill and she would have to return. "This is what
I've realised," scrawled Alya quickly, "which I must share with
you. We have to earn, by our lives, by such labour, tears and en-
durance, the blessing of being permitted to serve people like you.
I dared to say I would, but it was a flash in the pan. I gave you
hope, and deceived you. Forgive me, bless me, don't forget me
and pray for me!" Forgetting the censorship, weeping, she
finished the letter. But her tears did not burden her, as she stuffed
the letter into the envelope; there was no dead weight on her
breast.

Everyone sat down for a minute, to see Alya off. Even Ivan
Alexandrovich put his feet on the floor. When Liza and Alya
were already moving towards the door, he got up, holding on to
a chair, pulling on his galoshes, cut to fit his foot, and saying

"Well, I'll escort Alechka to the doorway," he walked along beside the wall, holding on to the hangings. A shudder of pity overcame Alya. This was the last time! She would never see him again! Perhaps she might meet Liza again, but him – never! This sick, good-natured grumbler, who had given uncle Pavel his son's coat without objections – she would never see him again. How much she had lived through at their house! She turned back to the large, bright, poorly-furnished but clean and orderly room. Here, not long ago, her 'room-mate' had slept on the narrow couch; there, she had stood looking out at the snowstorm, thinking of the delayed luggage. It was all over! Her suitcase and plaid bag were loaded on to the sledge. Liza would come with her to the station, it was not far on foot. In two hours, the train would be leaving the town ... It was not very cold, only 25 degrees of frost. Alya had an incomprehensible feeling of emptiness, or was it relief? – she did not know herself. Could it be that it was all over, for good, that she was going away ... not where her thoughts were tending ... where her sorrowing heart reverently longed to be, – but home? Now Ivan Alexandrovich was stepping back behind the door: "A safe journey! Go with God!" – Alya heard his last words and, turning round, shouted to him "Thank you for everything!". Liza was driving the hens back inside: "Where are you off to? Into the frost? The devil take you! Do you want to perish?" The grey bolt slipped back, the high gate opened. The sledge runners scraped along, the sledge slid after Liza and Alya and the boarded fence was left far behind them, that fence near which Alya had so recently bumped into her room-mate. Quickly, ever more quickly, the sledge flew over the road, which sparkled like diamonds; everything she had lived through was becoming 'the past.' Soon the shaky boarded footpaths of the roads near the station, the Angara and the station would be no more than a dream, would become part of her memories. Alya was silent, the sledge creaked along, but Liza could not control her tongue. Nekrasov was remembered once again. "What did I say, Alechka? Remember? Life's always like that: we are destined to have fine adventures, but it is not given to us to complete them!" Alya said nothing, but Liza, to sweeten the pill, whispered again to Alya, secretly, as if in the presence of the 'room-mate': "Down there on one side, in the basket, I've put in two dried salmon-fish for you . . . and a couple of eggs . . . and you'll manage some of yesterday's pies . . . and a piece of cheese. But you'd better not get out at the stations . . . You never know, the train might suddenly go . . . and you'll be left there . . ." Alya said nothing in reply to this either.

In the late evening, the train was approaching Tulun. Strange ornamental leaves and flowers, covered with grey beads of frost, were growing densely over the carriage windows. It was impossible to see the station as well as its surroundings. Alya did not lie down to sleep, waiting for Tulun. It was the connection to Bratsk, and from it a hundred kilometre land journey over hills and mountain ridges led to Ust-Vikhorevo, the village where Father Pavel was even now expecting her arrival.

A mad idea occurred to Alya when the railway carriages slowed down before Tulun and approached the station, with frozen wheels and chains screeching. They would stop for five minutes, enough time to throw down her things and, with 25 roubles left in her pocket, to reach her goal somehow. What sort of idea was this? Where did this impulse come from? It was the soul's last effort not to surrender its sacred, impossible dream. But the idea, although it was conscious, clear and obvious, found no point of support. It was driven back and smashed to smithereens by another, more powerful thought, sanctioned by life itself: "Mother, how is she? Will she recover?"

The full moon was illuminating the station, when Alya went out on the platform of the train, throwing on her coat and scarf. There was a small station building, with a typical Siberian fence leading away from it in opposite directions. Two windows were lit up, the third was dark. The bare poplar trees did not obscure the light from the windows, the shadow of their branches swayed weirdly on the station wall . . . blown by the wind . . . The train was still waiting. The girl's eyes stared longingly into the dim, snowy distance. She wanted to see, to pierce through two hundred kilometres: to achieve the impossible, to see what was happening there. He would only know in two weeks' time that she was not coming to him. Nekrasov had been right: "we are destined to have fine adventures . . ." Liza had been right, too, when she had reminded her of those words. She had been right, because . . .

A long, mournful whistle interrupted her thoughts.

"She was right . . . because . . . I'm leaving Tulun . . ."

The carriages moved off, creaking . . . And Alya remembered the Siberian woman from Ushakovka, who – after her first meeting with Father Pavel – had said to her outside the prison, firmly and admonishingly: "You might well have missed him, mightn't you?"

She, that simple woman, had been right. Her heart contracted painfully, Somehow, in some inscrutable way, Alya had missed him.

PART THREE

Chapter 1

UST-VIKHOREVO

The warm, windless autumn of 1931 kept the Angara open for navigation until the middle of October. The days stayed sunny and calm; before noon it began to get hot. From the twentieth of September onwards, the morning frosts called to mind the fact that the frosts of winter were near, but this misty veil would dissolve, the rosy-orange sun would rise, the sky turned blue, the sun beat down on open ground, and summer shone out all around. All the same, almost from the day Alya arrived in Irkutsk, the captains had been announcing on the jetty that the last passage from Irkutsk to Bratsk would be in a few days. One week went by, then another, but the tow-boats were still leaving the jetty as before, dragging behind them barges loaded with coal, grain and barrels of salmon-fish from the Upper Tunguzka. Finally the last but one return journey by steamer from Irkutsk to Bratsk was announced; on this steamer a transport of exiles was to be sent to Bratsk, for a further journey to the village of Ust-Vikhorevo. The two-day journey by water, just over 600 kilometres, did not scare people; they sighed "at last!" and there was rejoicing in the prison. From the stories of the residents, the prisoners certainly saw the 150 kilometres from Bratsk to Vikhorevo as the last trial they would have to undergo, or just as a terrible nightmare, but even a relative freedom cheered them up and made them glad. The cramped prison conditions had dragged on too long, weighing heavily on many people, some of them in solitary cells, some in communal cells, but nevertheless for all of them it was equally suffocating, dusty, separated from nature, from the sky and its lights, cut off from impressions of life, without friends, relatives or home. And now, when many of them were completely worn out and shaken by their experiences, by the sudden summonses from the cell and the night interrogations, when a man would be ordered to pick up his things and go out of the door, not knowing where he was going or what was in store for him, – now, a distant village beyond Bratsk, beyond the rapids on the Angara, surrounded by the *taiga* forest and cliffs, seemed an inviolable spot, a longed-for peaceful fireside, – like an unknown homeland. Almost all those going on the journey with Father Pavel were being exiled for short terms – 3 years or 5 years. His 25-year sentence* did not arouse either horror or contempt in his companions, nor was he even suspected of being some important criminal. On the contrary, they not only felt sympathy for the pale, stooping man, with a stick in his hand, but regarded him with simple, childlike curiosity as an older comrade, journeying with them into the distance, to lead a new existence. But people did get puzzled trying to guess what his crime had been and why he had been given such a long sentence. Everyone knew his own case and his own transgressions. Many hoped that they would be amnestied or have their sentences shortened. But what could this man have done? There did not seem to be any vices in his character. What were the terrifying 25 years for? The same accountant who was always short of breath, who was being sent to Ust-Udu for 5 years, wholly accepted his 5 years, not understanding Father Pavel's 25 years. Unable to restrain his curiosity, he began to talk to him about his sentence. The priest merely looked at him silently, smiling, but in his silence there was a trace of injured feeling. The accountant realised this, and apologised for his

* This is a mistake on the author's part. The 25 year sentence was introduced into the Soviet penal code only in 1937 and was a labour-camp term, not a period of exile. Father Pavel was serving a term of so-called "unrestricted exile" that is, he was allowed to live in a private house.

tactless question. However, Father Pavel immediately told him not to reproach himself and also relieved him of his thoughts about some great crime on the priest's part – he explained, as far as his companion could understand it, that a whole group of people, so-called servants of a religious cult, had come under surveillance at a particular historical moment, that was all ... We are bound to answer when asked what we believe, or how we have behaved. As for the rest – God's will be done! They had given him a 25-year term, but the Lord was powerful enough to release him at once, if He so willed it.

The accountant looked at Father Pavel with keen interest.

"So you're hoping for an amnesty just the same, Father Pavel?"

A bright look was his answer.

"Yes, I firmly hope that my case will soon be resolved!"

"Then, of course," thought the accountant, going away from Father Pavel, "if they give him an amnesty, ... But what if he's guilty of something anyway, or mixed up in something shady? What self-conceit!"

Liza's coat (the red sheepskin one) had arrived in time; they had brought it with a parcel on the day before he had to leave the prison. In addition to the coat, the parcel had contained soft boots, mittens, a scarf and everything he needed for winter.

During his last days in the prison, Father Pavel had become acquainted with a young man, twenty years old or a little older, who was going into exile with him – Fyodor Ukorov. He had come to feel an overwhelming sympathy for the priest. "Taken a fancy to you," said the guards affably, recognizing the exiles as free people already. What could the two of them have in common: the young man, a prisoner but still full of life and passion, and the man who was old and ill, in spite of being only 55 years old, who was a servant of a religious cult into the bargain, a "pope," as everyone called him here?

However, it is often impossible to explain why people like each other. Friendship is not always felt immediately or wholly, nor can anyone become a friend. Ukorov was sitting out his term in another block, but the exiles were already allowed some privileges; they met each other more often and more freely and could talk to each other for longer periods.

On the day before their departure, the ten going to Vikhorevo were issued their provisions for the journey: each of them got one kilogramme of rusks, made of roughly ground wheat, which looked like finely textured sponges, and 200 grammes of dried fish, – dried, bony fish. Nobody complained about being hungry on the journey, as almost everyone had received a parcel the day before, almost all of them had friends or relations in Irkutsk, and everyone turned out to have some brick tea, cucumbers, butter, dried cottage-cheese, sugar and eggs. Father Pavel was well-supplied for the journey, but how was he to carry his things? He could not lift them, or even walk, and he joked: "When they take me out, I'll sit down on the threshold; will you leave me by the wall, or drag me behind you?" But he was assurred that "there'll be transport for the sick, they won't abandon you." The coat was making things difficult for him. Father Pavel still had his old travelling cassock, which he had snatched up at home to take with him; he had worn it after arriving in Irkutsk, when walking from the station to the prison. Should he wear it, letting his weak legs get tangled up in it, making an absurd spectacle of himself in front of everyone? It would be difficult, unpleasant and cold . . . But would he not be hot, in the coat, when he had been warmed by the sun? He began to worry about how he was to carry the sheepskin coat across his shoulders. But all these worries disappeared with the advent of Fyodor Ukorov. He was young and strong and had something in him that swept aside all obstacles. "First of all you'll have to wear the coat round your shoulders. They'll give us a cart to the jetty – you'll be riding in it. We'll get there at about 6 o'clock in the morning – it won't be hot! The tow-boat will leave at 7.30, or 8 o'clock, while it's still cold. And on the boat it'll be really useful – as a pillow, or a blanket. You can roll it up or spread it out in a moment. Our destination, Bratsk, is quite far, and you don't know what the weather'll be like!" And Fyodor helped Father Pavel to pack his things, dividing the whole march into parts – he would carry the large sack on his back and the rest in his hands. "I haven't got much baggage," he boasted, "just this bag, and myself!"

However, Father Pavel was still worried – how would he manage to overcome the 115 kilometres to the village? How would they get there?

"As for that," said Fyodor, cheering him up, "they'll give us some carts in Bratsk, the ones they call "the little coffins." They'll give us two or three of those and some sort of small horse. We'll ride or crawl along the broken ground. I've already said I'll help you, and that's the end of it. As for this spiny dried fish, this gremille and perch, what's it good for? We're well provided. We'll just prick our tongues eating it. There's a fellow over there who's needy, we'd better give it to him, – that pale fellow, he's inside for murder. He's been in the camps a long time. He's employed here in the parcels section, they commuted his death sentence."

How could Father Pavel fail to recognize the "pale fellow"? During his month in Irkutsk, he had also been a helper and well-wisher to him . . . He was being held here before being sent to his second concentration camp. On parting from the priest, the pale prisoner burst into tears.

"You'll pray for me, pope, won't you," he said, shedding tears rapidly, "When you go tomorrow, I'll be watching you from the window. We walked here together when we arrived, remember? There's power in your prayers. If God exists – maybe He'll have mercy on me? Ask Him on my behalf . . . for so-and-so . . . You know my Christian name? I'm Vasily . . ."

"You could try to pray yourself," whispered Father Pavel loudly, "do try . . . After all, the thief on the cross . . . he was forgiven . . ." Tears choked him. Their parting was interrupted by Fyodor.

"They're definitely going to give us a cart!" – he reported joyfully, "I told them to put in a bit more straw, but they barked at me 'Who do you think you are, snotty-nose, and who are you ordering about? We'll be carrying dead meat in the cart, even if we do put more straw in it, but you, a young man, should be ashamed, look who you've taken up with!' But I don't care!" – concluded Ukorov, "They'll take you to the tow-boat and that'll be that. Just as long as they get you there!".

"Don't get involved for no reason," the priest shook his head. "I'm extremely grateful to you for your help and your efforts on my behalf, but you mustn't attract attention to yourself. I know your surname, I remember it's . . . Ukorov. But what's your Christian name?"

"Fyodor Ukorov. There are lots of Fyodors, but I was named after the warrior saint . . . St. Theodore Stratilates."

The pale lips gave a momentary smile.

"So you know of St. Theodore the Warrior. How is that?"

"Speaking for myself, I don't know anything about him," said Ukorov at once, "I don't remember my father or my mother. But I was told about the warrior by an old woman, a relative of mine. She christened me and used to visit me at the orphanage; they had these orphanages under Tsarism, like the children's homes they have now," – he informed Father Pavel plainly, "And I remember that she used to keep telling me, you're not just any kind of Fyodor, you're named after the Warrior saint."

"Well, that's wonderful! So you, Fyodor, should be a warrior by nature – he was a martyr, but in his lifetime he was a warrior."

"What, me?" laughed Ukorov, "what sort of warrior am I? First of all, I'm a thief. I was in a concentration camp, but they sent me here for other reasons, they nailed me with politics, I talked too much . . . back in the village . . . that happened when I was seventeen. And now I'm 22 already. Been working for three years now! Well, I won't die of boredom, will I? Then I was guilty, certainly, but now?" He was quite willing to tell the priest about his past; he did not remember his father, his relations were on his mother's side, but she had died early and if it had not been for his old grandmother, who visited him in the orphanage and at home, he would have been quite alone. He had gone off the straight and narrow path while he was still a boy. He had done time in a reformatory, then in a camp, but there, at work among new comrades, he had encountered words of life, about Eternal Truth, God and the New Way. Since then, he had eagerly sought the truth, taking part in arguments; he had been honest from then onwards, but he had landed up here– because he read spiritual books and knew religious believers, sectarians. Fyodor was an ardent seeker after truth and Father Pavel did not find it difficult to understand the young man and respond to his need; he was quite open and direct, accepting advice or explanations immediately, and it was not long before he was as close to him as a relative.

Chapter 2

They set off on their journey the day after the feast of the Intercession, early in the morning. The day promised to be fine. The
exiles arrived at the jetty at almost the same time as the cart
which provided transport for the sick Father Pavel and the guard,
sitting on the meagre layer of hay. Rattling over the stony wharf,
the cart came to a halt by the jetty, leaving its passengers with
well bruised sides and hips. Some of the exiles' luggage, such as
Father Pavel's little suitcase and bundle, was immediately thrown
off it and lay beside a heap of coiled rope. A merchant-passenger
steamer – towboat of the old type, with a paddle wheel, bearing
the naive inscription "Tiger Cub" on the bows, was rocking
gently on the waves by the shore. It stank of tar and oil, mixed
with a barely-distinguishable smell of baked bread and rusty
herring-barrels. The morning cleared, the rim of the sun's
shining head-band rose gradually above the horizon. The day
awoke; the outlines of the town appeared out of the mist, as if
from behind a fabulous, airy veil, which slowly faded and
vanished. Buildings, walls, church belfries emerged out of the
mist. The crests of the restless autumn waves were foaming and
turning grey on the river. The narrow gangway, white with the
morning frost, shook slightly under their feet. Ten people crossed
the creaking little bridge onto the steamer. They all settled down
in the stern, no-one wanted to go below, down to the smoke-
filled, four-bunk cabins.

There was still half-an-hour before the departure of the tow-
boat; the sailors checked the ropes attached to the barge and
tightened the tarpaulin over the sacks of coal. Meanwhile, on
the jetty, some people who had come to see them off had arrived

171

and were standing by the gangways in a small crowd . . . Father
Pavel glanced at them, and an almost unbearable premonition of
the distance ahead overcame him. Where was he being taken?
Why? What was he to do there? Irkutsk, Leningrad, – that was
a great distance of dry land, but could be reached by rail, – so his
thoughts followed each other, making his heart heavy, – but
now, he was being taken beyond the railway, he was being completely cut off, for ever, from all that was dear to him; 600 kilometres along the river and 115 more – past terrible steep cliffs – to
Vikhorevo itself, And the vastness of the Angara and its crested
waves penetrated his consciousness, like an image of eternity.

The first whistle sounded. Everyone on the boat came alive
and got up, someone on the jetty was sobbing, but the Tiger
Cub, still chained to the bank, went on rocking gently on the
dark, translucent water. A moment later, yet another passenger
threw himself on to the deck; he was drunk and could hardly
stand on his feet, but stopped himself from falling over, clasping
to his chest a large paper bag full of baked meat-pies. He was in
an extremely good mood, in very high spirits, and immediately
asked the captain when he would get to Makarevo. The
captain, screwing up his Buryat eyes, looked at him and smiled.

"You'd better go and lie down in a cabin, comrade, there's
room . . . You'll be able to sleep till we reach your stop – it'll be
10 hours, we'll wake you!"

"Comrade captain," the drunk insisted on going on, "allow me to
ask, will we be going straight up the river or zig-zagging about?"

The audience chuckled. Drunk before the boat had left, what
fun! However, the captain did not permit any familiarities or
jokes about his own Angara, even from a drunk, and immediately,
with dignity, came to the defence of his native river.

"Don't talk rubbish to me! Don't you know our water-
routes? What kind of Siberian are you then? Did you ever see a
snake, how it weaves from side to side? It goes straight to its
goal! Go below and sleep. Makes me ill listening to you!"

The boat's whistle sounded a second time, sending a cloud of smoke up out of the funnel. Everyone leant over the sides of the ship. Ukorov went up to Father Pavel, as if he had guessed how he was feeling. The captain stood, as if rooted to the spot, by the gangway. Meanwhile, the drunken man had turned round awkwardly to face Ukorov and Father Pavel, swaying on his unsteady legs; he came up to them, taking a piece of meat-pie out of his paper bag;

"Take it, for the love of God!" – he said, almost pushing it into Father Pavel's mouth, "Do me the honour, don't insult me, don't reject my bread and salt, – the meat-pies are still hot, straight from the oven, – do taste it!"

He had to take the piece of pie, in response to these insistent pleas. Taking the bread and salt, he asked the giver his name. 'Anisim!' Father Pavel was so taken aback by a coincidence of names that occurred to him, so lost in thought, that the third whistle, followed by a jolt, the grating noise of the gangway being removed, the order to 'cast away', the smack of a wet rope against the deck, – all sounded to him as if it was happening far away, as if in a dream ... Now the captain was shouting into a loudspeaker from the bridge, thickly, as if talking into a gas-mask, sending down the order 'slow speed!' Now the paddle-steamer had detached itself from the jetty and was off on its 600 kilometre journey, but Father Pavel, deeply sunk in his own thoughts, had missed the moment of unmooring and only awoke from an unknown dream when the "Tiger Cub" had already moved out into the wide stretch of water by Irkutsk, before starting on its way, leaving behind the city walls, the cathedral belfry, the outskirts and building sites, the station, the lines of goods-trains on the railway lines ... all this was changing colour, fading away into the distance ... The banks of Irkutsk became wreathed in a pinkish-grey film of mist; soon afterwards, the austere outlines of the Innokenty Monastery walls floated past, slowly melting away in the rays of the early sun.

All the exiles and guards were still in the stern; no-one wanted to go below to the cabins, in spite of the chill of the morning frost. Father Pavel was sunk in his own thoughts. Ukorov made as if to go up to him, but then went away, realising that his companion's thoughts were far away, while the piece of pie, wrapped up in a handkerchief, lay on the bench beside him ...

This was the picture which Father Pavel was seeing before his eyes, as if it were real: – the large, bright cell of the nun Anisya, the blessed elder sister of the Novodevichy Convent. The table was laid for a feast-day and Mother Anisya, together with her young novice, was herself serving the guests. Among the guests were Father Pavel himself, two nuns, the churchwarden from the Alexander Nevsky Lavra and two arch-priests from the cathedral. Each guest had his own plate, his own knife and fork, but Father Pavel was being skilfully by-passed by Mother Anisya. He had been given neither a plate, nor a knife and fork, but she had put a piece of freshly-baked cabbage-pie right in front of him, on the tablecloth, and was patting him on the head like a child, encouraging him: "Eat, eat up the pie, my little father, don't be bashful. You'll be glad of such a piece, when you travel down the wide river ... Take it in your hands, eat it, get used to it!"

Some of the guests had been embarrassed, others had laughed, – Father Pavel had eaten the pie with his hands, for the sake of obedience, and then had thought no more about it in those peaceful years. He knew that "Anisya behaves strangely," and that was all. And then she was a holy fool, why should she go by the same rules and norms of behaviour as ordinary people? When they had been drinking tea after the pies, she had taken a book and given it to the churchwarden from the Lavra: "Read to me, and I'll listen to what you read!" The churchwarden had read, she had kept on stopping him, correcting him, so keenly and with such lively humour, in her Rybinsk dialect, that the pie incident had been eclipsed and no one had remembered it then, or even paid any attention to it, as they should have. But now, in spite of the fact that there, in far-off Leningrad, and also in the Irkutsk distribution centre, he had been called "mentally disturbed" and unbalanced, he – the same "mental defective" – had again and again penetrated into the unattainable, had become deeply absorbed in the essence of things, passing into the mysterious world of revelation and prediction, beloved of the heart . . . How could the blessed Mother Anisya have known about the wide river? He was now sailing down the broad stretch of water, and beside him lay the piece of pie, given to him by "Anisim" . . . The coincidence of names was a mystery . . . Thinking and mediating reverently on this, he forgot himself, his troubles and the distant journey at that moment . . . All that was earthly had become as nothing. Through the alms he had received he had ceased to be a prisoner and a slave. The steamer's paddle-wheel was going round, gurgling, parting the crested waves . . . "Inconceivable are Thy ways, o God!" – and he crossed himself expansively, gazing into the distance. "Thy path is in the great waters" . . .

Quietly, Ukorov came and sat next to him. All this time he had been looking for an opportunity to talk about himself, but until now his secret wish had not been satisfied . . . He felt troubled and overcome by the home-sickness of an exile . . . He accepted the piece of pie he was handed and began to eat in silence.

"You're homesick, I see," asked Father Pavel tenderly, guessing at the young man's state of mind, "Well, never mind, we'll get rid of that in the village . . . You have work waiting for you . . . not like us old men."

Fyodor's voice sounded rough and grumbling, not like his usual friendly tone towards Father Pavel.

"How can I not be homesick? I hardly had time to begin life again after getting out of the camp – and I was off once more. They should have decided my fate at once. I've already told you how and why it happened ... I don't understand it myself. I was searching for the truth, and they nailed me with a political charge ... I've been looking for someone like you for a long time ... I want to have a heart-to-heart talk with you ... a sincere talk, about everything, without hiding anything."

"Only speak the whole truth, and don't lie," Father Pavel warned him, "Otherwise I won't even begin to listen ..."

"The whole truth, and nothing else!" – said Fyodor, and his sincerity sounded in his voice, to the point of tears. "Only talk to me as a friend. I'm not used to formality. I'll be like a son to you ... I never knew my own father ... How would that be?"

What had happened to Fyodor often happens to people, especially young people, when they have entangled themselves to the point of madness in the twisted mess of their life and then try to find a way out of this mess, deeply longing to open their heart to another human being, to empty their soul to the core and reshape it. And he had met just such a human being in prison, an exhausted, sick man, in his worn but priestly garb, with his special, bright outlook on everything, but Fyodor had known he would be going with him on the same transport, to the same village. The young man had spent the night in troubled dreams about the priest, thinking: "let him understand me!" And then he would retort defiantly: "if he doesn't understand and won't listen to me – all right, I don't need him!" "The whole truth" sounded out as an answer to his doubts; the sweet pain of repentance and the consolation that would follow filled his soul.

Chapter 3

The steamer travelled at an unhurried pace, puffing out white smoke, swaying almost imperceptibly on the broad waves and dragging behind it the fully loaded barge. People felt themselves to be free on the boat, the guards no longer bothered them. They were now "our own sort," whose business was just to deliver the required number of exiles to Bratsk, or 'Bratsk fortress' as they called it in the old fashioned style, and who would then return to Irkutsk on the last boat.

The day was turning out fine, everyone was still in the stern. The steep rocks overhanging the Angara stretched along the river banks, sometimes covered with moss, sometimes bare, in places adorned by a covering of conifer shoots or young forest plants: "It's just like a film!" – exclaimed one of the exiles. A solitary cedar, growing at the very edge of the river, was letting its cones fall into the water; a lightly-winged family of gulls, flying up from the waves, settled on the cliff; an eagle, with a sweep of its wings, soared high in the austere sky, Father Pavel took a deep breath, taking in the sounds around him, drinking in the majestic sights of a Siberian autumn – and whispered, unheard by anyone else, "This is my rest for ever, here will I dwell." The way of life he had known before had ceased to be a reality. The waters of the Angara enticed his soul onwards, on into the unknown distance, which he could not clearly distinguish yet. A change was taking place in him which an experienced doctor would have found easy to diagnose, when watching a seriously ill patient take a turn for the better. Everything that, in prison, had led him to collapse, grow numb and admit the triumph of death over the sources of life, had now disappeared, – had departed from him, like a serious illness. He woke up, sitting in the stern, in his huge sheepskin coat, with forgotten holy words lighting up his mind, his eyes gazing at new scenes, and that which must have been germinating inside him all this time was now maturing and putting out shoots. He could not analyse himself, as a man cannot check and analyse his own pulse correctly, but already the young Ukorov had been attracted to his personality, seeking his help and consideration; already the pale prisoner had wept on his breast at Irkutsk, asking for his prayers . . . and the mentally shaken convict-priest, the mental defective, as some called him, was now reviving here, on the steam-tug, his sick, troubled heart absorbing all that Mother Nature could give him of her healing power – and it was all summed up in the powerful words 'water – earth – sky'.

The chilly shadows of evening began to thicken. The 'Tiger Cub' wound its way along, avoiding small rapids from time to time. Lights were lit on the steamer. On the lower decks of the boat, people were already settling into their cabins. Ukorov brought a teapot of boiling water, and they boiled up some brick tea. He and Father Pavel kept their strength up by eating some of their provisions . . . and they were already getting ready to spend the night in their cabin, when Father Pavel suddenly expressed a desire to go up on deck again; the air was fresh in the stern, and he wanted to be near the sky, the stars, the foaming waves and the barely-visible, but guessed-at banks of the Makarevo stretch of forest. And so they went up on deck again.

The boat sailed on, slowing its pace, whistling mournfully.

"We're approaching Makarevo!" – came a voice from above.

"How long are we stopping there?" they asked the captain. About half an hour, as it turned out . . . "Makarevo is a big village – we'll unload our coal there" – the captain announced and then suddenly remembered something: "Wake the drunk up! This is his stop!" And the word went out all over the boat: "Anyone for Makarevo, get ready!"

"Stop!" – and the rope whipped through the air above them. The 'Tiger Cub' swayed slightly and knocked against the wall of the jetty. Voices sounded, the drunk disembarked, three collective farmers from Makarevo got on; another new passenger leapt lightly, almost youthfully, across the gangway, although he was not young; he had a small, greying beard and was wearing a long autumn coat, Russian high boots and a soft felt hat, – he had a small suitcase in his hand. "He looks like a foreign gentleman – you'd feel uncomfortable calling him a comrade," remarked Ukorov, and he moved away from Father Pavel at once, making way for the new arrival. "Sit down, there's a place here," he said roughly, but welcomingly. The man sat down beside them, shoving his suitcase under the seat, and took a deep breath, absorbing the full freshness of the evening, as well as the specific smell of the steamer smoke. After looking round, the new arrival glanced at his neighbour, and the latter in his turn looked at him ... A questioning look "Is it him?", unexpected joy, together with a kind of fear at the sight of the familiar, but changed, face; then, after such a gamut of 'impressions – "Is it really you, Father Pavel?" – rang out like a final chord.

The new passenger was Father Vladimir Lagovsky, a friend of Father Pavel's youth, a fellow-student at the Theological Academy. Father Lagovsky was serving out the last year of his exile, after a term of 5 years, but his charge was considered less dangerous and even now he enjoyed almost complete freedom of movement; he acted as a letter writer in the village of Makarevo, where he lived, but he was sometimes sent to Bratsk or Zayarsk, where he was now going with a report from the state grain farm. The old friends could spend 18 hours together, including the coming night. A short run! – But it seemed that there would be no end to their talking. Lagovsky talked most – he realised from Father Pavel's shortness of breath and his broken breathing, how hard he found it to move and speak, Somehow, they didn't dwell on their youthful memories. Father Vladimir gazed at him warmly, asking him about this, that and the other, and instead of having a great, all-embracing conversation, he merely threw out words like sparks, but like lightning-flashes, these lit up all that happened to the friend of his youth in recent years . . .

"So they're sending you to Vikhorevo?" – he sounded worried and somehow surprised, "It's a large village, a collective farm now. The church has been closed for two years. They tried to collectivise everything there, but it was difficult and everyone quarrelled, there's no sense in it. A lot still goes on in the old way. As for tractors and that sort of thing – that's for the future. It's a pity they didn't assign you to Bratsk, you could have settled in well there, got yourself a bit of work, always more pleasant that way."

"Bratsk . . . is some sort of centre, people like me aren't allowed there" . . . said Pavel, half saddened, half surprised by the inquiry.

"Centre or no centre, there are certainly no squirrels leaping through the trees there," smiled Lagovsky. "I've heard there are big plans for Bratsk in future. In a few years there's going to be a huge building project starting on the Angara. They're going to chop down the taiga and lay roads. Then Bratsk will be an important place . . . But your place of exile interests me. What are you going to do in Vikhorevo? Live on parcels? Keep the grain accounts? Lend out books, if there are any there?"

His companion was silent. The thread of their conversation had broken. What the one was saying and even thinking was not reflected in the mind of the other. Father Vladimir immediately understood this and fell silent. Casting a random glance at Father Pavel's face, in spite of the dull light of the fading day and the evening lights on the ship, he saw the shadows playing over his friend's brow, cheeks and lips, – ashy, wax-coloured and dark blue.

"I've decided not to think about it all . . ." began the broken voice again: "I'm ill . . . you see . . . I just want to get there. You remember in the Bible: And Jacob went on his way and the

angels of God met him?" That's like me. My clothes got held up
on the way, so some good people gave me their coat . . . I had
no strength left . . . they brought me to the jetty in a cart . . . The
young man there watches over me, helps me . . . like a son . . .
yes, like a son helps his own father."

Father Vladimir had known a different road into exile, a
smoother one, without fateful sentences and upheavals, – although it was true that at first the charge against him had sounded
terrible. Counter-revolution – by word of mouth: he was a
brilliant preacher. This was his fifth year here, near Bratsk. The
local authorities trusted him. At first he had been kept in prison
for a short time, in solitary, on a charge of "anti-Soviet tendencies
expressed in public – in a sermon." Now that was all behind him.
He was well-fed, he was paid according to official rates and his
sentence would soon be over. He began to assure Father Pavel
that the years would soon pass; he mentioned a possible "amnesty," trying to comfort him, although he himself did not
believe in the truth of his words, but he was overcome by a
boundless desire to give him comfort and cheer. Father Pavel
listened to him without interrupting, realising that his old friend
wanted to assuage his deep wounds, but he knew that those
wounds could not be healed. So they sat beside each other in the
stern, drinking in the blessed freshness of the approaching night
and reliving the joy of their meeting, occasionally glancing
at each other, while the boat sailed on and on, parting the
waves.

Although Father Lagovsky had met Father Pavel only rarely
five years ago, before he was exiled, he was well informed about
his home life and his divorce from his wife. Their last meeting
had been at the late-night service before Candlemas, in the
cathedral church of the Monastery. There had been a festal
litany, the sparkle of crosses and sacramental fans, and among the
priests in the cathedral had been Father Pavel – in a glittering
chasuble and tall mitre. Could it really be the same man – in a

Siberian winter coat, sitting beside him in the stern of a merchant tow-boat, with his head bent low, somehow hunched up between his shoulders? He had a dry cough and answered questions briefly, in a breathless, broken voice. There are times in life when a man lying on his bed in a fever dreams of a precipice, or mountains, or a vague, incoherent series of events; Lagovsky, a healthy man, not at all feverish, was now seeing such a dream. Any words of comfort, about work in the village or amnesties, were irrelevant here. Such words were lies, they might even offend the man sitting beside him. There was silence between them, waves splashed against the high stern, reflecting the ship's lights as golden sparks. It grew colder, night was falling, a frosty, almost winter night. It was already time to go below, to the cabins. Father Pavel seemed to rouse himself, raising his head.

"Everything is God's will. But I am greatly troubled. It will soon be two years since I was deprived of the spiritual sustenance of the sacraments and how can I depart without such protection? I'm sinful, weak and sick . . . It seems I'll have to pass away in my sins."

Lagovsky quickly interrupted him:

"My dear father!" – he said his voice choked by tears, "How fortunate you and I both are! What you have been longing for . . . I am carrying on me . . . I've just been to the collective farm on business, and there I was taken to see a sick man . . . and now, I've had this unexpected meeting with you. Here you are, take it . . . wait, I'll do it myself . . . Is nobody looking? I'll put it round your neck myself . . . The little tabernacle containing the elements is in the bag on the end of the ribbon. You'll find everything in it, for more than one occasion . . ." And, unbuttoning his worker's shirt, he carefully took off a thick silk bag on a ribbon, put it round Father Pavel's neck, hiding it beneath the folds of his clothes, helped him to fasten the collar of the coat and, bending down, he kissed the place where he had hidden his gift. All this happened quickly, skilfully, and just in time – Fyodor Ukorov and another exile were already coming up to call them down into the cabins – below, everyone had long since gone to bed and could be heard snoring.

"Let us go and rest as well, father," – Lagovsky said to him, in a quite new, joyful and bold tone of voice, but when he saw Father Pavel looking doubtful and troubled, he started to explain to him the full significance of what he had given him, as if he had not quite understood.

"Thank you, I understand," was the reply, "but what about you? What will you do? You're giving me life, but what about yourself?"

"Me? – Well, God will provide, I'll get some more. I'll soon be free! I'll go to Irkutsk to register my release. The cathedral there is still open . . . Don't worry about me!"

At this point, their conversation was interrupted by Fyodor.

"You must forgive me," he began, "but it's damp out here on the deck, and he's ill, and I'm trying to look after him; his health is more precious to me, perhaps, than to anyone else, and I'm going to take him to a cabin, even if I have to do it by force; we'll warm ourselves up there . . . come on, Father Pavel, let's go."

"Who's this that's so concerned about you? Tell me please, where's he from? Has he taken pity on you?" – asked Lagovsky, following Father Pavel and Fyodor below.

"This is Fyodor, named after the Warrior saint . . . that's why he's fighting the good fight," explained Father Pavel in the cabin, "He's been helping me on the way. We're travelling to the village together. He's going there to earn his daily bread, and I'm going to eat it up . . ."

Ukorov impulsively seized the speaker's hand and pressed it to his lips.

"You're an upright man, warrior," said Lagovsky, jokingly. "I'm so glad, father, that you won't be alone . . . Let's say goodbye, I have to get out in the morning at Zayarsk. Maybe

you can still get some sleep." And he gave his hand to Father
Pavel, in farewell.

"The Lord keep you!"

"Who's he, then?" – whispered Ukorov.

"The same sort as me," was the answer. "We studied together
once . . ."

The 'Tiger Cub' travelled on up the winding stretches of the
Angara for two days. At Zayarsk, early in the morning, Father
Lagovsky got off. Glancing at the cabin where he had spent the
night with Father Pavel and Fyodor, he went in quietly to say a
final goodbye. Both of them were sleeping. Father Vladimire
stood over the priest in silence, blessing him with the sign of the
cross. Fyodor opened his eyes sleepily, nodding to the departing
figure, but woke up completely when he heard the words
thrown out to him:

"Don't you leave the father, and the Lord won't leave you!"

Chapter 4

The journey by water had already lasted twenty hours. On the horizon, two high, sloping cliffs grew ever nearer and more clearly visible; symmetrically situated on opposite banks of the river, they looked like the wings of an enormous bird, – in a little while, the 'Tiger Cub' had entered the overhanging shadow of those wings, still straining forward along the river current flowing between them towards the jetty. The cliffs merged into rocky forests, the boat-whistle sounded, and wearily cutting through the waves, the steamer came into Bratsk . . .

The exiles walked out onto the shore with their bundles and suitcases. They had to wait until the next day before leaving on the last part of their journey – the 115 km. to Ust-Vikhorevo. The guards from Irkutsk were also leaving Bratsk the next day. The 'Tiger Cub' had to be restocked with coal and was then to make the journey back, with a strong risk of a snowstorm blowing up. The weather had taken a sharp turn for the worse, a north wind was blowing . . . Father Pavel and two other invalids were given shelter on board ship until their departure for the village. Three guards from the Bratsk NKVD, who knew the locality well, were assigned to escort the exiles to the village. The transport consisted of a hardy little Siberian horse and three box-like carts on high-rimmed wheels. Those who were strongest and not subject to dizzy spells were asked to walk, but in places the winding hill roads led over steep precipices and there was hardly anyone who avoided some travel in the carts; in accordance with the transport practice in those days, in dangerous spots the prisoners were taken over one by one, while the rest waited. The exiles walked almost half the distance from Bratsk to the

village along comparatively good trails, without making use of
the carts, which rattled idly over the frozen, stony soil.

Father Pavel was put on the horse from the start of the journey.
Awkwardly, with the help of his fellow-travellers, he kept his
seat on the shaggy mare, which was led on a rein by the local
guard, who was replaced now and then by Fyodor. The 'red
sheepskin' coat served as a saddle, while a soldier's greatcoat was
thrown over the traveller himself. Sitting on the coat was like
sitting on a soft cushion, but because of his unusually elevated
position he was seized with sick terror and then the inexperienced
rider would clutch at the horse's muzzle, feeling that he was
falling off. Suddenly he heard Fyodor's young voice: "Don't
look sideways, it'll make you dizzy!" When they had travelled
60 versts from Bratsk, the exiles camped down for the night in a
forest glade, in a safe place, surrounded by thickets of young
firs, pines and spruce. The bonfire was fed with dead wood and
fir-cones. That night the frost fell to 15 degrees; the horse was
resting, tied to a young pine; the soldiers were puffing out
tobacco smoke and Father Pavel even began to feel hot in his
coat by the fire. The stars radiated out across the heights of heaven.
In the morning, it was back to the winding, rocky path again,
with the taiga stretching out beyond the rocks, richly-coloured
autumn forests, orange-red, blue-green, with all the varied colours
bestowed by autumn on harsh nature.

In places, the footpaths themselves became more and more
dangerous. Carefully, step by step, Fyodor led the horse onwards.
The exiles changed their mode of transport. As soon as the
pathway allowed it, Father Pavel was taken off the horse and
transferred to a cart, where – scarcely breathing from weakness
and palpitations – he experienced the "coffin journey," while
another rider was loaded on to the horse. Riding in the cart with
its raised sides, not looking sideways so that he would not get
dizzy, was possibly more comfortable than on horseback, but
the cruel jolting was torture. The roads sometimes got wider and

the travellers would sigh in relief, but then the trials being endured by the people on horseback and in the coffin-carts began once more.

In enduring the difficulties of the journey, Father Pavel painfully remembered Alya and her intention of following him, and prayed that she would be spared the hill roads, the horses and all that hindered his path. He prayed that she would not have to experience the rocky precipices, the coffin boxes or the dizziness.

"After the winter feast of St. Nicholas, the roads will be better," said one of the guards, "but now, if there's a snowstorm, it'll be really awful. We'll be swept into an abyss!"

The paths gradually began to lead downwards and reverted to the usual, reasonably wide hill road. Its borders glistened with hoar-frost, white with snow-covered juniper bushes and shoots of pine, spruce, cedar and fir. An unbelievably beautiful and spacious view opened up before their eyes. In the distance, the Vikhorevka river wound its way into the left bank of the Angara. The zigzagging road led past a lake and up to a little old church, closed long ago, with the typical conical dome of all northern churches. It was surrounded by the crosses of a cemetery, overgrown with bird-cherry and alder bushes. To the right and to the left stretched offshoots of the darkening taiga. Not far away, the outlines of roofs were visible; smoke was rising above them, and the barking of dogs could be heard – they were coming to the village.

Chapter 5

Almost at the very edge of the large Siberian village, jutting out
a little from the row of firmly constructed huts, sparkled the
cleanly washed windows of a house belonging to Yevgraf
Zakharov, a well-to-do but nowadays slightly dispossessed
peasant. The outer huts were bordered, like a natural decoration,
by spruce, pine and fir trees, the forecourt of the adjacent forest.
It was divided from them by a cleared patch of land; beyond
that, the young shoots of the taiga began. The trees along the
village borders, because of their massive trunks, thick branches
and foliage, had until quite recently been known as 'Yevgraf's
wood' and had been regarded as part of his personal property.
Zakharov had watched over Ust-Vikhorevo; he had loved his
little wood and had been proud of it, and had gnashed his teeth
somewhat when part of this wooded border had been taken over
by the village Administration. Yevgraf had been left with only a
few trees behind his house; every now and then squirrels would
jump from branch to branch, scattering fir-cones on their way.
Zakharov had renovated his house on a large scale about twenty
years ago, and in recent years he had also added a cosy verandah
and a spacious barn. The soundness of the timber, the high
foundation posts, the wooden porch with its four steeply-
ascending steps, the ingenious carvings above the stoutly-made
shutters – all showed that the owner was well-off. In spite of his
somewhat taciturn character and his gloomy appearance, people
respected him and took his views into consideration. Not so very
long ago he had been the church warden, and had been accorded
a place of honour among the peasantry. However, in the same
way as the words can't be thrown out of a song, so it was

impossible to eradicate a firmly established conviction from the peasant's heads: namely, that Yevgraf had not acquired his riches by way of inheritance, as his family had never risen higher than the middle ranks of the peasantry. Everyone knew that in his youth he had gone to look for treasure in the mines and had returned with a fortune; after getting married, he had taken possession of a small estate and farm and, although he did not break off his ordinary, friendly business ties with any of the villagers, he did put a certain distance between them and himself. "Yes, Yevgraf's got gold" – said the Siberian peasants of Vikhorevo to each other, and sometimes they allowed themselves to remark, in a friendly way, while gossiping, that there was something dark in the rich peasant's past, say what you will, something evil he had done in the forests, thanks to which Yevgraf had returned a different man, grown rich all of a sudden, – and then again, in church matters he was so zealous and enthusiastic that no-one could match him . . . Often, in the course of conversation on church feast-days, after his fifth glass of brick tea, Zakharov would sit and talk wisely about Holy Mount Athos, about Kiev, saying that the human soul yearns constantly for those places, but its sins weigh it down, as if its legs had grown into the ground, and will not let it go. "He must be talking about himself!" – thought those around him, but no-one spoke; they all sighed and nodded in agreement at their host.

Yevgraf's family was not large: it consisted of himself and his wife Tatyana, a staid, religious woman, like himself, and also their daughter a young married woman with a daughter of her own, who was now living with them, while their son had been sent to Bratsk for a long period on a business trip by the collective farm. It was not long ago, less than a year, since the law on collective construction had affected Vikhorevo. It was difficult for the new order to be grafted onto this remote corner of Siberia, but people like Yevgraf Zakharov were nevertheless made to feel the pinch, as far as was possible; some of their property was requisitioned, they were deprived of a few cows, sheep and horses, while their houses, after some stormy disputes and even scandals, were transformed into cottage-libraries, shops or even dispensaries. There was no such dispensary in Vikhorevo, although Vasilisk Petrovich, an exiled medical assistant from Omsk, who had arrived two years ago to serve a five-year term of exile, was fighting for one and, although he had no voice in administrative assemblies, he was always trying to persuade Yevgraf Zakharov that it would be advantageous and just for him to act generously, by handing over the lower floor of his house for medical purposes; he had even asserted eloquently that such an act would be remembered in the history of Bratsk territory. It would be hard to explain how Yevgraf got out of this situation, untouched by water, unscorched by fire. He was censured, called a "good-for-nothing," a bourgeois, a "petty proprietor element," but his cottage, sturdy, two-storeyed, with its bright windows in their blue frames, did not become either a dispensary, or a shop, or a library, or a nursery. All such institutions were housed in other cottages. Yevgraf's wood was condemned to be felled. Besides the cattle, the Zakharovs had some of their farm implements confiscated, as well as some harness and a few provisions, but even this had been accompanied by furious interference from Tatyana; abandoning her sobriety, she had turned into a lioness, and after the battle and the victory she loved to describe it to her fellow-villagers. But the master of the house behaved as if nothing had happened. After suffering some impoverishment, he did not humble himself or beg for alms, he behaved quite peaceably and sensibly, remaining among the most influential people in the administration of the collective farm, as before, accepting all the decrees and novelties introduced by the chairman . . . Still, the spacious, bright rooms of Zakharovs house continued to trouble people in the large village, and soon the village soviet suggested to Yevgraf that he should squeeze into a smaller living space and give shelter in his house to some residents from the huts of poor peasants, the Sidorov family, for example, who brewed illegal spirits and were always fighting among themselves. This suggestion put Zakharov in a position where he had his back against the wall. Having saved his house from becoming a library, a nursery or clinic, he now realised that he could not get away with just the farm implements, two or three horses and some of the agricultural goods, or part of the uncultivated land. He had to show an example to others: he even had to show a little gratitude for the fact that he had been disturbed less than many others, and then more politely. But to take Sidorov and his family into his house, so that they could pollute the place with the smell of illegal spirits? Never! The village was awaiting the arrival of new exiles from Irkutsk. They would be here today or tomorrow, and would have to be housed. How many already spent time here; some were still serving their sentence! Something occurred to Yevgraf Zakharov; he went to the Administration and told the chairman, Pimen Semyono-vich, that he was willing to allow residents to settle in his house, that he would give them the upper storey – the attic with the large store-room and the side-bedroom, while he and his wife and daughter would move downstairs, making the large room into two, as they had discussed, but he was asking the Administra-tion to give him the new exiles as lodgers. He would be free to take two or three people. Pimen Semyonov was surprised. All the exiles to this distant village of Irkutsk-Bratsk territory were, after all, considered unsuitable for anything, they were credited with various vices and were often regarded with suspicion.

"What are you thinking of, Zakharich*, – an exile?" Semy-onov's question even sounded friendly, after the recent battle over the house. "But we wanted to make things a little easier for you, in this difficult situation; you yourself were grumbling about

---

* Zakharich – peasants often use only a man's patronymic to address him respectfully, though it is even more polite to use the Christian name and patronymic e.g. Yevgraf Zakharich.

them sending such greenhorns into the wilderness! Let everything take place calmly and quietly, in an orderly way. We haven't been oppressing you lately, just knocking off a few of your chattels, but that's according to the law, isn't it? We managed without your residence. We took pity on an old friend. You must understand that!"

"I thank you humbly . . ." – and Yevgraf stroked his beard, "but all the same . . . won't you give me the exiles? A pair of them? Or three?"

"But whatever do you want them for? We wanted to help you, mate, and you're putting a noose round your own neck! We could have split up the Sidorovs, stopped them fighting among themselves. They'd have known some peace and you wouldn't have been disturbed at all. And if you don't want them, we could give you old man Kuzma and his nephew, who works in the shop; we'd make you a present of them, but look what sort of elements you want! We could house the exiles here and there, with somebody or other, Somewhere close to the authorities – it's quieter that way. Understand that – you don't live in the centre of the village, but near the border . . ."

But Yevgraf insisted on having his own way:

"I want the exiles," he said firmly, "I have to think of my soul now, that's what. Do you understand?"

Yevgraf's keen glance, from under his hairy eyebrows, seemed to scorch Semyonov. The chairman even felt a bit awkward.

"I understand . . . But what kind of people are they now? You want them to relieve you of a bit more property, do you? They will, but not legally."

"Why should they relieve me of anything? Where would they take it? Into the taiga, or under a pine tree. Oh, Pimen Semyonich, they're completely crushed, that's the sort of people they are."

"Oh indeed . . . You can wash a snake once or twice, but one half of it still wriggles, and the other half's not far behind; it's just like an exile. The trouble we have with them! Now there are ten of them coming, and we have worries enough for a hundred – you'll see for yourself!"

"However," said Yevgraf, not giving up, "they've been living here in the village, with five-year sentences, working. And how they work! We should mix with them more – yes, that's how it is."

Yevgraf's request was granted . . . The request was even convenient for the chairman.

They arrived in the village after two nights in the woods, tired after their third day's journey from Bratsk, at midday on a serene October day. At the edge of the village stood the smithy, the sound of hammer blows could be heard from afar and they could see the fiery ring of the red-hot forge. The wholesale shoeing of farm animals in preparation for the winter was going on. Horses were being brought in all the time from the village, and people were looking distrustfully, even fearfully, at the ten new arrivals and their guards. One of the exiles, who had just been taken off a horse, was leaning heavily on the arm of a young man and having trouble breathing.

"Sit down on the logs, friends, wait a bit, we've got to shoe the horse, she's limping, see . . ."

This was their last rest before the approaching end of their nomadic existence. They settled themselves on the fallen logs near the smithy. The dark, smoke-blackened figure of the smith appeared in the doorway. Four horses, besides the fifth one from Bratsk, were waiting in line. The smith took charge:

"Bring yours up, guard, and wait a bit. When do you have to get back? How did she get this far with a nail like that?"

"She's used to it . . . We're going back tomorrow. How's the weather?"

"So-so. Just hold her a bit, straighter . . ."

The weary mare trustingly gave him her hind hoof.

"That's it, that'll do . . . get going . . . good luck to you . . ."

They wanted to put Father Pavel back up on the newly-shod bay horse, but he refused.

"I'll walk there somehow, with Fyodor's help; it's not far."

They went through the village; it took a long time to reach the administrative hut. The windows glittered, the heads of women and children could be seen behind them, staring at the new people; children ran out onto the porches. The wide road, hardened into cracks and ruts as a result of the first frosts, seemed almost unpopulated. The men of the collective farm were working – some felling trees in the forest, some stacking timber, repairing and rearranging the household effects in the barns, others crawling about on their own roofs, making them warm by repairing gaps in preparation for winter. Finally they came to the village soviet, where the chairman of the collective farm had been assigned a large room, and there the new arrivals sat down again on benches, letting their baggage drop. They cast glances at the table, with its cover of dusty red cotton, at the poster "All for one goal – collectivization of the country!", unfurled between two windows, and at the two profiles side by side in the big frame under the poster, one flesh-coloured, with a black moustache, the other deathly – lilac in hue*. Someone lit a cigarette, one guard went off to the shop, another was cleaning his rifle. They asked for water, as all of them were thirsty. A woman brought them a bucket which had just been drawn up, creaking, from the well, together with a ladle; all of them drank eagerly, almost unable to wait their turn. The shaggy little horse, which had served them so well on the road and had just been shod, was tied up in the courtyard by the shed. It was resting, waving its tail from time to time and softly munching hay from a trussed-up sack. The coffin-carts now looked like large children's toys and were resting by the barn too. People were dozing off, leaning up against each other, but all of them were thinking only one thing: when would they be assigned to their lodgings? The woman who had brought

* Lenin and Stalin.

the bucket of water came in again and told them: "he's coming!"
Pimen Semyonov entered, carrying a piece of paper, sat down at
the table and began to write everyone's names down in turn –
their Christian names, patronymics, and surnames, where they
had worked before their imprisonment, and so on. Everybody
came to life. Local people, especially women, gathered at the hut.
Ivan Mamayev, an exile from last year, now working at the mill,
pushed the crowd aside and put his head in at the door:

"Where are we going to put the sick old man? He's worn
out . . . they dragged him here on the back of the horse most of
the way. He's sitting on the mound by the Maksimovs' place,
scarcely breathing. He should be the first to be placed! He's
almost dead."

Everyone went out to look at the sick man. Father Pavel was
leaning against the wall of a house, breathing heavily. People
shook their heads and gestured helplessly, women sighed and
gasped; when they found out they were looking at a priest, each
of them invited him to her house.

"However did you get here, my dear? The road to our place
is something awful!"

Fyodor was hovering anxiously over Father Pavel. He had been
scared by the priest's sudden attack of breathlessness; he brought
him a ladle of water, undid the hooks at the collar of his coat and
splashed water on his face from the ladle, but everyone shouted at
him: "You'll give him a chill, it's not summertime, we should
get him inside."

"No, I beg you, I'm better here," protested Father Pavel in a
clear, but quiet voice. "I often have these attacks . . . it'll pass . . .
it's from the journey . . ."

In answer to their insistent inquiries about the journey, Fyodor
explained how the sick priest had been transported – part of the
way in the 'coffin-cart', like the others, partly on horseback;
part of the way he had walked, slowly, with someone supporting
him, – and as for himself, his name was Fyodor Ukorov, and he

had been the father's companion since as far back as Irkutsk,
since they had left the prison.

"So good people still exist!" – murmured the Siberians of
Vikhorevo, looking at Fyodor.

"I'm not good at all, but I was so sorry for him, he's touched
me to the depths of my soul," said Fyodor, explaining in a rapid
whisper, turning away from Father Pavel, who had gone quiet
again, "Look how we respected them before! Like our own
fathers . . . And now? Bad times have come on us, and it's worse
for them . . . they can't escape misfortune . . . Is he coming to,
did anyone hear him say anything?" And he moved towards
Father Pavel again.

"Where are you from, yourself? Bratsk?" – Fyodor was asked.
"Where were you put inside? What did they do you for?"

"I'm from Omsk, from the transit prison," said Fyodor, unwillingly, "They slapped a political charge on me and sent me
here for three years, what's the point of saying more? We'll have
to get my invalid settled in somewhere as quickly as possible,
there's not much to say about me."

Yevgraf Zakharov was now coming towards them; he had
been in the forest and had not heard about the new arrivals at
once; hurrying round the side of the administration building,
he almost ran into the group of people surrounding Father Pavel.
It was explained to him that the sick man was a political exile, a
priest from Leningrad, that they had hardly managed to get him
here alive, and that he must be found a place quickly, so that he
could rest, lie down and get warm.

"Well, what about it? You wanted some exiles? Will you take
this one?" – asked Pimen Semyonov, joining the crowd.

"Yes, I'll have him," said the other, briskly.

Some roughly-constructed stretchers were stacked in the
entrance-hall of the administration building. They had been
made, not so very long ago, by some of the exiles at the orders of
the medical assistant, Vasilisk Petrov, the one who had dreamed

of setting up a dispensary and had picked on Zakharov's house for that purpose, but the authorities had not given him permission to work professionally in the village, as he wished, which somewhat depressed him. He did not lose heart, however; he wrote a declaration to the Supply Distribution Centre and was expecting a positive reply in the spring; meanwhile, he had decided that, whatever happened, he would go on with his studies to complete his medical training, even if it was only little by little, and that he would run a successful practice. His relations sent him medicines in parcels. A pharmacist he knew also provided him with necessities, but his stocks quickly ran out; at all events, he was now left with his medical bag, bearing a faded cross, which he had taken with him into exile, and the stretchers. Father Pavel was put on one of these and carried to Zakharov's house, swaying gently from side to side because of the holes in the wide road. Fyodor walked ahead. When they got there, he touched Yevgraf's shoulder confidently:

"Don't separate us, sir," he begged, "I told the chairman that as well, he rang up . . . The sick man can't get on without me. I bring him things and look after him, and keep things in order. And I can't do without him either. Allow me to stay, I'll work for you and serve you – just tell me how I can help. Tell me what to do – and I'll get it done, whatever it is."

Yevgraf's gaze pierced through the young man.

"All right, you'll do," he decided, "Who knows what kind of person you are? But if you respect such men . . . Only remember, no vodka drinking! Otherwise I'll chase you out at once and take on someone else, understand that . . ."

The sick man was carried into the house, into the spacious hall on the ground floor, to the accompaniment of the shaggy watch-dog's yelps and barks. From there, Father Pavel walked upstairs with the help of the mistress of the house and Fyodor; he was put in the side bedroom, a large, bright room, with a roomy lumber-room next to it; here he could sleep undisturbed, while a small door from the lumber-room led out into the hall. Tatyana Fyodorovna, Yevgraf's wife, helped Father Pavel to get into the large bed with its mound of pillows and its homespun linen sheets, elegantly trimmed with lace. At this he began to apologise for having to use their linen for the time being, but assured them that his things would soon arrive, parcels would be sent and then ... Tatyana dismissed his words with a wave of her hand and refused to listen. "Oh just be quiet, my dear man," she repeated, "they haven't deprived us of our linen as yet, and we can't drag it along with us to the next world anyway ... there'll be enough for us all ..." She brought up some soap, a wash-tub, a bucket and a stool and all other necessities, arranged it all in order and nailed a hanging wash-stand to the wall, but Father Pavel was so exhausted from the journey that he merely wiped his face and hands with a wet linen cloth, still lying down, and let himself drift into sleep. However, as soon as it became known in the village that a priest from Leningrad had settled in at Yevgraf's, people began to assemble in the side bedroom, most of them women. They brought their children to be blessed and pushed all others aside, in getting through to the priest. Tatyana begged them all not to push, to give him some rest, Zakharov himself lost his temper with the womenfolk; meanwhile, Fyodor had run to collect their documents from the village soviet, where they had handed them in to be checked, and on his return, had been alarmed by the crowds of people in the side-bedroom. He wanted to drive them out as well, but was opposed by Father Pavel himself. He had woken up, looked around and smiled at the people, then raised himself as comfortably as he could on the high pillows and began to bless these who had come; when they had all gone, he started to ask his hostess's pardon for the trouble he had caused her. However, any annoyance she might have felt was made up for by the joy which truly shone out of the eyes of those who had received the blessing. A few minutes went by – then a new torrent of visitors arrived, this time with offerings: one woman held out a jar of bird-cherry jam to him, another thrust five eggs into his hand, while a third asked "couldn't he baptize her youngest, when he's better, that is . . . The church has been closed for near on two years now, and they took our priest away to God knows where, and so my little son was left without the Holy Sacrament . . ."

At long last they went away. The priest dozed off again, while Fyodor nestled down with his head at his feet; it was in vain that Tatyana called him to come and rest in the lumber-room, where she had made up a bed for him. The thick blue darkness was already falling when the medical assistant peeped into the room – wanting to meet the sick man. "After all, it'll keep me in practice concerning the heart," he mused, "otherwise I'll die of boredom, and forget everything I've learnt . . . Yes, but how am I going to behave towards such an illegal element, and a religious cult-servant at that? Shall I call him "Father?" But what sort of "father" is he to me? Address him by his first name and patronymic? But how can I – it's not as if he's an old friend of mine. Just call him by his surname? No, that sounds awkward too. Comrade? That's even worse. No, I'll simply call him "you," that'll be best . . ." So thinking, he went up to Father Pavel and introduced himself again, asking if he had been comfortable lying on the stretcher he had thought of. Taking his pulse, he pressed down painfully with his finger in two or three places on his swollen leg and winced openly at the sight of the deep marks he left on it.

"I'm going to give you some medicine," he said, entering Father Pavel's surname in his notebook. "It's a good drug, from herbs, no-one's got it, but I have. It's called "adonis." It has to be infused, strained and taken at the rate of four spoonfuls a day. In addition, you need rest, sleep, milk, and light meals. I hope you'll be better soon . . . Our climate's harsh but healthy. So remember, sleep, rest, milk and yoghurt. After that, I'll be glad to see you at my place. I lodge not far from here. Yevgraf Zakharich knows me – I can be here in a moment." He disappeared behind the door.

Evening finally brought the peace and quiet he longed for. They closed the shutters. Fyodor refused to spend the night in the lumber-room. There he would fall asleep so soundly, after the journey, that no sound would rouse him. And what did he need such an honour for? He would lie down here, at the feet of the sick man, or beside him – he would be able to look after him and assist him. Tatyana Fyodorovna wanted to hang a wide cloth canopy round Father Pavel's bed, but he begged her not to make it more difficult for him to breathe. They decided that if the frost began to bother him, a homespun curtain would at once be put up. He talked to Zakharov about the most important matter of payment for his lodgings, and in spite of the fact that the master of the house and his wife did not even want to mention money, insisting that they were voluntarily taking in Father Pavel because of the law on giving up living space, and that therefore he would count as one of their family, in the end they all agreed to the following exchange. Father Pavel would give them the contents of his parcels, handing everything over to Tatyana and putting it at her disposal. In return the lodgers would not do any cooking or prepare their own meals – the priest, because he was an invalid, Fyodor because he would be busy – after all, from tomorrow he would be wholly subordinate to the collective farm and would only be able to spend a few hours, if that, at his sick friend's side. That was decided ... But just as they were getting ready to go to bed, the front door bell – a possession peculiar to rich peasants – rang. In addition, someone kept knocking at the door. "Have you no shame? Coming so late!" – Tetyana grumbled at the two women there, "Are you going to keep it up until tomorrow morning? He needs his sleep after a journey like that, while you – well, God forgive you!" – Suddenly, she stopped short, seeing that they were carrying a generous gift in their hands: the women quickly unwrapped their bundles. There was fragrant, porous honeycomb, and under it, a bowl of oatmeal pudding; the other woman placed an earthenware jug of cream and curd cheese, freshly made and just out of the oven, in front of Tatyana.

"Don't be angry, we're just going," they whispered, "Just give the father our pudding to taste. Tell him to get well, he's our benefactor. We felt as if we'd been given a new lease of life when we saw him . . . And we ask your pardon, Tanya dear, for bothering you."

"Little by little and quietly – then he'll get well, you'll see," said Tatyana on parting, now quite friendly, echoing the women themselves.

Chapter 6

Silence fell. Fyodor stared round at the new walls and the freshly painted white ceiling, the mirror, the lamp and the ikon of the Saviour in the corner. "You've got a lovely place here!" – he exclaimed, thoughtfully. "It's like paradise for us!"

"Eh, my lad, we got to this paradise by way of hell," said the indefatigable Tatyana, sitting down at the spinning wheel and twisting a thread, "We even agreed to be de-kulakized*, all our property was integrated with the village; nobodies became all-powerful. If we're kulaks, all right – that's the way it is. But why have some people turned on their own kind, like that Pimen Semyonov? He's oppressing his own, isn't he? And how! Our son had left home, and the old man himself wasn't at home. And then they descended on our house! "Hand over the cottage! Get out, clear off, kulak brood!" There were three of them. Pimen had trained someone else, got them to follow him, so that we could be dispossessed at one blow. So there they were, the three of them . . . and I was alone . . . They walked round the house, as if they were the masters, – making plans: here we'll have the nursery, and if not, well – maybe it would be better as a reading-room, and it'll be useful for medical purposes as well . . . they discussed it aloud, the anti-Christs, but I didn't despair, realising I still had strength in my hands! l took up the poker and whispered my Sunday prayers aloud, then l advanced on them with the poker first – and they; our village authorities, grabbed a shaft. The shaft had been standing in the hall, we'd just made a new

* "De-kulakized" peasants were well to do peasants who had been deprived of their land and property in the interests of revolutionary equality and collectivism.

one, with blue flowers painted on it, – and so they advanced on
me in their turn. "What are you rushing into?" – they yelled,
"You're a woman, after all!" Well, woman or man, I let them
have it! They weren't going to see the cottage theirs, any more
than they could see their own ears! We came to blows! I was
teaching them with the poker, and they were watching for an
opportunity to crush my bones with the shaft . . . This hair of
mine they pulled out by the roots! They gave me a couple of
bruises on my face, rainbow-coloured they were – changed
colour too, and they bruised my ribs; the skin on my shoulders
was grazed to the bone, but they got a good beating too! I
showed them what kind of wife Yevgraf has! I don't know how
it happened, I lay down until morning, pressing a wet cabbage to
my head, but the cottage has remained ours. The next day they
came again, five of them this time, to see my husband and carry
out a peaceful requisition. They still turned us inside out. Took
away some of the cattle, put aside this and that from our belongings, and turned the wood over to the Administration. "You've
got a fine woman there, though," they shouted, "You won't
lose out with her!" – And what do you think, my lad? They left
us alone from that moment, and our cottage stayed ours; it's not
a reading room, or a dispensary, or a nursery – it stayed as it
was: Yevgraf's house . . . Well now, lad, you'd better go and lie
down, tomorrow you've got to go to work, you're not a visitor
here . . . and you're tired after your journey. He was saying your
friend there, that his niece was coming to be with him? But who
will she find to take her, a woman, to such a fearful hole? You're
here: you'll be working and dropping in, looking after him,
we'll keep an eye on him too, everything'll be all right . . . Give
me the lamp, I'll light the way for you, or you'll get lost in the
passage on your way into the hall . . ."

Father Pavel had long since gone to sleep during their conversation, and was in a dreamless sleep, the reward of his hard
journey, undisturbed by any voices, sounds or noises. He had

reached his goal. He was in Vikhorevo. The first day of his 25-year sentence was over. At first he imagined he was still on the steamer, because of the humming noise in his head. Then an abyss opened up in his consciousness and peace and silence engulfed him.

Fyodor settled down on the floor for the time being, though a folding bed had been put up for him in the lumber-room. He wanted to be beside the father, to continue his journey with him further and further. Before going to bed, he had gone round the upper hall of the whole attic with Tatyana, where wormwood garlands hung under the very roof and ropes and lime covering the beams were visible in the half-darkness. It was cold here, almost frosty. A sturdy ladder led down to the huge barn, where cows were sleeping in the hay, softly chewing the cud; their stalls were separated from the sheep by a wooden barrier; there was also a stall for a goat and her kid – everywhere the hand of the true farmer could be seen, the abundance of stores . . . Above, through the thatch on the barn roof, stars were visible in the blue, already frosty sky.

In this way, Father Pavel found himself a settled place to spend his exile.

Chapter 7

Tatyana Sidorovna was laying a small table in the side bedroom. The short autumn day had come to an end: it was dusk. Father Pavel had just woken up and was gazing at the simple tablecloth with its pattern of squares, at the loaf of wheaten bread, at all that was new around him, – and, finally, he asked the mistress of the house if it was "afternoon or evening?"

It turned out that he had slept the whole night through and had been dozing during the day. This had happened to him before – in his youth – when he had exhausted himself doing exams or, later, after lengthy services and lectures. Then, as now, he had not realised immediately where he was, on waking. Seeing that her guest was awake, Tatyana went up to him:

"Shall we have some tea, father, or shall I bring you a little warm milk? Have you rested from your journey? Would you like a wash? Go on sleeping for the time being, but tomorrow, when you're a bit stronger, we'll go down to the living-room. We're simple people here. Our own masters ... Look, here's Fyodor as well! How are things going, lad?"

Fyodor had been working half the day chopping firewood in the barn of Pimen Semyonov himself; there he had been well-fed and given the rest of the day off; from the next morning, he would be working on the collective farm, like all the other exiles. Without such work, the new arrivals would not have been able to survive for a day ... All the new inhabitants of Irkutsk province immediately started work in preparation for winter – some at the mill, others felling trees in the forest, or pouring out and calculating the weight of the grain. Pimen Semyonov could tell a person's abilities and knew what kind of work to give him.

Fyodor still could not believe that he was really in the village, that his friend the priest was with him and had completed the journey more or less safely, that their days in prison were over. "You'll become a real human being, necessary to others, Fedya, only through work and prayer" – so Father Pavel had told him while they were still on the steamer. And when Fyodor was hewing and chopping firewood for the chairman, he remembered these words, and his hands – weak after his spell in prison – regained their former strength. Now he only had to get really involved in the work of the collective farm, find some way of making his own living. "Honest labour!" – he said to himself, taking off his leather mitten and wiping his eyes. Everything around him was new: the solid peasant huts, built to last for centuries, the sunny, windblown day, the dust or first snow flakes whirling along the streets, tiny white specks that had been flying through the air since morning. From the moment he had entered Yevgraf's house, Fyodor had begun to feel cheerful and had hopes that the priest would recover. The young, strong exile heard the voice of life in all of this: in the friendly welcome they had received at their new home, in the fact that they had managed to settle in with worthy, well-off peasants; he was also cheered by the thought that rich milk and cheese would help the sick man to get well. And then there was the fact that they had settled in together, in the same place. Surely that was a sign that his weariness and illness would soon disappear! A great, child-like joy, which he had never known, seized him at the thought of this abundance. He ran home, as if on wings! How was the father? Had he slept well? Were these new people not bothering him and tiring him out?

No letters had come yet, nor could there be any so soon. Father Pavel thought of Alya, of her journey. How would she get here, if she kept to her resolution? Hair-raising roads, the November blizzards, when you could only crawl over the hills. At the moment, he felt so weak, he was only really comfortable in the presence of Fyodor. Against his will he sensed something inconvenient and unnecessary in the idea of Alya coming to this place – the thought came to him that he had become a burden and a hindrance to his beloved sister Masha ... She must have been so worried by her daughter's absence, and what about her actual journey to join him? Alya's possible arrival weighed heavily on him, but he also prayed for her journey and its safe outcome, accepting it and worrying about it at one and the same time, so that he had already discussed his misgivings with Tatyana even before Fyodor returned.

Tatyana Sidorovna was a wise woman by nature and not one to give quick answers. She fell silent for a moment, crossed herself and said softly, in her sing-song voice:

"May God help her to get here. You saw what the roads are like for yourself ... What guide could she travel with? Just the postman, perhaps. Write to the girl, – tell her to wait till it freezes, not to hurry. Perhaps after the winter feast of St. Nicholas? You, our welcome guest, got here without a blizzard, but when such a blizzard blows up, what then? And if you look at it honestly, there's no reason why she should come at all! We'll do everything for you. But if she comes, we can always find a place for her. We'll put Fyodor in with you and her in the lumber-room ... Don't you worry about it, my dear ... And there'd be work for her too. In the shop, or the nursery – maybe Vasilisk will still get permission for his clinic. Did you say she knew something about chemist's shops?"

Her balanced words quietly calmed his troubled soul. On entering, Fyodor caught part of their conversation. He looked curiously at Tatyana after her story of yesterday about the fight, the poker and the shaft. ...

He gazed at her with the careful stare of a man who had seen more evil than good since his childhood. How would she feed the priest while he, Fyodor, was out at work until the evening? The father shouldn't have promised her the entire contents of his parcels so generously, in return for a share in their meals. Siberian women could be mean, their husbands too. They were generous in words, but in deeds? And Fyodor, frowning somewhat, but not daring even to hint at his thoughts and notions to the priest, sat down beside Tatyana, as near to the samovar as possible.

Chapter 8

A hard sparkling Siberian frost had still not come in the middle of December. The winter feast of St. Nicholas was almost upon them and the roads had frozen hard long ago. Near Ust-Vikhorevo they were wide and mountainous. One of them ran from the post-office to the village – two kilometres, not more. At its beginning it followed the river bank as far as the little church, which was more like a chapel; the hill it stood on was covered by the village graveyard, half of which had grown wild and was in a picturesquely neglected state. Only a few recent graves stood out in the clearing . . . To right and left, the fields stretched away to the uneven crests of the forest in the distance. From the top of the hill, immense distances opened up, covered by the young forest of the taiga. Down below, on the frozen lake, a solidly-made sledge was travelling along, the horse resiliently picking its way on its shaggy hooves – in the distance a narrow bridge could be seen, dark against the sky. The right hand fork in the road led to Ust-Vikhorevo. The young lad in his winter coat and ear-muffed hat had been walking along it for more than an hour. It was Fyodor Ukorov, carrying a parcel to the village. This was already the fourth parcel which had arrived addressed to the priest! Eight kilos altogether, and how heavy they were! His legs had still not recovered after the camp and the year in prison – he still found it a bit difficult to walk . . . But, nevertheless, he had to work and keep up in every way: he chopped wood and dealt with the grain on the collective farm, and occasionally acted as postman. He stopped, adjusted the ropes and hoisted the parcel higher onto his shoulder.

"Father Pavel, my poor martyr," he addressed himself aloud

to the sky and the taiga, "I admit I've grown greedy, but I'm greedy on your behalf, not anyone else's. What does it matter to me? At the farm I'm well-fed, I stuff myself with milk, but Tatyana just has to see a parcel and she'll deprive you of groats and sugar again . . . and in return she'll give you some good-for-nothing meat jelly, and you won't be seeing your own good stuff again . . ."

He stopped himself, halted and again adjusted the box on his shoulders.

"Lord God, what kind of thoughts are these? . . . Away with them! May they vanish! . . . It's his business, not mine, to share out his parcels. And it's not my business to judge Tatyana either!"

He still had to follow a blazed trail through one more small wood before he reached Ust-Vikhorevo. Fyodor stopped for a moment, partly resting, partly having a look round. Snow-covered pines and fir-trees surrounded him. A fabulous silence breathed mysteriously round him; he felt the magnificence of white-haired frost. A rabbit flew out of the bushes and, desperately flashing its white paws, rushed past him. Tree-stumps stood around like huge mushrooms, with mounds of snow pulled over their heads like caps. Thin twigs of bird-cherry and wild berry bushes wove their silvery lace all around. A kind of bright joy sparkled the traveller's heart. He had known it in his adolescence, when he had not yet committed any crimes or transgressions, and had not emerged from the common round of life. Now, in this Siberian wood, he was visited once more by that fleeting guest, but there was a new meaning in this sensation, a new desire – to share its return to his life with the man who was patiently awaiting his arrival on the wide couch at home, with whom he had travelled as a friend to the end of the prisoner-transport, and to whom he had revealed his whole life and the transgressions that had brought him here, whom he trusted as a son, as a child trusts its father. These thoughts and feelings completely banished his earlier enmity and spite towards Tatyana, and Fyodor hurried homewards with cheerful step.

At the door, the strident barking of the master's black dog rang out; the chained mongrel in the yard barked back menacingly and howled at the man entering. Fyodor patted the dog, who had recognised him, took off his boots in the hall, brushed snow off them with a brush, and leaving them there to dry, put on some tattered slippers and went upstairs with the parcel.

Father Pavel was asleep, but he heard Fyodor at once, roused himself and opened his eyes, half-hidden by his heavy eyelids.

At first glance, anyone might have asked – is he dead? Or dying? The mauve colour of his nose, ears and lips hinted at least that the end was near. But when he awoke and came to himself, when he talked to people, his sharp, always attentive eyes reflected an essential life which did not accord with the idea of his dying soon. He lay on the large flower-embroidered pillow given to him by his hosts and on his thin pillow from Leningrad – this helped him by giving him added support. The coat, the 'red sheepskin', which had served him as a pillow, a saddle and as a blanket at the campfire during the recent journey, was now rolled up conveniently, supporting his feet.

"Are you frozen? Worn out?" – he asked Fyodor kindly. The latter put the parcel on the stool and carefully adjusted the heavy, ragged blanket round the sick man.

"There's nothing wrong with me," he replied, after a pause, "And the woods! I can't get enough of looking at them! They're so beautiful! Father dear, we don't have any like that back where I come from! It's like in a theatre, at a show. There's any number of rabbits and foxes. Get well for spring, and we'll go to the woods together, – and see the taiga too!"

An answering smile – benevolent, pitying and crafty – showed fleetingly on the priest's face . . .

"We'll go, Fedya, we'll go! But in the meantime, open the box. What have we been sent from Leningrad?"

Fyodor's natural interest in the contents of the parcels had been blunted and even replaced by a feeling of annoyance. At the sight of the box that he had brought, the four-year-old Nonka would not leave the side-bedroom – she kept edging towards the parcel. Tatyana or her daughter in law, if she was nearby, would appear at once. If anyone met Fyodor on his return from the post-office, it was all over; the side bedroom would be besieged by Yevgraf's family, they themselves would offer to open it, and anyway, until everything had been taken out they would not go away. Receiving and opening what was sent in front of people was painful and distressing for Fyodor. He knew that, according to the agreement made at first, everything was to be handed over to Tatyana and her husband, while in return for the parcels they were to pay for the upkeep of their lodgers and provide them with food and drink, but surely they had also agreed to share their meals? However, for about two months now their shared meals had not included semolina pudding or stewed fruit, or jelly, or sweets, or white pastry-cakes or biscuits – none of the things that had been sent. At table, they had served up pork in gelatine, oatmeal pudding, potato flan, lean mutton, thick millet porridge with pieces of fried mutton in it, or they gave them fat-laden cabbage soup, or salmon-fish and salted cucumbers, if any barrels of salmon-fish reached the village. This was obviously how they had understood the agreement – as an exchange? Fyodor was shaken by caustic, spiteful, simply furious thoughts. "Greedy, mean people – God, they're real kulaks!" – he tormented himself. "It was clear from the first; it wasn't mine but theirs, all the same I should have interfered. I took care of him on the road, but I haven't looked after him here. He gave away what was his, like a small child, surrendered his own property and didn't touch a thing himself; he was hungry, he couldn't make do on oatmeal pudding and milk, but he touched nothing – and I thought we had landed in paradise!" – And the young man couldn't stand it any more: he revealed all that he was thinking to the priest, but

Father Pavel strictly forbade him to interfere in any way:

"I don't need much, do I? If they give me some oatmeal porridge and milk, that's quite enough . . . Did we even get that, back "there?" Just be quiet, Fedya, it'll come out all right," he said severely, but cheeringly, calming him down. And it did turn out all right! It was only three days after they received the last parcel that the master of the house, Yevgraf himself, happened to sit down to a meal with Father Pavel and Tayana in the side bedroom; usually he was late and ate his meals downstairs. The meal consisted of thick porridge, cabbage soup and mutton; Father Pavel took nothing and finally confessed, apologising, that he could not now eat anything fatty or thick-boiled – he just couldn't get it down!

Tatyana pricked up her ears; her husband glanced at her out of the corner of his eye and told her to boil up some thin semolina pudding and milk for the father at once, and whatever else he could eat. Yevgraf did not interfere in the housekeeping, had not noticed precisely what food was shared at supper and had not kept track of the parcels, but his wife, after receiving from Father Pavel the bags and packets of groats, prunes, sugar, vermicelli and sweets, had put them all in her own store room and, not intending to distribute them for general use, was going to keep them till they were needed, as many hard-fisted peasant women did. She did not even think about whether she was doing right or wrong. Her lodger was refusing food – that meant he was ill, and sick people have no appetite, while all that she had been serving at table was tasty nourishing and filling for a healthy man and she had been quite sincere in replacing the contents of the parcels by her own cooking. But the sick priest had eaten less and less . . . and he had sometimes been asking for milk products . . .

"What's the matter with you, lad, couldn't you say anything to us, keeping quiet all this time?" – Tatyana turned on Fyodor, as if he were the guilty one. "I'll just boil him up some semolina pudding and stewed fruit. That's no way to behave – the man isn't eating and you say nothing . . ." At this point she cast a keen glance at her husband. "I'll catch it now!" – she felt the words resound in her head – "oh, misery me, and how!"

Towards evening, Fyodor summoned up all his courage. "Now I won't be doing wrong if I finish the conversation we had at the table." – And when he was alone downstairs with Tatyana that evening, he could no longer restrain himself from speaking out, especially when Tatyana started to praise the pudding, licking the spoon.

"Yes, that's the sort of pudding you should be making him," he began without ceremony, "He didn't get enough to eat in prison, now he should eat. But he'll starve to death if we give him our food. You can see what he's like. Do you think he'd say anything? And he doesn't need much, does he? He can't eat more than three spoonfuls at a time. It'll all remain yours anyway, for the future, but he doesn't need your food at all."

"You should have explained that to us long ago, dear," intoned Tatyana meekly, "We agreed on an exchange with him – ours in return for yours, and we're quits . . . What a business! Doesn't want to eat! Tomorrow I'll make him more white semolina, and I'll boil up some porridge oats as well."

"But not thick porridge," directed Fyodor, now in a bold, masterly tone, feeling that, as the priest had said "it would come out all right," "Make it thin, with milk. If you make it so thick you can stand a spoon upright in it, like lime, so that it won't fall, – it'll be no good to him, it'll just make him ill."

The same day, late in the evening, Yevgraf returned from work thoughtful and morose. He always came home tired, he had no time to follow household matters, as he was doing the chairman's grain accounts, regaining his former important and influential position. He sat on the bench for a long time, taking off his boots and listening to Tatyana's familiar words about the shared meals and people having no appetite. Then he went into the storeroom himself and looked at everything in it before going to bed; then he went upstairs to the side bedroom, still morose. The words of evening prayers could be heard through the door. Fyodor was reading them aloud, out of the prayer-book, Father Pavel was listening though half asleep; four-year-old Nonka was sleeping on a couch by the wall. Yevgraf decorously stood in a corner of the room. Afterwards, Fyodor went up to the bed.

"Yevgraf Zakharich has come to see you, father."

"Ah, Yevgraf Zakharich?" – Father Pavel turned to him, "It's a long time since you've been to visit us in the evening . . . Give him a stool, Fyodor."

But something strange was happening to the master of the house. He fell on his knees and hid his face in the folds of the coverlet. His head shook with sobs.

"Whatever's happened? Fedya, leave me alone with him," directed the sick man, "What's the matter, Yevgraf Zakharich? What's this about?"

"Accursed wretch that I am!" – His words flew out one by one. – "I've sinned before God and you, my father! We've been tempted by what's lawfully yours, your daily bread! And that bread's lying there in the store-room, rotting away. And you're not eating . . . How greedy we've been! Real kulaks! Now I understand at last what a "kulak" is! . . . Oh, father, I wanted to do my soul good by helping you, and just look how we've served you! Taking away all you need and shoving what you don't need down your throat! The shame of it! Sin after sin . . . Dear father, I'm worn out, take my burden away. I'll open it all up to you. Take it all back . . . We've got enough, and to spare. You're welcome to it! Eat your food and ours, but go on living!"

Father Pavel wept with him and comforted him. He tried to calm him by saying that he had never thought of reproaching them, that there could be no accounts between them; he himself asked forgiveness for not being able to eat the same meals as everyone else, because of his illness . . . In a word, he turned the conversation so that it became unclear who was the most to blame – though he probably came out of it as the most sinful of them all, but Yevgraf kept sobbing out his own troubles, whispering some kind of secrets, bringing out all that had long lain heavily on his conscience, repeating over and over again "forgive me, forgive me." There was nothing to be done: Fyodor was called in and told to fetch from the suitcase the priest's stole, carefully wrapped in a large towel, which he had received in the first parcel from home . . .

Chapter 9

So the frosty days went by, one very much like another. Father
Pavel had long since learnt that Alya had gone back to her sick
mother, from a letter she had sent him in November, after the
holiday. From the hurried lines, which did not quite make sense,
he saw at once what was going on in her soul and touched his
lips to the traces of her tears, praying fervently for the warm-
hearted girl. She was now at home! His great worries and doubts
about her coming immediately disappeared and he involuntarily
whispered the words of the prayer he loved: "Now lettest Thou
Thy servant depart in peace'. Now he only had to pray, endure
his infirmity and wait – for what? The coming of spring? But his
feet, swollen by dropsy, kept throbbing and would not let him
rest at night. The drugs brought by the medical assistant were of
little help. His strength was failing, clearly and noticeably. In
the first days of his stay in the village he was still finding it easy
to get up and, with Fyodor's help on one side and the support of
his stick on the other, he would go out into the lumber-room and
the hall, and descend to the lower part of the house to see his
hosts, to sit down for a while, talk and make them happy by his
visit. At other times, Fyodor would help him out into the yard
behind the house, where Yevgraf stacked his pine logs, in level,
snow-covered piles, giving off a sharp, aromatic smell of resin.
There was also a high-backed little bench and a small table in the
courtyard garden; there, they would drink tea in summertime.
The remnant of Yevgraf's forest rustled drowsily, showering
down snowflakes. They could not sit out in the frost for long;
they feated their eyes on the sky, the taiga, blue in the distance,
then Father Pavel would go back upstairs – "I've been in my

hermitage for a while!" – he would say, smiling, to Fyodor. "This is my resting place for ever, here will I dwell." He wrote these words in his first postcard to Alechka in Irkutsk. Letters from his wife in Leningrad came regularly, always good-natured, friendly, asking the business-like question: what was he in need of? They were full of school events and greetings from friends. Other letters came – whimsical, confused, but always sincere, letters from Arseny, and – at last – letters from his sister Masha and Alya. Maria Petrovna had recovered from severe typhus and was now getting better. Alya was working in a chemist's shop; she was thinking of going on to higher education and was keeping up her diary, as before. He found it difficult, but answered them all, if only on single pages; he wrote soothingly about his health, saying that he was well, that he was surrounded by sincere people, who were looking after him; he begged his Nina to think more of herself, not to worry about him, to put her trust in God, as she had formerly, in her childhood, and always signed himself "your unworthy intercessor Pavel" at the end of the letter. At the end of January, Alya received a reply to her own letter from him and found some passages in it disquieting, when she thought it over. "What's happened to him?" she wondered. He had written: "My health is reasonably good, but I am very tired and worn out, I've been overcome for the time being by neurasthenia and I've become very weak; I now understand that external means cannot help me – I am trying to lie in silence for long periods, alone if possible; I read, think and generally give myself over to spiritual exercises, and I feel better for it. I try to pray, but to pray with faith, patience and humility, as the holy fathers taught us, to entrust everything to Almighty God, the Lord and his great Saint Nicholas, as we should be moved to do in our hearts." The letter ended: "I send you my humble blessing, as your spiritual father. Please pass on my heartfelt regards and gratitude to Yelizaveta Pavlovna* for her services to me. She took on

* Liza. (Yelizaveta Pavlovna was her Christian name and patronymic).

trouble and exertion on my behalf. Once again, may the Lord bless you!" Your devoted, humble Pavel A."

The letter did not comfort her, as the first one had, but worried and puzzled her. Moreover, it gave rise to a penetrating, lightning thought: "this is his last letter, we won't get any more letters from him." What was this temporary neurasthenia, that he was fighting by non-external means? What he says about being tired and worn out doesn't apply to his life in Vikhorevo, of course. He tired himself out before, out 'there', but now something else had happened . . . Alya could not imagine the sick man's state to herself. What she had to do, what would determine her path from now to the end of her life, was to pray for him – not in the way she had prayed in Irkutsk, but as he had indicated – with faith, patience and humility.

Father Pavel had written this letter to Alya about his neurasthenia and weariness with great difficulty, when embarking on a new period in his vagrant life. After suffering a severe heart attack at the end of January, he decided to hide it from his dear ones – in vague, imprecise terms. After the attack, he finally took to his bed. No violent shocks or disturbing experiences could be permitted in this last part of his exile; the days flowed by peacefully, as if there had been no storms in the recent past. On his arrival in the village, he had begun to live a static life and, like a wandering sailor, had reached a quiet harbour. He was surrounded by care and attention from simple, upright and sincere people; Fyodor had become a true spiritual son to him. He watched over the priest's every glance and breath. The Siberians of Vikhorevo invaded Father Pavel's room at every possible opportunity, greeting him in the age-old way "dear, welcome guest of ours!" They would push a pair of salted cucumbers, a cabbage or a freshly made cheese into his hands or Tatyana's. Siberia was miserly in its men, but the women overcame all difficulties and shared whatever they could spare.

Chapter 10

On the day before the heart attack, which was on the eve of Tatyana's namesday, Yevgraf was visiting Father Pavel in his room. He often looked in on him now, and would tell him about his youth, Lake Baikal, the gold mines and much else, of the kind that people consciously and repentantly reveal only to spiritual confessors. The priest listened to him, growing tired and drowsy from the twilight, the monotonous voice and his own weakness. Sometimes he forgot himself and uttered some words in his sleep. Yevgraf went out, trying not to make a noise with his boots, but Father Pavel awoke in spite of his efforts. "Are you going away already, Yevgraf Zakharich? Forgive me for dozing off and interrupting your story," he excused himself in embarrassment.

However, on Tatyana's namesday* there was no-one upstairs – neither Yevgraf nor Fyodor, nor the object of the celebrations herself. She was boiling up the samovar for her guests, while the master of the house had gone out on business. Fyodor was chopping firewood for some neighbours nearby. Father Pavel was lying on the bed alone. In truth, it began – or seemed to begin – from a feeling of weary tedium, called forth partly by the closed shutters, partly by thoughts which had wandered off the path of prayer. A heavy, lowering sense of melancholy and weariness entered, like an ancient old woman, crawled inside him, sat on his chest and pressed immediately on his jawbone. There was such a terrible pain behind his ears, which prevented him from opening his mouth or calling people . . . But whom could

* Every Orthodox Christian has a namesday – the feast day of his patron saint. A namesday is celebrated like a birthday.

he call? Everyone was downstairs, he could hear doors slamming – those were the guests arriving. He tried to groan, but couldn't; someone had his face in a painful and suffocating grip, pressing down on his ears, but moving their bony fingers lower and lower, until his upper ribs and his breathing as a whole were affected by the pain and fear of death. The hand slipped down further: now the tormenting pain was not all coming from under his ribs, or from his elbows, which were circled by cast-iron bracelets. It was on the left, moving towards the stomach, and on the right, along his lower ribs, that this unbearable pain was situated, not allowing him to remember or call on the Sacred Name for aid. The attack was bringing pain and death with it. Nevertheless, he remembered and spoke that Name, not aloud, not even in a whisper – his voice and breath were in the power of the iron hand – but in some state of consciousness beyond the powers of the body, which seemed to be hovering outside his being; unable to breathe in or out, he cried out – powerfully, but silently, – to the Sacred Name ... He heard the sound of Fyodor's footsteps. He was coming in with a small piece of meat-pie from Tatyana. A weak groan came from the bed ... A moment later, the whole household was aroused. Tatyana hurriedly kindled a second samovar, thinking that boiling water would come in useful one way or another, her guests offered all kinds of advice, mostly sensible, but difficult to put into practice in a hurry, while the exiled medical-assistant, who had been among the guests, abandoning his advice to "keep his feet warm" until summer, ran for his medical bag, which was in the administration building. It was not that he had hopes of helping the sick man by means of its contents, but he felt uncomfortable arriving on a call without the bag bearing the faded red cross; the bag itself, which had long since been emptied out and had not been restocked by anyone, contained some scissors, two dusty bandages, a wad of cotton wool, two phials of camphor, a long-unsterilised syringe with a thick needle, a bottle of dried-up iodine and some miraculously preserved stomach drops. Running at lightning speed to Yevgraf's house, Vasilisk was counting on the effect of these drops, as they contained both valerian and opium. The medical man who had lost his rights was helpful by nature, but he was also like a veteran war-horse, running at once to the fray, even with the most ineffectual weapons, making up his mind what to say to comfort the sick man and avoid disgracing himself in the eyes of society. There were rumours that he was to have his civil rights restored to him and would be given professional work here for the remaining years of his exile – otherwise he would forget all he had learnt; he had studied a long time ago and there were more and more new facts to learn! For example, this heart case – it had been all right all the time and now, suddenly, something had gone wrong. But what could he, Vasilisk, do to help? Keep his feet warm and give him the stomach drops, but then what? So thinking, he arrived at the bedside, out of breath, letting the strap of his bag slip off his shoulder: from it dangled a worn piece of hemp twisted into a horseshoe shape and two splints. The patient was finding it difficult to speak – his voice had gone, Drops of sweat were flowing copiously down his forehead; the medical assistant took his pulse . . . Father Pavel's pain had almost gone: it had weakened and dispersed, dying away in his back, under the shoulder-blades; he smiled at the young man whose hand was pressing on his wrist. After questioning him about what had happened, Vasilisk considered it appropriate to sigh deeply and inform the patient:

"Your pulse rate is "celer."*

"Is that dangerous?" – asked the priest in a whisper, but already showing a lively interest.

"Well, n-no, how can I explain it to you? It's usual in such cases. Inside you the heart vessels are shaking themselves up, but it'll be all right." – He checked the pulse again and announced delightedly "There, you see, I'm right. It's settling down . . . it's

* Latin: fast.

not "celer" any more, there's just a bit of – how shall I put it? – "celerity" left. Would you like some tea now? – Good. Anything that'll warm you up. Ah, a hot iron at his feet, that's a marvellous idea, Tatyana Sidorovna, but don't burn him. And here are some drops for you, as well, – they're slightly bitter, as they've got narcotics and all kinds of stuff in them . . ."

He counted out twenty drops of the stomach medicine into a jug. Father Pavel obediently swallowed the dose, bitter as worm-wood. "I should really give him an injection now," thought the medical assistant, " but who knows what this syringe is like? The chairman has a good one, the new "Record," which he ordered from Bratsk and keeps at his place. But is it worthwhile to potter about with this monstrosity and sterilise it, always supposing it still comes to pieces? You have to do these things properly."

He began to say goodbye to Father Pavel, advising him to sleep, and take some very light nourishment the next day. "What's this, Ukorov? Don't be silly," he said, pushing away Fyodor's hand, which was trying to slip a bar of "Golden Anchor" chocolate into his pocket. "I won't take it, this is my duty as an ordinary human being!" But Fyodor pushed the chocolate even deeper, in spite of him, and held the pocket shut by force.

Father Pavel was feeling better all the time. He pressed the medical assistant's hand and whispered to him, on parting:

"You're not at all that "Vasilisk"* that should be trodden underfoot . . ."

But the medical assistant did not understand him and assumed an air of superiority:

"I shall not allow anyone to tread on me," he said, and went away, carrying his bag, fully conscious of his own worth and the fact that he had done his duty.

---

* "Vasilisk" means serpent, or basilisk in Russian. The reference is to Satan.

Chapter 11

After that memorable night, Fyodor tried as far as he could, not to leave his beloved priest alone, but this was difficult for him – either he was delivering the post, or doing piece work in the nearby wood, the felling and uprooting of pine-trees had begun, and then the logs had to be sawed and chopped. Father Pavel lay in bed, without getting up any more, without speaking or complaining, without even the smallest grumble. He still had continuous attacks of pain, almost every day, although it was bearable, not severe, just momentary contractions, but he was growing weaker. Fyodor would come home worried and anxious, his heart thumping; he would sit down beside him, take his hand and press it to his lips. How fervently he wished he could warm those cold fingers and get rid of their bluish colour. One day at the beginning of February, when Fyodor had dropped in for a moment from the neighbour's house, where he had been chopping wood, and had come to Father Pavel's bedside as always, the priest took his hand out of his grasp and placed it on Fyodor's head . . .

"Love God more than anything else, Fedya. Man? What is man – even those who are closest to us? Grass! Straw! It is cut down – and withereth. It withereth, that's all – and it's gone."

"Who are you talking about – that withers and is gone?" – Fyodor gave a start, raising his head.

"Who? Well, why not myself? . . . Fight on, Fedya, my Warrior! However we try to avoid it, we'll have to part . . ."

"I won't let you go!" – The young man felt a hot lump rise in his throat and chest. He grabbed Father Pavel's shoulders with both hands, so tightly that the latter winced involuntarily.

"I won't let you go!" – Fyodor insisted, through his tears, "I've said I won't allow it and that's all there is to it . . ."

Alarmed by such an unexpected frenzy, the priest freed his hand with some difficulty and patted Fyodor on the head.

"What will I be without you?" – mumbled Fyodor, "I've surrendered my soul, become a real human being, – and now am I going to be alone again? Among strangers? I shan't go back to what I was before, but how can I live without you, father, in a far-off place like this, in the taiga? – I just don't know."

"You don't need to know. It's all clear. You don't have a long term of exile. Only you'll have to live in a new way, as an honest man. There are good people everywhere. Yevgraf here, for instance, he won't push you out . . ."

"Yevgraf?" – Fyodor echoed, questioningly, "But he's a real beast of prey. He's got the look of a wolf."

"He's no wolf, Fedya. You'll see that he's not. I can calmly leave you in his charge. Anyway, won't we be together any more? We will! As we are now. Only we won't be able to see each other or touch each other; you won't be able to squeeze me half to death, as you did just now . . . You really did almost finish me off . . . She's suffocating me, and then you started to suffocate me too, though you're like a son to me."

"Who's 'she'?" Fyodor asked, guardedly.

"Who? Why, my illness . . . Calm down, my friend. You mustn't go on like this. Do you know, I feel a little better today . . . the sun's shining outside, I really feel somewhat revived."

A timid hope flickered in the young man's mind.

"Perhaps 'she' might leave you?"

"Everything is in God's hands, Fedya. Perhaps you're right . . ." – Yevgraf knocked angrily at the door.

"What, have you stopped work for today, Fyodor? The Chechulins have got a pile of wood as high as heaven, but he's at home! Get out and start chopping, it's a long time to supper. We don't need any idlers here!"

"It's my fault, Yevgraf Zakharich . . . I detained him," came a whisper from the bed.

The master of the house immediately exchanged his angry tone for a gentle one. His severe face was lit up by a smile.

"Are you a little better, father?" – and he came up to the sick man. "You've caught a cold in the throat, by the way you're whispering. I'll tell Tatyana to rub some mustard on your neck, and you'll have a glass of rum after dinner. It's good for you! You'll feel better at once."

He got the same smile in reply. People smile like that at children, when they have to be humoured and something has to be hidden from them.

"You don't know anything about me, but I know" . . . whispered that smile in reply to all Yevgraf's words, questions and worries. Father Pavel gave his host a bright glance and blessed Fyodor, when the latter came up to him before departing.

Chapter 12

In the absence of Fyodor and Yevgraf, their place by the sick man's bedside was taken by Tatyana, as her husband and the lodger always worked until the evening. Tatyana would sit down in the side-bedroom, with her yarn, or the socks she was knitting, but as soon as Father Pavel opened his eyes, she would begin to chat to him, not to amuse him, but to find some relief from living continuously with her taciturn husband. She mixed up superstitious ideas with religion. She called to mind cases of children being ill-wished, when they had been turned into werewolves in the taiga or the swamps, how sometimes mothers had succeeded in re-christening and regaining such a child, and even in bringing it back home. There was an ancient, half-pagan superstition concealed in her, unconquered by the present system or by the religious principles she had imperfectly learnt as a child. Tatyana could read slowly, but couldn't spell; she was always trying to introduce the priest to *The Dream of the Mother of God*. But he only asked her to read the Gospels to him. She would read aloud the passages he indicated in a monotonous, soothing chant, interrupting to give her own interpretations.

"That's true, father dear! Elijah will come, must come. And then all things will come to an end. There have been rumblings all this summer. We, sinful wretches that we are, were fighting, middle peasants and rich peasants, fighting each other, you can't hide sin – but the Terrible One, he just kept thundering and thundering. Revealing his presence. Saying "Don't forget yourselves, my people, I'm here." The day of wrath is coming – brimstone, burning up everything. It says so in the Bible! Now in Daniel the prophet . . . Are you sleepy, father?"

The priest did not answer her. He was asleep . . .

The days passed, quiet, calm and frosty, as if specially selected. A week before Candlemas, there was a hint of a thaw, but towards nightfall, the frost hardened to over 20 degrees below freezing point again. Candlemas had been a Communion feast-day in Vikhorevo not so very long ago. Even now the house-wives who had formerly been devotees of the church baked pies, eating them on the eve of the feast-day, as they had done in the old days, but if the 'feast-day' did not fall on a Sunday, they all went to work as they did on ordinary days. On 10 February, Father Pavel was given a letter from his wife. "My dear, I'm worried about you," she wrote to him, "Do you have all you need? Write to me about everything, tell me all your wishes and desires. I have great hopes of the summer holidays. Spring's not far away now, I'll be coming to visit you . . . wait and we'll see each other."

The clock struck twelve o'clock. He had read the letter and hidden it under his pillow . . . The window-pane was reflected by the sun, in the shape of a cross, upon the door. For the moment, his breathing was free and unimpeded. His illness had given him rest for two and a half days, now he put one foot out of bed, then the other, and quietly began to dress, fearing to move about too much; when Fyodor came in, the priest was sitting on the bed, as if recovered, stretching out both hands to him.

"Fedya, help me to get up! Where's my cassock, my coat? – Father Pavel was giving directions in his usual whisper, but in a stronger, more cheerful tone, as if the whisper would soon develop into a voice. In response to Fyodor's alarm, doubts and protests, he went on repeating that he was longing to dress as quickly as possible and go out in the sunshine, to his favourite corner in Yevgraf's courtyard, which he called his 'cell' or 'hermitage'. It was in vain that Fyodor tried to dissuade and hinder him. The priest, always so co-operative and submissive in matters relating to his illness, was now unrecognisable. He was hurriedly trying to put on his boots, but his own would not fit him and he had to put on Yevgraf's huge ones, with their cracks and leather gaiters, kept behind the Russian stove, – the master of the house used them for going to the forest, but now they were resting, roasting in the warmth; he had gone to work in other boots, which were lower and more comfortable.

"Give me my cross!" – asked Father Pavel in the same intense whisper. They got it from under the pillow, where it was lying wrapped up in the stole. "Now everything's ready for our walk."

"It's no good, father," began Fyodor again, "how will I drag you down the steps, you're so weak? Tatyana Sidorovna, help us!" – he shouted from upstairs. "Is it him?" – a voice came from below, and Tatyana came to their aid. Father Pavel put his arm round Fyodor's neck, Tatyana supported him from behind, and they safely negotiated the stairs. Downstairs, Tatyana took over care of the priest, while Fyodor opened the stiff door into the yard, still muttering "how will we get him back upstairs? It's easier to come down, but going up again?" But Father Pavel was far away from them all. "Sunshine!" he whispered, "Every kind of creature . . . the fresh air! The hermitage I've longed for!" Fyodor sat down first and, leaning back on the wall behind the wooden bench, supported the full weight of the priest's body leaning against his own. The frosty air, as clear and transparent as a mirror, permeated with the scent of pine, filled his lungs. In the spaces between the branches of larches and fir-trees, the snow covered fields were sparkling like jewels. The round midday sun was painful to look at, almost blinding him. Father Pavel leaned back against Fyodor's chest, as if on a board, resting his head on his right shoulder, pressing against his neck somewhat, resting his hands on Fyodor's. The fresh air, the silence and the hours he had not slept at night had the sudden effect of making Fyodor drowsy. He forgot his surroundings, drifting into a fresh, youthful sleep, and even when a fir-cone on a twig fell on him from above, he did not react, and when the familar whisper and a groan sounded next to him, he did not respond. Father Pavel groaned again, a second time, and only then did Fyodor wake up.

"Lift me up, . . . faster . . . Fedya! It's the same . . . as before . . . the end, that's all . . ."

He was now a dead weight, leaning on Fyodor; the latter raised his burden with difficulty, laid the sick man on the bench; taking off his sheepskin coat, he placed it under his head, and rushed into the cottage. Soon people came running – Tatyana, Yevgraf's neighbours; combining their strength, they dragged Father Pavel upstairs, sent for Vasilisk and warmed up some water. The medical assistant came running, this time with all the necessary equipment. He had got the new syringe from the chairman and immediately gave the priest an injection. Father Pavel gradually obtained relief from his painful shortness of breath, his face faintly regained the colour of life; sweat appeared profusely on his brow and neck. Pressing Fyodor's hand with his moist fingers, he was continuously murmuring something. Tatyana and Fyodor bent down to listen. "Why did you have to wake me?" whispered the pale lips, "To suffer more torments? Again? I was going away so happily . . . and you prevented me . . ."

"Who woke you, who prevented you, father dear?" asked Fyodor, agitatedly, drying his hand, then hiding it under the blanket.

"You stopped me . . ." Father Pavel insisted, almost inaudibly, "Over there, where the sun is . . . On that side. The rosy sky . . . The rose-coloured light . . . yes, I saw it. But you pulled me back . . . shouting, and everything was hidden again . . . Don't hinder me any more – it was so, so good . . . rosy . . . the whole sky. Truly . . . I saw it . . ."

On leaving, the medical assistant explained to those who had gathered there:

"Before the end, you know, some people are like this . . . They have these wishes, like he did, "to go into the garden, into the fresh air." But what is there in the garden? Oxygen and ozone, as well as the other substances ... His blood-vessels contracted – that's why it happened ... He must have complete quiet ... and his pulse isn't even "celer" any more, it's like a thread. Yes ... for him, the end would be best ... He's an outcast from society, what else is there to say? My regards, Yevgraf Zakharich! Always happy to serve the sick! If you need anything, just call me, I'll come at once."

Chapter 13

It was the beginning of hours of drowsiness. The shutters had been closed long ago, it was night, but Father Pavel slept on. Trying not to knock against anything or step on a creaking floorboard, Tatyana or her daughter-in-law would come in, glance at the sick man and go out, telling someone "He's sleeping." On the ground floor of the house it was stuffy and smoky; the stove had been heated late to bake bread – Tatyana had not managed to do it in the morning. Sitting round the teapot were Yevgraf, who had just come back, and his young married daughter Zina, with the four-year-old Nonka. The little girl had a wild nature and was shy with everyone, hiding in the folds of her mother's dress, and as soon as anyone spoke to her or started to joke with here, she would shut her sky-blue eyes; then she imagined no-one could see her. "But I can see you all the same – so there! And I'm going to eat you!" – her grandfather would joke. The rosy face would turn away at once and Nonka would disappear completely in the ample folds of Zina's skirt.

The Zakharovs also had visitors from the neighboring collective-ive farm, and Vasilisk had also dropped in that evening to inquire about his patient.

"Our respects to you, representative of medicine!" – said Yevgraf. "Sit down and have some tea with us. It says it's 'Indian, First Class', but it's never been in India."

Vasilisk Petrovich liked to visit people. Firstly, he counted on hearing all the news there, getting to know this and that, other-wise life there was empty. Secondly, he could show what kind of person he was himself – his standard of education, his politics. He could show off his medical knowledge as well: people asked you questions, you answered them – that was elementary medical education. Perhaps he would be allowed to work here officially for the last years of his sentence, then these conversations could be accounted for and he would report them honestly, without lying, not from a superior point of view, so to speak. So and so many discussion-lectures, so and so many question-and-answer sessions, suggestions, . . . and he stirred his tea, thinking of the future. Round the table they were discussing 'current 1932 topics: the pressing and complex matter of collecting shares and deposits in the co-operative. Yevgraf was getting excited and angry.

"Let's say I don't refuse to pay my deposit, I take them as much as they want, and then they give me dried cod, or a few sugar-candies or bullseyes with dust on them, so what good are they to me? What sort of shares are those? In return for my hard-earned . . . my precious . . . what I've worked for in the sweat of my brow . . ."

"Well, now, how much is the sweat of your brow worth?" – his neighbour interrupted, "You've sweated little enough . . . Yevgraf Zakharich . . . Everyone knows where you got it from, do you think the older people don't remember how you went looking for gold dust in your younger days? . . ."

"Yes, I did go looking," Yevgraf persisted, "but have you searched in my drawers or trunks? Do you know for certain that I brought back any gold dust? Perhaps I was a different man then and I've changed now? Perhaps I recognized the former authorities then and now I've done away with them?

"You're just a chameleon, are you, Yevgraf Zakharich?" asked his brother-in-law, smiling a little mockingly.

"All right, let me be a chameleon then, but once the wind's blown me in this direction, I'll stay that way. You've got a lot of imagination, haven't you? You're like a brown bear from the taigs, you're that ignorant. Consider yourselves critics, do you? Doesn't like the sweat on my face! Well, if you want to know, I had to sweat then too, for the gold dust, and now I need to sweat even more, the way I work . . . it's not easy providing bread for the people. Or do you think it is?"

Everyone fell silent, drinking up their tea . . . The conversation ended at once, but it was to Yevgraf's credit that, although he expressed his feelings, he had not poured oil on the flames, but had snuffed out the quarrel. However both the brother-in-law and the neighbour, as well as the master of the house himself, felt somehow uncomfortable. Only the medical assistant was still in a good mood and tried to change the subject.

"The way we twist and turn!" he said, indignantly, "I'm not the gentleman I was, of course, but I'm wholly against the kind of excesses that have taken place, in your house, for example. It horrifies me to remember your hand-to-hand fight with the poker and shaft, Tatyana Sidorovna! I can't bear to think of it! What kind of enlightenment was that? It was the dark ignorance of Ostrovsky's "Storm!"* First we must educate the population in culture, give them instruction . . . There were posters hanging up everywhere, that the youngsters had put up. But where were they educated? In the Young Communist League – and they immediately began brawling! Is that what they sent him here for, along our coffin trails from Bratsk? A man with understanding – he'd have come here himself and given what he had to give, – he'd have said, "Take what's mine to give, whatever you need for the good of the people and our homeland.""

"Look what happened to Feofanikha!" – Yevgraf's brother-in-law interrupted him, with a kind of strange delight, "The old woman was sitting alone in her hut, and they started yelling at her through the window 'Get out, you old crow, you old-fashioned element, give us your hut for a nursery!" – Five of them, two stout collective farmers and three Young Communists to help them, – Feofanikha nearly lost her mind! It's a good thing Pelaga managed to get rid of them, she's got her father's character, she's just like Feofan when he was alive! She broke two clay

* Ostrovsky's "Storm" depicts the tragic results of dark peasant ignorance.

pots over their heads and threw the pieces after them, besides hammering them with her fists."

"I had to bandage them all afterwards, five face bandages," Vasilisk couldn't help mentioning, as his own contribution.

"But they still took half the hut away from her?" inquired the neighbour.

"How could they do without that? – And in the Bratsk paper they wrote:" Collectivisation passed off cheerfully. People gave away their property happily. All of them were united, as one!" All quiet and peaceful! Makes you sick to listen!"

With these words, Yevgraf got up: "I think I'll go upstairs and have a look . . . See if he's still breathing."

Silence fell round the table . . .

Chapter 14

Yevgraf went upstairs with a heavy heart. He did not feel himself any more. It was only a short time ago that he had been freed from his burden of many years and had wept out his troubles by the priest's bed; he had resolved to control his fits of rage and indignation . . . and now, all of a sudden . . . What had he gained from quarreling with the collective farmers? Had he not deserted peace and quiet for a mundane row, even bringing up the past? However, he was acquiring an inner peace, and he had resolved to preserve it and to curb his former bursts of anger. In this state of confusion, he entered the priest's room. Father Pavel was not asleep and gave his visitor a keen, attentive glance. He had not regained his voice after the attack in the garden. He spoke in a whisper, but quite clearly, with a touch of hoarseness that had been distinctly audible when he was still quite well.

"Is it evening or night time? I'm a little mixed up . . ." – and he turned his face towards Yevgraf. "Yevgraf Zakharich, you know, the day after tomorrow is Candlemas. I would like to fast. When Fyodor comes home today, we'll think about what would be proper . . . And you join me too. Tomorrow, don't say no . . . I shan't be getting up any more, but – please God – I'll live till the feast-day . . . I don't want to leave you without support . . . we'll be together . . . for the last time . . ."

Yevgraf did not answer at once, he was thinking about something.

"As God wills, father dear . . . But what can we do? After all, it's not so long ago that . . . Then I told you everything . . . the whole truth . . ."

He broke off in confusion. Father Pavel understood what he was trying to say.

"I still have one gift, the Holy Sacrament!" – he whispered, his voice trembling with joy. "I'll give it to Fedya too, one day soon . . . soon . . ."

He began to breathe rapidly and unevenly. Yevgraf bent over him, fearing another attack. But the sick man continued, after a fit of coughing:

"It's a miracle that I have it . . . When we were on our way here, along the river, I met someone I knew . . . also a priest, he recognised me and entrusted it to me. He gave it just to me, but I can't partake of it alone! There'll be enough for us all."

However, Yevgraf was now even more embarrassed:

"How can I take the last crumbs of the bread you need? It would last out; you could take it once or twice more, at least . . ."

"I? Well, as it says, I will not drink henceforth of the fruit of the vine . . . Praise be to God for everything!"

They decided that Yevgraf would come up tomorrow, as soon as it was light. "I can't today, I'll make my confession tomorrow," he explained. "We were sitting over tea today, chattering unnecessarily, quarrelling because of those same shares."

"And do you think you'll be better tomorrow?" – asked the priest, smiling shrewdly.

"Not better, father, but all the same, a night removes you from your sins a little. Forgive me, for Christ's sake."

So began an unforgettable evening, when Yevgraf's whole character opened up and he left the cares and petty scandals of life behind for the peace of the faintly-lit attic and the sound of evening prayers and readings from the church calendar. Fyodor was reading them aloud, indistinctly but fervently, confusing the pronunciation of Church Slavonic words. It seemed to Yevgraf that he was listening to an angel. He fell on his knees and, repeating the prayer of the publican, bowed low to the ground from time to time.

"Pray for me, father," he begged the priest, on parting from him until the morning. "God knows I want to become a new man, like a little child, but my old skin won't let me, everything goes wrong . . ."

"Become a new man?" smiled Father Pavel, "You are a new man; don't pay any attention to your old skin, it'll always bother you. But you just keep going – and you'll get there in the end, only be repentant . . ."

Shortness of breath was making it difficult for him to whisper more.

"I want to ask you . . . don't say no, Yevgraf Zakharich, . . . don't leave my Fyodor. I've found a son on my difficult road. I never had any children of my own, and he came so suddenly into my life. He's not lazy, he works hard, he has a simple, child-like faith, but he needs supervision and looking after. You yourself understand what sort of life he's led so far? Now go . . . Never fear, I'll live till the feast-day, please God!"

It was the evening before Candlemas. The lamp was burning low, crackling; the objects in the room were just distinguishable. Fyodor added oil to the lamp and adjusted the wick, then went away, promising to look in later that day. The master of the house was left alone with Father Pavel. After Yevgraf had confessed and been absolved, he got up off his knees and kissed the Cross and the Gospels; then Father Pavel asked him to sit down next to him. Both of them were silent for a long time; Yevgraf moved the glass of water closer and got ready to listen to the Communion prayer, – but instead, he heard the priest tell him, clearly and plainly, "Now I'm going to make my confession . . . Hear me and receive my sins, for the sake of Christ crucified." "Father!" – begged Yevgraf, weeping, "What are you saying to me? Are you in your right mind, sir? You know my sins now, but how can I do this? I don't dare! Remember, my light, what I confessed to you, the things I've done! Ask Fedya, he's still a child . . ."

"You are a man, a husband," insisted Father Pavel in a firm whisper, using an authoritative tone no-one had imagined he possessed, "Don't desert me like this . . . Even the minutes are numbered for me . . . Take this on yourself as an act of obedience. Listen! I'll read a prayer. Then, when I've finished my confession, all you have to say is "God forgives you – and you too, forgive me, a sinner."

With heartfelt anguish and a sense of dread he had never experienced before, Yevgraf took in the secrets of the pastor's confession. He felt as if the floor were moving beneath his feet. His head bent down almost to his knees. At first he tried to stuff his fingers in his ears – but the priest gently touched his hand and he opened his ears to the words which reached him, as if from a distance. Father Pavel went on whispering and whispering, easing not only his own burden, but also that of his hearer. How long did this last? Anyway, what had lain for years like a stone on the soul of the man hearing the confession, what had already fallen from his shoulders during his first act of repentance, breathed its last in these moments, releasing him completely, restoring to him his peace of mind and his ability to sleep, destroying his old nickname of "beast of prey."

Finally, the priest fell silent. Yevgraf was silent too, wiping his nose, eyes and cheeks with his sleeve.

"I think that's all," breathed the man confessing. "Now tell me how well I taught you . . . God forgives you – and you too, forgive me, a sinner."

After these words, Father Pavel immediately began to read the prayer before Communion.

Chapter 15

After the severe attack of breathlessness in the courtyard, the priest's intense pains left him. He was visited by short-lived, mild pains, which were bearable and did not show. A dreamlike weakness, which lasted for hours, overcame him; this lasted till the evening of 13 February, when it left him for a short while and he regained some of his strength, so that he was able to prepare quite consciously for the day he had been long awaiting and on the morning of 14 February he celebrated the Holy Sacrament.

At ten o'clock precisely, Fyodor ran in, saw him sleeping and rejoiced: "Let him sleep, sleep cures everything! It can't be otherwise, he'll get over his illness from this day; he's had no attacks since the one in the courtyard!" With such cheerful thoughts, he was preparing to leave, but first he went up to the bed – and the sleeper opened his discoloured eyes for a moment, glanced at Fyodor and then closed them again.

"Remember, father, how you promised to come to the taiga with me in the spring? I can see you're better already!" – said the young man, his words falling into the unresponsive silence of the room. "Sleep cures everything, don't contradict me!"

At the door, he turned towards the bed again – he could not bring himself to leave.

"Your hands are cold again, as if they'd been out in the snow! Keep them under the blanket, until they warm up again. Well, I'm off now . . ."

On his way out, he asked Tatyana to take up a hot iron to warm the father's feet.

At four o'clock, Tatyana went to look in on the sick man. He was asleep. He had a tranquil, peaceful expression on his face; she touched his feet, but the iron would not warm them – they were cold as far up as the knees.

It was getting dark, evening was approaching; it was the time when the late night service would have begun, if the tiny church had not been closed.

Downstairs, Tatyana had just taken the festive pies out of the oven. Then she began to prepare supper for the father – a bowl of oatmeal pudding with milk and a piece of pie – and called Fyodor, who had just come in, to take it upstairs. He was in time to hear the quiet sighs coming from the barely-moving lips and, leaning over the priest, he managed to catch his last whisper ". . . according to Thy word . . ." He froze, seeing that Father Pavel had just given a start and was now looking, not at him or at anything in particular, but somewhere else: his gaze was now fixed on a point beyond the wall, piercing through it.

The grief of the orphaned Fyodor was so great that the Zakharovs did not leave him alone for a long time. However Yevgraf comforted him or tried to talk him round, in those first hours all was vain.

"He loved you very much, lad, but we've come to like you too, Fedya. Live with us, like a son, don't go away anywhere, d'you hear?" – said Yevgraf, himself grieved, trying to cheer him up. "Just work honestly, don't get involved with flighty women, don't beat about like a windmill in the wind. And if you get bored, we're one family now, our son'll be coming to see us, you'll have a friend. You won't be bored then." Meanwhile, Tatyana kept reminding them of the amnesty, saying that if Fyodor's case, which he had not hidden, was deprived of its political charge, leaving only the religious charge, then he could be released altogether and sent to study and work in Bratsk or Irkutsk. It was rumoured that a big construction project would soon be developed here as well, that there were plans to clear the

taiga and move it aside, to cut wide roads through it and build a
"sluice" on the Angara, so that the journey in the coffin-carts
would not be necessary any more.

"Thank you for your good words," answered Fyodor, "Don't
you leave me. I'm just an orphan now, so to speak. You help me,
uncle Yevgraf, help me – I'll tell you how." – He smiled, but
there were tears in his eyes. "To pass an examination like an
honest man."

The same vening, when Father Pavel's death became known,
half the collective farm came to the Zakharovs' house. The priest
had lived there for about four months, but for many people he
had become their "adviser," "benefactor" and "dear father." In
her trunks Tatyana had found some linen and gold braid, left
over from the church ornaments – it had been used for veiling
the cross on the feast of the Intercession. Vasilisk Petrovich immediately ran to the chairman and asked him for three metres of
muslin from the household stores to filter the milk – and brought
the muslin to the Zakharovs. The house was already full of
people; among the crowd of women and children, who had
come to bid farewell to the deceased, his assured voice rang out:

"I was always surprised at him – a pleasant, educated man!
That his delicate organism should have suffered so much: hunger,
prison, exile! Terrible! He could have been a doctor, an engineer,
even a professor. And why did it all happen? In his childhood the
harmful influence of religion was overlooked. If he had been
given the right kind of education, he would have become a real
human being. Instead of a servant of a religious cult! An unnecessary element! Not a man, so to speak, but a "myth.""

At this point, he almost collapsed on the floor – Yevgraf's arm
descended on his shoulder like a bear's paw.

"You're a 'myth' yourself, if you want to know! Don't speak
evil of good people, don't you dare! Better look after your bag,
you've got plenty of 'myths" in that—goodness knows what
you've got in there! You could pack it with hay, it would be

more useful than running round the sick with those sort of 'myths'! It looks as if the satchel was full to the brim, but all you've got in it is empty phials and elastic bands, and those aren't good for anything. Couldn't even give an injection in time! Shame on you!"

He stopped himself, fell silent, he seemed to feel a sudden, quiet breath flow through him, and he went on, no longer angrily, but persuasively, even peaceably.

"You've got relations, Vasilisk Petrovich, they send you parcels; get them to send you a complete medicine chest, and let the chairman give you a proper Red Cross medical bag. In the spring they'll let you start treating people, so go ahead, and I'll do all I can to help you. I'll even give you the side-bedroom for your good works, or somewhere downstairs, in his memory – then you'll have your own 'surgery'! I promise you!"

The medical assistant muttered, in embarrassment:

"We've still got to get the medical chest and fill up the bag. We'll put it all in perfect order, Yevgraf Zakharich."

Meanwhile, people were still arriving at the Zakharovs'. Women besieged the medical assistant with their questions: how did he die, what was it from, where was the pain? Vasilisk Petrovich looked round to see if the fault-finding master of the house was anywhere nearby, – but then launched into a militant educational lecture on medicine:

"A man's heart is like a pump," he explained, "Our blood flows round a system of tubes. The tubes broke down, narrowed, the heart failed, his pulse was no longer even "celar," as they call it, which is dangerous too, but was like a thread ... and that was the end of it ...."

The women wept regretfully and sighed, not understanding anything about the tubes, and then streamed upstairs, to see the father and bid farewell to him.

Chapter 16

In the little garden behind the house, the father's 'hermitage', as he had called it, where he had gone for his last walk, Fyodor and two exiles were finishing his coffin. There was a sharp smell of pine-wood shavings. His 'abode' was deeply cut and made to measure – everyone felt the father would be comfortable in it. It was lined with fine linen; a muslin frill – handmade by Tatyana – was pinned to it with tiny nails, and on the lid was a gold braid cross. Right there in the courtyard, the coffin was sprinkled with holy water, which had been carefully preserved by the believers of Vikhorevo, and was carried upstairs. Father Pavel was lying there in his summer cassock, which he had received from home only a few days ago, under a new sheet, with his face open to the air. They sewed a gold cross onto the topsheet as well. In the country, unlike the town, there's not much fuss about funerals. The officials of the Village Soviet were informed that such and such an exile had died on such and such a date, then everyone went off to the cemetery to dig the grave, early in the morning on Candlemas day. The priest had already been placed in his coffin; people had brought all kinds of conifer branches – red fir, pine and cedar twigs, juniper – to lay on top of it. Everyone who knew how to read was reading the Gospel over the deceased. They couldn't bury him on Candlemas, as they would have had to carry him out in good time, before darkness fell, but unprecedented discussions had arisen: one of the villagers had suggested that such a man should be buried to the accompaniment of church bells. Others agreed; they began to discuss whether they should restore to the belfry the bell which had been taken down two years ago and was now lying in the cellar of the

Vikhorevo chapel. – "Couldn't we combine our forces for this, mates? It's not such a heavy bell, and we'll find the strength, as believers, – then we'll be able to ring out a farewell to the father, in the proper way, and we'll sing over his grave – and back in the homeland they'll sing the funeral service for him in his absence ... Chairman Pimen Semyonov won't come to the funeral – he'd feel uncomfortable, as a Party member, and the sound of the bell won't be heard as far as Bratsk; everyone's forgotten about our bell anyway, they wanted to take it for the ferry, but to this day it's still there ..."

"All right, get the bell!" – shouted Yevgraf, feeling himself to be the elder once more, "It's my decision, I've decided instead of the chairman, and I'll take the responsibility!" The exiles and villagers – about 30 people altogether – rushed towards the church, to help or look on. The bell was raised by all of them together. It still had all its chains, ropes and pegs beside it; they dragged it out of the cellar onto the raised porch, and from there to the belfry, with the help of the chains and ropes. But could they raise it without a song, on such an occasion? And what were they to sing? It wouldn't do to sing a folk song like "Dubinushka."

Some one decided to set an example to everyone:

"For we are now to receive the King of all! ..."

Everyone took up the chorus; the bell was now in place, it had been pulled up to the top, taken up to the massive hook and securely attached to it ...

In the frosty air, the song was still dying away:

"invisibly escorted ... by ... the angels ..."

When they had finished raising the bell, Yevgraf shouted down:

"Now give it a ring, and we'll see what it sounds like!"

The sound they had not heard for so long throbbed through them and rang out over the countryside around them.

The father was carried out of the Zakharovs' courtyard on the feast day of St. Symeon the God Receiver, at around midday. A grave near the altar awaited him, with a young bird-cherry tree growing over it. The coffin was carried by Fyodor Yevgraf and the exiles who had arrived with the priest. The newly raised bell rang out monotonously and mournfully. His whole journey was made to the accompaniment of constant singing of "Holy God." They sang the litany, then the "Eternal memory" rang out; the coffin swayed on its linen and was lowered into the embrace of the eternally frozen ground; one after another, clods of frozen earth hurtled down on top of it, knocking dully against the roof of the coffin. People standing round wept. Taking off their hats, new men – Yevgraf Zakharov and Fyodor Ukorov – took their stand on the fresh mound.

People don't stand about for long in the frosts of Siberia! It was three kilometres there and back, they had to return to the village before twilight. Many headed for Yevgraf's house, as he had invited anyone sent by God to visit them for the wake. Tatyana was waiting for the guests at home, with pancakes and fruit jelly. "We're your grateful guests!" – answered those accompanying him, one by one, in response to this invitation.

Fyodor was the last to tear himself away from the grave. In the last two days he had wept out all his tears and was now over-come by a feeling of supernatural peace. It was a comfort to acknowledge that many other people had truly felt the loss of the father, the man he had held so dear, that traveller to an unknown land, like himself. "Remember, Fedya, work and pray, make yourself pray – prayer is the light of your soul – so said one of the saintly elders," – that was what the father had taught him. "You must become a new man, an honest man.! Now you're not alone. The Lord will help you in all things." It was in such simple, clear terms that he had been instructed by this former academic, this bookish but always humble man. "I must do everything that the father prayed for!" – decided Fyodor, bending down to the arm of the cross and giving it a filial kiss – and then he hurried home.

A light wind was whirling dust over the new grave-mound and flying up into the branches of the bird-cherry bush. The wind would grow stronger and wilder towards night, perhaps a snow-storm was blowing up? . . .

So the story of the exiled pastor came to an end . . . But though the storm blows over the new and old grave mounds, covering them with snow, though the snowstorm whirls over the distant cemetery, wrapping it in a mantle of white snow, though time goes by and the years disappear, though no-one comes there any more and the small cross with its worn inscription falls off its base and collapses onto the ground . . . still the bird-cherry tree will go on arraying itself anew in its wedding colours every spring, and the path of remembrance, prayer and veneration, which leads to such graves, will never be overgrown . . .